MOST REQUESTED

Taste of Home

Ground Beef

TASTE OF HOME BOOKS • RDA ENTHUSIAST BRANDS, LLC • MILWAUKEE, WI

MOST REQUESTED

Taste of Home

Ground Beef

VERSATILE, BUDGET-FRIENDLY AND ALWAYS SATISFYING, GROUND BEEF IS THE PERFECT GO-TO INGREDIENT!

34

145

© 2022 RDA Enthusiast Brands, LLC.
1610 N. 2nd St., Suite 102, Milwaukee WI 53212-3906
All rights reserved. Taste of Home is a registered trademark of RDA Enthusiast Brands, LLC.
Visit **tasteofhome.com** for other *Taste of Home* books and products.

ISBN: 978-1-62145-749-7
LOCC: 2021938565
Component: 119200106H

Executive Editor: Mark Hagen
Senior Art Director:
Raeann Thompson
Editor: Hazel Wheaton
Designer: Jazmin Delgado
Deputy Editor, Copy Desk:
Dulcie Shoener
Copy Editor: Cathy Jakicic
Contributing Designer:
Jennifer Ruetz

Cover Photography
Photographer: Mark Derse
Set Stylist: Melissa Franco
Food Stylist: Josh Rink

Pictured on front cover:
Sloppy Joe Slider Bake, p.19

Pictured on title pages:
Zesty Horseradish Meat Loaf,
p. 111; Beefy Cabbage Bean
Stew, p. 52

Pictured on back cover:
Cheeseburger Pepper Cups, p.136;
Beef Taco Chili, p.37; Spicy Beef
Satay, p. 9

INSTANT POT is a trademark
of Double Insight Inc. This publi-
cation has not been authorized,
sponsored or otherwise approved
by Double Insight Inc.

Printed in China
1 3 5 7 9 10 8 6 4 2

AMERICA'S FAVORITE BEEF IS GROUND BEEF!

The most popular cut of beef, hands down, isn't a cut at all, but simple, delicious and oh-so-versatile ground beef! Satisfying breakfast skillets, hearty chilis, savory stews and comforting casseroles—ground beef does it all. Need a crowd-pleasing appetizer for your next party? A main course salad to serve friends? A slow-simmered soup that has your family coming back for more? Freezer-friendly and quick to cook, ground beef is the answer to nearly all your kitchen quandaries.

The team at *Taste of Home* collected our favorite top-rated ground beef recipes for this brand-new cookbook, **Most Requested Ground Beef.** With more than 325 recipes to choose from, you'll always find a dish to complete your menu.

To make meal planning even easier, we included five handy icons throughout the book so you can get the most out of your valuable time.

5i These recipes require no more than five items (minus water, oil, salt, pepper and optional ingredients), so they're ideal when you're watching both the clock and your budget!

❄ Stock your freezer with the comfort foods you enjoy most. These meals freeze well, and reheating instructions are included along with the recipes.

🍎 Keep your commitment to eating right while serving the foods you crave! This apple icon spotlights recipes that are on the lighter side.

🍲 Let your slow cooker do the work when you need a family-friendly dinner that's ready to eat when you are.

🍲 Heat up the Instant Pot®—these hearty meals are a busy cook's dream come true!

So whether you're looking for a quick and easy 30-minute skillet dinner, a special lasagna meal, spicy smothered nachos for a weekend party or the perfect burger for a backyard cookout, you'll find plenty of great choices in *Taste of Home* **Most Requested Ground Beef.** What's for dinner tonight? It has to be ground beef!

23

92

27

124

TABLE OF CONTENTS

45

Ground Beef

PARTY FAVORITES

Bulk up the appetizer buffet with beef! After all, this kitchen staple is far too popular, tasty and convenient to reserve for entrees alone. Turn the page to see how you can serve up the hearty bites friends and family crave most.

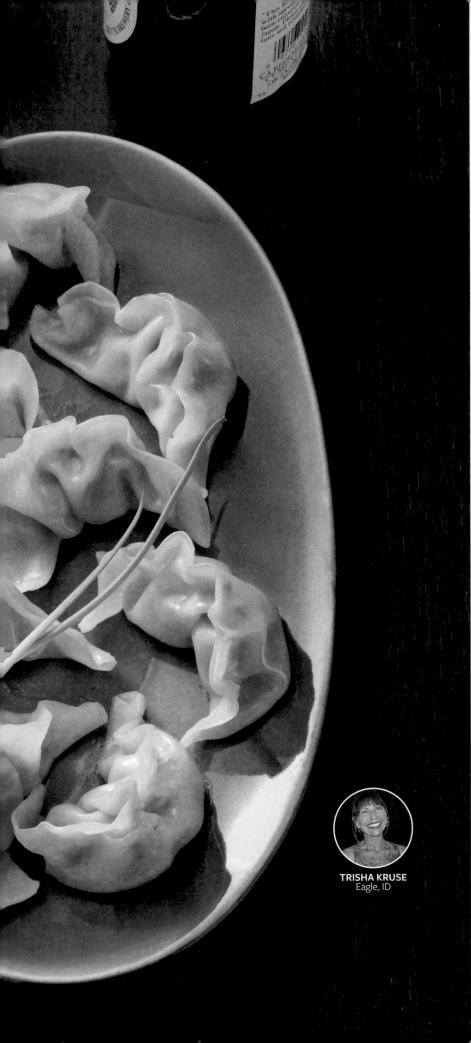

STEAMED BEEF & GINGER POT STICKERS

These dumplings have a hearty filling that's easy to make and a dipping sauce that's too irresistible to pass up. I prepare them in advance and freeze them.
—*Trisha Kruse, Eagle, ID*

- -

PREP: 1 hour • **COOK:** 5 min./batch
MAKES: 4 dozen

4	green onions, thinly sliced
2	Tbsp. reduced-sodium soy sauce
2	garlic cloves, minced
1	Tbsp. rice vinegar
1	Tbsp. minced fresh gingerroot
¼	tsp. coarsely ground pepper
1	lb. ground beef
48	pot sticker or gyoza wrappers

DIPPING SAUCE

¼	cup reduced-sodium soy sauce
2	Tbsp. rice vinegar
2	Tbsp. ketchup
1	Tbsp. minced fresh gingerroot
2	tsp. sesame oil
1	garlic clove, minced

1. In a large bowl, combine the first 6 ingredients. Add beef; mix lightly but thoroughly. Place a scant 1 Tbsp. filling in center of each wrapper. (Cover remaining wrappers with a damp paper towel until ready to use.)

2. Moisten wrapper edges with water. Fold wrapper over filling; seal edges, pleating the front side several times to form a pleated pouch. Stand pot stickers on a work surface to flatten bottoms; curve slightly to form crescent shapes if desired.

3. In a 6-qt. stockpot, place a greased steamer basket over ¾ in. of water. In batches, place dumplings in basket. Bring water to a boil. Reduce heat to maintain a low boil; steam, covered, 4-5 minutes or until cooked through.

4. Meanwhile, in a small bowl, combine sauce ingredients. Serve with dumplings.

1 dumpling with ½ tsp. sauce: 37 cal., 1g fat (0 sat. fat), 6mg chol., 115mg sod., 4g carb. (1g sugars, 0 fiber), 2g pro.

TRISHA KRUSE
Eagle, ID

READER REVIEW
"Wonderful, easy to make! Outstanding recipe!"
SARWIE28, TASTEOFHOME.COM

SPICY BEEF SATAY

The fragrant spices and full flavors of North African cuisine make these appetizers a popular party food.
—*Roxanne Chan, Albany, CA*

- -

PREP: 35 min. • **BROIL:** 5 min.
MAKES: 2 dozen (½ cup sauce)

   1 cup white wine vinegar
   ¾ cup sugar
   ½ cup water
   1 Tbsp. orange marmalade
   ¼ tsp. grated orange zest
   ¼ tsp. crushed red pepper flakes
   ½ cup finely chopped salted roasted
       almonds
   2 Tbsp. minced fresh mint
   1 green onion, finely chopped
   1 Tbsp. lemon juice
   1 garlic clove, minced
   ¼ tsp. each ground cinnamon, cumin
       and coriander
   1 lb. lean ground beef (90% lean)
       Minced fresh parsley

1. In a small saucepan, combine the first 6 ingredients. Bring to a boil. Reduce heat; simmer, uncovered, 25 minutes or until reduced to ½ cup.

2. Meanwhile, in a large bowl, combine the almonds, mint, onion, lemon juice, garlic and spices. Crumble beef over mixture and mix lightly but thoroughly. Divide into 24 pieces. Shape each piece into a 3x1-in. rectangle; insert a soaked wooden appetizer skewers into each.

3. Broil 6 in. from the heat 2-4 minutes on each side or until a thermometer reads 160°. Arrange on a serving platter. Drizzle with sauce mixture and sprinkle with parsley.

1 appetizer with 1 tsp. sauce: 74 cal., 3g fat (1g sat. fat), 12mg chol., 25mg sod., 8g carb. (7g sugars, 0 fiber), 4g pro.

GREEN OLIVE DIP

Olive fans will love this dip. It's cheesy and full of beef and beans. It could even be used as a filling for taco shells.
—*Beth Dunahay, Lima, OH*

- -

PREP: 30 min. • **COOK:** 3 hours
MAKES: 8 cups

   1 lb. ground beef
   1 medium sweet red pepper, chopped
   1 small onion, chopped
   1 can (16 oz.) refried beans
   1 jar (16 oz.) mild salsa
   2 cups shredded part-skim
       mozzarella cheese
   2 cups shredded cheddar cheese
   1 jar (5¾ oz.) sliced green olives with
       pimientos, drained
       Tortilla chips

1. In a large skillet, cook beef, pepper and onion over medium heat until meat is no longer pink, 5-7 minutes, crumble meat; drain.

2. Transfer to a greased 3-qt. slow cooker. Add beans, salsa, cheeses and olives. Cover and cook on low 3-4 hours or until cheese is melted, stirring occasionally. Serve with chips.

¼ cup: 96 cal., 6g fat (3g sat. fat), 21mg chol., 262mg sod., 4g carb. (1g sugars, 1g fiber), 7g pro.

TEST KITCHEN TIP
Filling out a tasty southwestern buffet? Serve this dip alongside quesadillas, nachos, guacamole, salsa, chili con queso, taquitos sangria, white wine, margaritas and/or lemonade.

NACHO TRIANGLES WITH SALSA-RANCH DIPPING SAUCE

These nacho bites are a fun fusion of Greek appetizers and flavors of the American Southwest. The simple dipping sauce is a perfect match—the ranch balances out the heat of the jalapeno and chipotle peppers— and takes the recipe to the next level.
—*Angela Spengler, Niceville, FL*

- -

PREP: 45 min. • **BAKE:** 15 min./batch
MAKES: 4 dozen

½	**lb. ground beef**
¼	**cup finely chopped onion**
½	**cup shredded pepper jack cheese**
½	**cup shredded cheddar cheese**
¼	**cup frozen corn, thawed**
¼	**cup canned diced tomatoes**
2	**Tbsp. taco seasoning**
2	**Tbsp. finely chopped seeded jalapeno pepper**
1	**Tbsp. finely chopped chipotle peppers in adobo sauce**
32	**sheets phyllo dough (14x9-in. size)**
¾	**cup butter, melted**
½	**cup ranch salad dressing**
½	**cup salsa**

1. In a small skillet, cook beef and onion over medium heat until the beef is no longer pink and onion is tender, 5-7 minutes, breaking up beef into crumbles; drain. Stir in the cheeses, corn, tomatoes, taco seasoning, and jalapeno chipotle peppers; set aside.

2. Preheat oven to 375°. Place 1 sheet phyllo dough on a work surface; brush lightly with butter. Cover with another sheet of phyllo; brush with butter. (Keep remaining phyllo covered with a damp towel to prevent it from drying out.)

3. Cut the 2 layered sheets into three 14x3-in. strips. Place 1 Tbsp. filling about 1 in. from corner of each strip. Fold 1 corner of dough over filling, forming a triangle. Fold triangle over, forming another triangle. Continue folding, like a flag, until you reach the end of the strip. Brush end of dough with butter and press onto triangle to seal. Turn triangle and brush top with butter. Repeat with remaining phyllo and filling.

4. Place triangles on greased baking sheets. Bake until golden brown, 12-15 minutes. Combine the ranch dressing and salsa; serve with triangles.

Freeze option: Freeze cooled triangles in freezer containers. To use, reheat triangles on a greased baking sheet in a preheated 375° oven until crisp and heated through.

Note: Wear disposable gloves when cutting hot peppers; the oils can burn skin. Avoid touching your face.

1 appetizer: 77 cal., 5g fat (3g sat. fat), 13mg chol., 143mg sod., 5g carb. (1g sugars, 0 fiber), 2g pro.

MINI BEEF TOURTIERES

Here's a twist on the traditional tourtiere recipe. Ground beef replaces pork, and cream cheese pastry takes the place of pie pastry. The filled mini cups make a melt-in-your-mouth addition to any buffet.
—*Cheryl Bruneau, Winnipeg, MB*

PREP: 1¼ hours + chilling
BAKE: 15 min.
MAKES: about 2½ dozen

- ½ cup butter
- 4 oz. cream cheese, softened
- 1½ cups all-purpose flour

FILLING
- 1 Tbsp. canola oil
- 1 lb. lean ground beef (90% lean)
- 1 medium onion, minced
- 2 garlic cloves, chopped
- 2 Tbsp. chopped fresh parsley
- 1 Tbsp. Dijon mustard
- 1 tsp. dried savory or sage
- 1 tsp. poultry seasoning
- ½ tsp. dried thyme
- ½ tsp. celery salt
  Dash salt
  Dash pepper
- ½ cup soft bread crumbs
  Optional: Chopped tomatoes and additional minced fresh parsley

1. Cream butter and cream cheese. Add flour, a little at a time, until a dough forms. Shape into a ball. Cover and refrigerate 1 hour.
2. Meanwhile, for filling, heat oil in a large skillet over medium-high heat. Add ground beef and onion; cook, crumbling meat, until beef is no longer pink, about 5 minutes. Add garlic; cook 1 minute more. Add the next 8 ingredients. Stir in bread crumbs to absorb meat juices. Let stand about 10 minutes.
3. On a lightly floured surface, roll out the dough to ⅛-in. thickness. Cut with a floured 2¾-in. round biscuit or cookie cutter. Press crust on bottom and up sides of 30 ungreased mini-muffin cups, rerolling dough as needed.
4. Preheat oven to 375°. Spoon 1 Tbsp. filling into each prepared muffin cup. Bake until crust is golden, about 15 minutes. If desired, top with tomatoes and parsley.

Note: To make soft bread crumbs, tear bread into pieces and place in a food processor or blender. Cover and pulse until crumbs form. A slice of bread yields ½-¾ cup crumbs.

1 appetizer: 96 cal., 6g fat (3g sat. fat), 21mg chol., 128mg sod., 6g carb. (0 sugars, 0 fiber), 4g pro.

MINI CRESCENT BURGERS

A friend first brought these snacks to a Sunday school party. The original recipe called for pork sausage, but I substituted ground beef with taste-tempting results.
—*Pam Buhr, Mexico, MO*

PREP: 20 min.
BAKE: 15 min./batch
MAKES: 4 dozen

- 1 lb. ground beef
- 1 cup shredded cheddar cheese
- 1 envelope onion soup mix
- 3 tubes (8 oz. each) refrigerated crescent rolls

1. In a large skillet, cook beef over medium heat until no longer pink, 5-7 minutes, breaking up beef into crumbles; drain. Stir in cheese and soup mix; set aside.
2. Preheat oven to 375°. Separate crescent dough into triangles; cut each triangle in half lengthwise, forming 2 triangles. Place 1 Tbsp. of the beef mixture along the wide end of each triangle.
3. Roll up; place pointed side down 2 in. apart on ungreased baking sheets. Bake for 15 minutes or until golden brown.

1 appetizer: 79 cal., 4g fat (1g sat. fat), 8mg chol., 178mg sod., 7g carb. (2g sugars, 0 fiber), 3g pro.

CHEESY MEATBALL SLIDERS

These meatball sliders are a fun way to serve meatballs at your party without using a slow cooker. Made on mini Hawaiian rolls, they have a hint of sweetness to balance out all the wonderful Italian seasonings.
—Taste of Home *Test Kitchen*

- -

PREP: 1 hour • **BAKE:** 30 min.
MAKES: 12 servings

- 2 lbs. lean ground beef (90% lean)
- 1 cup Italian-style bread crumbs
- 3 Tbsp. prepared pesto
- 1 large egg, lightly beaten
- 1 jar (24 oz.) pasta sauce
- 1 pkg. (18 oz.) Hawaiian sweet rolls
- 12 slices part-skim mozzarella cheese
- ½ tsp. dried oregano
- ¼ cup melted butter
- 1 Tbsp. olive oil
- 3 garlic cloves, minced
- 1 tsp. Italian seasoning
- ½ tsp. crushed red pepper flakes
- 2 Tbsp. grated Parmesan cheese
- 1 cup shredded part-skim mozzarella cheese or shredded Italian cheese blend
  Minced fresh basil

1. Preheat oven to 350°. Combine ground beef, bread crumbs, pesto and egg; mix lightly. Shape into 12 meatballs; place on a greased rack in a 15x10x1-in. baking pan. Bake until browned and a thermometer reads 160°, about 35 minutes. Toss the meatballs with pasta sauce; set aside.
2. Meanwhile, without separating rolls, cut horizontally in half; arrange bottom halves in a greased 13x9-in. baking dish. Place half of cheese slices over roll bottoms; sprinkle with oregano. Add meatballs and sauce. Top with remaining cheese slices and bun tops.
3. Combine the butter, olive oil, garlic, Italian seasoning and red pepper flakes; brush over the buns. Bake, covered, for 20 minutes. Uncover; sprinkle with Parmesan and shredded mozzarella.
4. Bake, uncovered, until the cheese is melted, 10-15 minutes longer. Sprinkle with the basil before serving.
1 slider: 514 cal., 25g fat (12g sat. fat), 120mg chol., 856mg sod., 39g carb. (15g sugars, 3g fiber), 33g pro.

EASY TACO CUPS

These zesty little cups rank high on my list of faves because they combine three things I look for in a recipe: fast, easy and delicious! They make a simply fantastic finger food for game-day parties, and my guests have fun selecting their desired toppings.
—Ashley Jarvies, Manassa, CO

- -

PREP: 30 min. • **BAKE:** 15 min. + cooling
MAKES: 12 servings

- 1 lb. ground beef
- ½ cup chopped onion
- 1 envelope taco seasoning
- 1 can (16 oz.) refried beans
- 2 tubes (8 oz. each) refrigerated seamless crescent dough sheet
- 1½ cups shredded cheddar cheese
  Optional: Chopped tomatoes, sliced ripe olives, shredded lettuce, sour cream, guacamole and salsa

1. Preheat oven to 375°. In a large skillet, cook beef and onion over medium heat, 6-8 minutes or until beef is no longer pink, breaking meat into crumbles; drain. Stir in taco seasoning and refried beans; heat through.
2. Unroll each tube of dough into a long rectangle. Cut each rectangle into 12 pieces; press lightly onto bottom and up sides of 24 ungreased muffin cups.
3. Fill each muffin cup with a rounded tablespoon of beef mixture; sprinkle each with 1 Tbsp. cheese. Bake 14-16 minutes or until dough is golden brown. Cool taco cups in pans for 10 minutes before removing. Serve with toppings as desired.
2 taco cups: 291 cal., 15g fat (7g sat. fat), 37mg chol., 819mg sod., 25g carb. (4g sugars, 2g fiber), 15g pro.

MEXICAN FIESTA PLATTER

This recipe proves you don't need to fuss to prepare an appetizer for a crowd. With generous layers of beef, rice, corn chips and cheese, it's a nacho lover's dream!
—Ann Nace, Perkasie, PA

- -

PREP: 15 min. • **COOK:** 35 min.
MAKES: 20 servings

2½ lbs. ground beef
2 cans (16 oz. each) kidney beans, rinsed and drained
2 cans (15 oz. each) tomato sauce
1 envelope chili seasoning
1 pkg. (9¼ oz.) corn chips
3 cups hot cooked rice
2 large onions, chopped
2 cups shredded Monterey Jack cheese
1 medium head iceberg lettuce, shredded
4 medium tomatoes, chopped
1½ cups chopped ripe olives
Hot pepper sauce, optional

1. In a Dutch oven, cook beef over medium heat until it is no longer pink, 5-7 minutes, crumbling beef; drain. Add the beans, tomato sauce and chili seasoning; simmer for 30 minutes, stirring occasionally.
2. On 2 serving platters with sides, layer chips, rice, onions, meat, cheese, lettuce, tomato and olives. Sprinkle with hot sauce if desired.
1 serving: 340 cal., 17g fat (6g sat. fat), 45mg chol., 663mg sod., 28g carb. (4g sugars, 5g fiber), 19g pro.

MEDITERRANEAN HUMMUS NACHOS

My husband once piled all the Middle Eastern dishes I made on top of pita chips. It was delicious and fun, so we've kept doing it! We love this combination with ground lamb, too. I am half Lebanese, so we usually call these Lebanese nachos. Whatever you call them, they are outstanding.
—Gina Fensler, Cincinnati, OH

- -

TAKES: 30 min. • **MAKES:** 6 servings

½ lb. lean ground beef (90% lean)
1 Tbsp. pine nuts
¼ tsp. salt
⅛ tsp. pepper
6 Tbsp. plain yogurt, divided
1 pkg. (7.33 oz.) baked pita chips
1 cup prepared tabbouleh
½ cup hummus
1 large tomato, chopped
¼ cup sliced ripe olives
1 Tbsp. minced fresh parsley
1 Tbsp. minced fresh mint
Chopped red onion, optional

1. In a small skillet, cook beef over medium heat until no longer pink, breaking it into crumbles, 4-6 minutes; drain. Stir in the pine nuts, salt and pepper; cool slightly. Stir in 2 Tbsp. yogurt.
2. Arrange pita chips on a serving platter. Layer with the beef mixture, tabbouleh, hummus, tomato, olives, parsley, mint, the remaining 4 Tbsp. yogurt and, if desired, onion. Serve immediately.
1 serving: 299 cal., 14g fat (4g sat. fat), 27mg chol., 624mg sod., 29g carb. (2g sugars, 4g fiber), 13g pro.

FAVORITE CHEESEBURGER PIZZA

My sister-in-law used to own a pizza restaurant and gave me this awesome recipe that features ground beef, cheddar and Thousand Island dressing. We like it on whole wheat crust.
—*Katie Buckley, Wyoming, DE*

- -

TAKES: 25 min. • **MAKES:** 8 servings

- 1 lb. ground beef
- ¼ tsp. salt
- 1 prebaked 12-in. thin pizza crust
- ½ cup Thousand Island salad dressing
- 1 small onion, chopped
- 2 cups shredded cheddar cheese
- 2 cups shredded lettuce
- ½ cup sliced dill pickles

1. Preheat oven to 450°. In a large skillet, cook beef over medium heat, until no longer pink, 6-8 minutes, breaking it into crumbles; drain. Sprinkle beef with salt.

2. Place crust on an ungreased pizza pan or baking sheet; spread with salad dressing. Top with beef, onion and cheese.

3. Bake 6-8 minutes or until the cheese is melted. Top with lettuce and pickles just before serving.

1 slice: 394 cal., 24g fat (9g sat. fat), 65mg chol., 706mg sod., 22g carb. (3g sugars, 1g fiber), 21g pro.

KATIE BUCKLEY
Wyoming, DE

MINI BURGERS WITH THE WORKS

I started preparing these mini burgers several years ago as a creative way to use up bread crusts accumulating in my freezer. Their tiny size makes them simply irresistible.
—*Linda Lane, Bennington, VT*

- -

TAKES: 30 min. • **MAKES:** 1 dozen

- ¼ lb. ground beef
- 3 slices American cheese
- 4 slices white bread (heels of loaves recommended)
- 2 Tbsp. prepared Thousand Island salad dressing
- 2 pearl onions, thinly sliced
- 4 baby dill pickles, thinly sliced
- 3 cherry tomatoes, thinly sliced

1. Shape the beef into twelve 1-in. patties. Place on a microwave-safe plate lined with paper towels. Cover with another paper towel; microwave on high for 1 minute or until meat is no longer pink. Cut each slice of cheese into fourths; set aside.

2. Using a 1-in. round cookie cutter, cut out 6 circles from each slice of bread. Spread half the bread circles with dressing. Layer with the burgers, cheese, onions, pickles and tomatoes. Top with the remaining bread circles; secure with toothpicks.

1 burger: 68 cal., 3g fat (1g sat. fat), 11mg chol., 153mg sod., 5g carb. (1g sugars, 0 fiber), 4g pro.

HEARTY RYE MELTS

When we moved from the Midwest to Kentucky, we were invited to a neighborhood gathering where this appetizer was served. Hanky panky, as it's often called around here, is traditionally served at Derby Day parties, but at our home it's become a year-round favorite.
—*Melanie Schlaf, Edgewood, KY*

- -

TAKES: 30 min. • **MAKES:** 2 dozen

- ½ lb. lean ground beef (90% lean)
- ½ lb. bulk pork sausage
- 1½ tsp. chili powder
- 8 oz. Velveeta, shredded
- 24 slices snack rye bread
  Fresh parsley sprigs, stems removed

1. In a large skillet, cook the beef and sausage over medium heat until no longer pink, 5-7 minutes, breaking into crumbles; drain. Add chili powder and cheese; cook and stir until cheese is melted. Spread a heaping tablespoonful on each slice of bread. Place on a baking sheet.
2. Bake at 350° for 12-15 minutes or until edges of bread begin to crisp. Garnish with parsley. Serve warm.
1 piece: 88 cal., 6g fat (2g sat. fat), 20mg chol., 231mg sod., 4g carb. (1g sugars, 0 fiber), 5g pro.

FREEZER BURRITOS

I love burritos, but the frozen types are so high in sodium, I created these. They're a perfect option to have on hand for quick dinners or late-night snacks—I've even had them for breakfast sometimes!
—*Laura Winemiller, Delta, PA*

- -

PREP: 35 min. • **COOK:** 15 min.
MAKES: 12 servings

- 1¼ lbs. lean ground beef (90% lean)
- ¼ cup finely chopped onion
- 1¼ cups salsa
- 2 Tbsp. reduced-sodium taco seasoning
- 2 cans (15 oz. each) pinto beans, rinsed and drained
- ½ cup water
- 2 cups shredded reduced-fat cheddar cheese
- 12 flour tortillas (8 in.), warmed

1. In a large skillet, cook beef and onion over medium heat until meat is no longer pink, 5-7 minutes, crumbling beef; drain. Stir in salsa and taco seasoning. Bring to a boil. Reduce heat; simmer, uncovered, for 2-3 minutes. Transfer to a large bowl; set aside.
2. In a food processor, combine pinto beans and water. Cover and process until almost smooth. Add to beef mixture. Stir in cheese.
3. Spoon ½ cup beef mixture down the center of each tortilla. Fold ends and sides over the filling; roll up. Wrap each burrito in waxed paper and foil.
Freeze option: Freeze burritos for up to 1 month. To use: Remove foil and waxed paper. Place 1 burrito on a microwave-safe plate. Microwave on high for 2½-2¾ minutes or until a thermometer reads 165°, turning burrito once. Let stand 20 seconds.
1 burrito: 345 cal., 11g fat (4g sat. fat), 36mg chol., 677mg sod., 40g carb. (3g sugars, 3g fiber), 22g pro. **Diabetic exchanges:** 2½ starch, 2 lean meat, ½ fat.

CHILI QUESO DIP

I've had this recipe for more than 42 years and have updated it from time to time. This is an easy party favorite, and everyone loves the taquito dippers.
—*Joan Hallford, North Richland Hills, TX*

- -

PREP: 20 min. • **COOK:** 2 hours
MAKES: 40 servings (2½ qt.)

- 1 lb. ground beef
- 1 lb. bulk pork sausage
- 1 small onion, chopped
- 2 jalapeno peppers, seeded and finely chopped
- 1 garlic clove, minced
- 1 can (15 oz.) chili con carne (without beans)
- 1 can (10¾ oz.) reduced-fat, reduced-sodium condensed cream of mushroom soup, undiluted
- 1 can (10 oz.) diced tomatoes and green chiles, drained
- 1 jar (4 oz.) diced pimientos, drained
- 1 pkg. (2 lbs.) Velveeta, cubed
  Prepared taquitos, tortilla chips or corn chips

1. In a large skillet, cook beef and sausage with the onion, jalapenos and garlic over medium-high heat until meat is no longer pink, 5-7 minutes, crumbling the meat. Using a slotted spoon, transfer the mixture to a 5-qt. slow cooker. Stir in the chili, soup, tomatoes, pimientos and cheese.
2. Cook, covered, on low until heated through, 2-3 hours, stirring halfway through cooking. Serve warm with taquitos or chips.
¼ cup dip: 147 cal., 11g fat (5g sat. fat), 39mg chol., 473mg sod., 4g carb. (2g sugars, 0 fiber), 8g pro.

SLOPPY JOE SLIDER BAKE

Simple ground beef has been turned up a notch by party sliders that are sure to please your crowd. I love how easy they are. Be sure not to skip the glaze. It's what takes these sliders over the top!
—*Rashanda Cobbins, Milwaukee, WI*

- -

PREP: 20 min. • **BAKE:** 15 min.
MAKES: 1 dozen

- 1 pkg. (18 oz.) Hawaiian sweet rolls
- 12 slices cheddar cheese
- 1½ lbs. lean ground beef (90% lean)
- ½ cup chopped onion
- 1 can (15½ oz.) sloppy joe sauce
- 1 Tbsp. packed brown sugar
- 1 Tbsp. soy sauce
- ¾ tsp. pepper

GLAZE

- ¼ cup butter, melted
- 1 Tbsp. packed brown sugar
- 1 Tbsp. Dijon mustard
- 1 tsp. soy sauce
- ½ tsp. garlic powder
- 1 tsp. sesame seeds
- 1 tsp. black sesame seeds
- 1 tsp. dried minced onion
  Dill pickle slices, optional

1. Preheat oven to 350°. Without separating rolls, cut rolls in half horizontally; arrange bottom halves in a greased 13x9-in. baking pan. Top with half of cheese slices; set aside.
2. In a large skillet, cook beef and onion over medium heat until beef is no longer pink and onion is tender, 6-8 minutes; break up beef into crumbles; drain. Stir in sloppy joe sauce, brown sugar, soy sauce and pepper. Cook and stir until combined, 1-2 minutes. Spoon beef mixture evenly over rolls; top with remaining cheese. Replace top halves of rolls.
3. For glaze, stir together butter, brown sugar, mustard, soy sauce and garlic powder. Brush over rolls; sprinkle with sesame seeds and minced onion. Bake, uncovered, until tops are golden and cheese is melted, 15-20 minutes. If desired, top with pickle slices.
1 slider: 392 cal., 19g fat (10g sat. fat), 91mg chol., 668mg sod., 32g carb. (15g sugars, 2g fiber), 23g pro.

MARINA
CASTLE KELLEY
Canyon Country, CA

RAMONA'S CHILAQUILES

A dear neighbor shared this recipe. She used to make it from scratch, but my version takes a few shortcuts.
—*Marina Castle Kelley, Canyon Country, CA*

- -

TAKES: 30 min. • **MAKES:** 4 servings

- ½ lb. lean ground beef (90% lean)
- ½ lb. fresh chorizo
  or bulk spicy pork sausage
- 1 medium onion, finely chopped
- 1 garlic clove, minced
- 1 can (14½ oz.) diced tomatoes
  with mild green chiles, undrained
- 1 can (10 oz.) diced tomatoes
  and green chiles, undrained
- 4 cups tortilla chips (about 6 oz.)
- 1 cup shredded Monterey Jack cheese
  Chopped fresh cilantro
  Optional: Sour cream, diced avocado
  and sliced red onion

1. Preheat oven to 350°. In a large skillet, cook beef and chorizo with onion and garlic over medium heat until beef is no longer pink, 5-7 minutes; crumble meat; drain. Stir in both cans of tomatoes; bring to a boil. In a greased 1½-qt. or 8-in.-square baking dish, layer 2 cups chips, half of the meat mixture and ½ cup cheese; repeat layers.
2. Bake, uncovered, until cheese is melted, 12-15 minutes. Sprinkle with cilantro. If desired, serve with toppings.
1 serving: 573 cal., 35g fat (14g sat. fat), 110mg chol., 1509mg sod., 28g carb. (5g sugars, 4g fiber), 33g pro.

TEST KITCHEN TIP
Chilaquiles are indulgent any way you fix them, but they can easily be lightened up a bit. Simply use chorizo chicken sausage and baked chips to lop off 15grams of fat.

SOUTHWESTERN APPETIZER TRIANGLES

A clever cross between wontons and tacos, these triangles are fun to serve. My mom created the recipe years ago, much to the delight of my family. Since I began making them, my husband insists we have them on Sundays during football season, as well as on special occasions.
—*Sheila Pope, Preston, ID*

PREP: 25 min. + cooling
COOK: 40 min.
MAKES: about 7½ dozen

- 1 lb. ground beef
- 1 medium onion, chopped
  Salt and pepper to taste
- 1 can (16 oz.) refried beans
- 1½ cups shredded cheddar cheese
- 1 cup salsa
- 1 can (4 oz.) diced jalapeno peppers, drained
- 2 pkg. (12 oz. each) wonton wrappers
  Oil for deep frying
  Additional salsa

1. In a large skillet over medium heat, cook the beef, onion, salt and pepper until meat is no longer pink, 5-7 minutes; crumble beef; drain. Add the beans, cheese, salsa and jalapenos. Cook and stir over low heat until the cheese is melted. Remove from the heat; cool for 10 minutes.

2. Place a teaspoonful of beef mixture in the center of 1 wonton wrapper. Moisten edges with water. (Keep remaining wrappers covered with a damp paper towel until ready to use.) Fold wonton in half, forming a triangle; press edges to seal. Repeat.

3. In an electric skillet or deep fryer, heat oil to 375°. Fry wontons, a few at a time, until golden brown, 2-3 minutes. Drain on paper towels. Serve the appetizers warm with additional salsa.

1 appetizer: 65 cal., 4g fat (1g sat. fat), 6mg chol., 91mg sod., 5g carb. (0 sugars, 0 fiber), 2g pro.

MOIST MEXICAN CORNBREAD

Our family enjoys this beef-stuffed cornbread for a snack or even a simple entree.
—*Elizabeth Sanders, Obion, TN*

PREP: 15 min. • **BAKE:** 30 min.
MAKES: 10 servings

- 2 large eggs, room temperature
- 1 cup sour cream
- ⅔ cup canola oil
- 1½ cups cornmeal
- ¼ cup all-purpose flour
- 2¼ tsp. baking powder
- ¾ tsp. salt
- 1 can (4 oz.) chopped green chiles, drained
- 2 Tbsp. chopped green pepper
- 2 Tbsp. chopped onion
- 2 Tbsp. chopped pimientos
- 1 lb. ground beef, cooked and drained
- 1½ cups shredded cheddar cheese

1. In a bowl, combine eggs, sour cream and oil. In another bowl, combine the cornmeal, flour, baking powder and salt; fold in chiles, green pepper, onion and pimientos. Add the egg mixture; mix well.

2. Pour half into greased 13x9-in. baking dish. Top with beef. Sprinkle with ½ cup cheese. Spoon remaining cornmeal mixture over top. Sprinkle with the remaining cheese. Bake at 350° for 30 minutes or until a toothpick comes out clean.

1 piece: 448 cal., 32g fat (9g sat. fat), 88mg chol., 490mg sod., 23g carb. (2g sugars, 1g fiber), 16g pro.

BEEF & ONION PIROSHKI

When I lived in Seattle, one of my all-time favorite places was a small stand that sold piroshki—Russian stuffed pocket sandwiches. Whenever I'm missing my former town, I make my own batch.
—Julie Merriman, Seattle, WA

PREP: 30 min. + cooling • **BAKE:** 15 min.
MAKES: 32 appetizers

- 1 lb. lean ground beef (90% lean)
- 1 cup finely chopped sweet onion
- 2 garlic cloves, minced
- ½ tsp. salt
- ¼ tsp. pepper
- 1 cup chopped fresh spinach
- 1 cup shredded Havarti cheese
- ¼ cup sour cream
- 2 Tbsp. snipped fresh dill
- 1 pkg. (17.3 oz.) frozen puff pastry, thawed
- 1 large egg
- 1 Tbsp. water

1. In a large skillet, cook the beef, onion, garlic, salt and pepper over medium heat until the meat is no longer pink; crumble beef; drain. Cool to room temperature.

2. Stir the spinach, cheese, sour cream and dill into the beef mixture. On a lightly floured surface, roll a puff-pastry sheet into a 12-in. square. Cut into sixteen 3-in. squares. Repeat with remaining sheet.

3. Spoon 1 Tbsp. beef mixture onto the center of each square. Fold dough over filling, forming a triangle; press the edges with a fork to seal. Transfer to greased baking sheets. Whisk egg and water; brush over tops. Bake at 400° until golden brown, 14-16 minutes.

1 appetizer: 115 cal., 6g fat (2g sat. fat), 18mg chol., 118mg sod., 9g carb. (0 sugars, 1g fiber), 5g pro.

BARBECUED PARTY STARTERS

These sweet and tangy bites are sure to tide everyone over until the main course is ready. At the buffet, set out some toothpicks to make for easy nibbling.
—Anastasia Weiss, Punxsutawney, PA

PREP: 30 min. • **COOK:** 2¼ hours
MAKES: 16 servings

- 1 lb. ground beef
- ¼ cup finely chopped onion
- 1 pkg. (16 oz.) miniature hot dogs, drained
- 1 jar (12 oz.) apricot preserves
- 1 cup barbecue sauce
- 1 can (20 oz.) pineapple chunks, drained

1. In a large bowl, combine beef and onion, mixing lightly but thoroughly. Shape into 1-in. balls. In a large skillet over medium heat, cook meatballs in 2 batches until cooked through, turning occasionally.

2. Using a slotted spoon, transfer meatballs to a 3-qt. slow cooker. Add hot dogs; stir in preserves and barbecue sauce. Cook, covered, on high or until heated through, 2-3 hours.

3. Stir in pineapple; cook, covered, until heated through, 15-20 minutes longer.

⅓ cup: 237 cal., 11g fat (4g sat. fat), 36mg chol., 491mg sod., 26g carb. (20g sugars, 0 fiber), 9g pro.

READER REVIEW

"This is one of the dishes I made for a Super Bowl party we had. I loved how simple it was to make. Everyone seemed to enjoy the sweet BBQ flavor."

ROBBRD, TASTEOFHOME.COM

BLUE-RIBBON BEEF NACHOS

Chili powder and convenient jarred salsa season a zesty mixture of ground beef and refried beans that's sprinkled with green onions, tomatoes and ripe olives.
—*Diane Hixon, Niceville, FL*

- -

TAKES: 20 min. • **MAKES:** 6 servings

- 1   lb. ground beef
- 1   small onion, chopped
- 1   can (16 oz.) refried beans
- 1   jar (16 oz.) salsa
- 1   can (6 oz.) pitted ripe olives, chopped
- ½   cup shredded cheddar cheese
- 1   green onion, chopped
- 2   Tbsp. chili powder
- 1   tsp. salt
  Tortilla chips
  Optional: Sliced ripe olives, chopped green onions and diced tomatoes

1. In a large skillet, cook the beef and onion over medium heat until the meat is no longer pink; crumble the beef; drain. Stir in the next 7 ingredients; heat through.

2. Serve over tortilla chips. Top with olives, onions and tomatoes if desired.

1 serving: 294 cal., 14g fat (6g sat. fat), 53mg chol., 1353mg sod., 19g carb. (5g sugars, 9g fiber), 20g pro. uncovered, for 5 minutes.

Note: Wear disposable gloves when cutting hot peppers; the oils can burn skin. Avoid touching your face.

TEST KITCHEN TIP
This recipe prevents soggy nachos by adding the heavy toppings right before serving. It also uses real cheese instead of Velveeta, which can help prevent mushy chips.

COWBOY BEEF DIP

In a foods class, a group of us developed this recipe for the North Dakota State Beef Bash Competition. We won the contest!
—*Jessica Klym, Dunn Center, ND*

PREP: 20 min. • **COOK:** 25 min.
MAKES: 12 servings (3 cups)

- 1 lb. ground beef
- 4 Tbsp. chopped onion, divided
- 3 Tbsp. chopped sweet red pepper, divided
- 2 Tbsp. chopped green pepper, divided
- 1 can (10¾ oz.) condensed nacho cheese soup, undiluted
- ½ cup salsa
- 4 Tbsp. sliced ripe olives, divided
- 4 Tbsp. sliced pimiento-stuffed olives, divided
- 2 Tbsp. chopped green chiles
- 1 tsp. chopped seeded jalapeno pepper
- ¼ tsp. dried oregano
- ¼ tsp. pepper
- ¼ cup shredded cheddar cheese
- 2 Tbsp. sour cream
- 2 to 3 tsp. minced fresh parsley
  Tortilla chips

1. In a large skillet, cook beef, 3 Tbsp. onion, 2 Tbsp. red pepper and 1 Tbsp. green pepper over medium heat until meat is no longer pink; crumble the meat; drain. Stir in the soup, salsa, 3 Tbsp. ripe olives, 3 Tbsp. pimiento-stuffed olives, chiles, jalapeno, oregano and pepper. Bring to a boil. Reduce the heat; simmer, uncovered, for 5 minutes.

2. Transfer to a serving dish. Top with the cheese, sour cream and parsley; sprinkle with the remaining onion, peppers and olives. Serve with tortilla chips.

Note: Wear disposable gloves when cutting hot peppers; the oils can burn skin. Avoid touching your face.

¼ cup: 116 cal., 7g fat (3g sat. fat), 26mg chol., 336mg sod., 4g carb. (1g sugars, 1g fiber), 8g pro.

ITALIAN APPETIZER MEATBALLS

Store-bought spaghetti sauce speeds up the preparation of tender homemade meatballs. Leftovers make terrific sub sandwiches.
—*Rene McCrory, Indianapolis, IN*

PREP: 40 min. • **COOK:** 2 hours
MAKES: 4 dozens

- 2 large eggs, lightly beaten
- ½ cup dry bread crumbs
- ¼ cup 2% milk
- 2 tsp. grated Parmesan cheese
- 1 tsp. salt
- ¼ tsp. pepper
- ⅛ tsp. garlic powder
- 1 lb. ground beef
- 1 lb. bulk Italian sausage
- 2 jars (24 oz. each) spaghetti sauce
  Minced fresh parsley, optional

1. Preheat oven to 400°. In a large bowl, combine the first 7 ingredients. Crumble beef and sausage over mixture, mix lightly but thoroughly. Shape into 1-in. balls.

2. Place the meatballs on a greased rack in a shallow baking pan. Bake until no longer pink, 15-20 minutes.

3. Transfer meatballs to a 4-qt. slow cooker; add spaghetti sauce. Cover and cook on high for 2-3 hours or until heated through. Garnish with parsley if desired.

1 meatball: 67 cal., 4g fat (1g sat. fat), 20mg chol., 264mg sod., 4g carb. (2g sugars, 1g fiber), 4g pro.

BEEF TRIANGLES & CHUTNEY DIP

When I brought these crisp, golden brown triangles to a friend's housewarming party, they were gone in minutes. The spices in the beef make them unusual and delicious.
—*Carla DeVelder, Mishawaka, IN*

PREP: 45 min. • **BAKE:** 10 min./batch
MAKES: 56 appetizers (1 cup sauce)

- 1 lb. ground beef
- 1 small onion, finely chopped
- ⅓ cup dried currants
- ½ tsp. salt
- ½ tsp. ground cumin
- ¼ tsp. ground cinnamon
- ¼ tsp. ground nutmeg
- ⅛ tsp. cayenne pepper
- ⅛ tsp. pepper
- 1 Tbsp. cornstarch
- ½ cup water
- 28 sheets phyllo dough (14x9 in.)
  Butter-flavored cooking spray
- ½ cup plain yogurt
- ½ cup chutney

1. In a large skillet, cook beef and onion over medium heat until meat is no longer pink; crumble meat; drain. Stir in currants and seasonings. Combine cornstarch and water until smooth; gradually stir into beef mixture. Bring to a boil; cook and stir for 2 minutes or until thickened. Remove from the heat.
2. Place 1 sheet of phyllo dough on a work surface with a short end facing you; spray sheet with butter-flavored spray. Place another sheet of phyllo on top and spritz with spray. (Keep remaining phyllo covered with a damp towel to prevent it from drying out.) Cut the 2 layered sheets into four 14x2¼-in. strips.
3. Place a rounded teaspoon of filling on lower corner of each strip. Fold dough over filling, forming a triangle. Fold the triangle up, then fold triangle over, forming another triangle. Continue folding, like a flag, until you come to the end of the strip. Spritz end of dough with spray and press onto triangle to seal. Turn triangle and spritz top with spray. Repeat with remaining phyllo and filling.
4. Place triangles on baking sheets coated with cooking spray. Bake at 400° until golden brown, 8-10 minutes. Combine yogurt and chutney. Serve with warm appetizers.
1 triangle with ¾ tsp. sauce: 41 cal., 1g fat (0 sat. fat), 4mg chol., 51mg sod., 5g carb. (2g sugars, 0 fiber), 2g pro.

SESAME-BEEF POT STICKERS

I enjoy these pot stickers as a late-night snack. They also work well as a quick appetizer for family parties.
—*Carolyn Turner, Reno, NV*

PREP: 20 min. • **COOK:** 10 min./batch
MAKES: 2 dozen

- ¾ lb. lean ground beef (90% lean)
- 2 Tbsp. reduced-sodium soy sauce
- 1 Tbsp. sesame oil
- 2¼ tsp. chili garlic sauce
- 2 tsp. onion powder
- 1 tsp. garlic salt
- ¼ tsp. dried parsley flakes
- 24 pot sticker or gyoza wrappers
- 1 large egg, lightly beaten
- 3 tsp. sesame or olive oil, divided
- ½ cup water, divided

1. In a large bowl, combine the first 7 ingredients. Place 1 Tbsp. beef mixture in center of each pot sticker wrapper. (Cover wrappers with a damp towel until ready to use.)
2. Moisten wrapper edges with egg. Fold wrapper over filling; seal edges, pleating the front side several times to form a pleated pouch. Stand pot stickers on a work surface to flatten bottoms; curve slightly to form crescent shapes if desired.
3. In a large skillet, heat 1½ tsp. sesame oil over medium-high heat. Arrange half of the pot stickers in concentric circles in pan, flat side down; cook 1-2 minutes or until bottoms are lightly browned. Carefully add ¼ cup water (water may spatter); reduce heat to medium. Cook, covered, 3-5 minutes or until water is almost absorbed and filling is cooked through.
4. Cook pot stickers, uncovered, 1-2 minutes or until the bottoms are crisp and the water is completely evaporated. Repeat with remaining pot stickers.
1 pot sticker: 50 cal., 2g fat (1g sat. fat), 14mg chol., 164mg sod., 3g carb. (0 sugars, 0 fiber), 3g pro.

CHEDDAR & ONION BEEF SLIDERS

My girlfriend and I threw an outdoor party for our friends, and these sliders were a hit. Caramelized onions with wine are the secret.
—*Kirk Brooks, Tucson, AZ*

- -

PREP: 1¼ hours • **COOK:** 10 min.
MAKES: 8 servings

- ¼ cup butter, cubed
- 1 medium red onion, halved and thinly sliced
- 2¼ tsp. Montreal steak seasoning, divided
- 1 cup dry red wine
- 1 lb. ground beef
- 2 slices cheddar cheese, quartered
- 8 dinner rolls, split

1. In a large skillet, heat butter over medium heat. Add onion and ¼ tsp. steak seasoning; cook and stir 6-8 minutes or until onion is softened. Reduce heat to medium-low; cook 40-45 minutes or until deep golden brown, stirring occasionally. Stir in wine. Bring to a boil; cook 10-12 minutes or until liquid is almost evaporated.
2. In a bowl, combine beef and remaining steak seasoning, mixing lightly but thoroughly. Shape into eight ½-in.-thick patties.
3. In a large nonstick skillet, cook burgers over medium heat 3-4 minutes on each side or until a thermometer reads 160°; top with cheese during the last 1-2 minutes of cooking. Serve on rolls; top with onion.
1 slider: 320 cal., 17g fat (8g sat. fat), 75mg chol., 499mg sod., 20g carb. (2g sugars, 2g fiber), 15g pro.

KOREAN WONTONS

Korean wontons (called mandoo) are not hot and spicy like many of the traditional Korean dishes. Filled with inexpensive vegetables and beef, the fried dumplings are very easy to prepare and so tasty!
—*Christy Lee, Horsham, PA*

- -

PREP: 35 min. • **COOK:** 5 min./batch
MAKES: 3 dozen

- 2 cups shredded cabbage
- 1 cup canned bean sprouts
- ½ cup shredded carrots
- 1½ tsp. plus 2 Tbsp. canola oil, divided
- ⅓ lb. ground beef
- ⅓ cup sliced green onions
- 1½ tsp. sesame seeds, toasted
- 1½ tsp. minced fresh gingerroot
- 3 garlic cloves, minced
- 1½ tsp. sesame oil
- ½ tsp. salt
- ½ tsp. pepper
- 36 wonton wrappers
- 1 large egg, lightly beaten
- 3 Tbsp. water

1. In a large cast-iron or other heavy skillet, stir-fry cabbage, bean sprouts and carrots in 1½ tsp. oil until tender; set aside.
2. In a small skillet, cook beef over medium heat until no longer pink, crumbling the meat; drain. Add to the vegetable mixture. Stir in the onions, sesame seeds, ginger, garlic, sesame oil, salt and pepper.
3. Place about 1 Tbsp. of filling in the center of each wonton wrapper. Combine egg and water. Moisten wonton edges with egg mixture; fold opposite corners over filling and press to seal.
4. Heat the remaining oil in a large cast-iron skillet. Cook wontons in batches until golden brown, 1-2 minutes on each side, adding more oil if needed.
1 wonton: 47 cal., 2g fat (0 sat. fat), 8mg chol., 86mg sod., 5g carb. (0 sugars, 0 fiber), 2g pro.

CHILI CUPS

Nothing tickles appetites quicker than these spicy bits. They're like eating chili in a muffin. I like to prepare and freeze them ahead of time for the Christmas season.
—*Diane Hixon, Niceville, FL*

PREP: 45 min. • **COOK:** 10 min./batch
MAKES: about 5 dozen

- 1 **lb. ground beef**
- 1 **medium green pepper, diced**
- 1 **medium onion, diced**
- 3 **garlic cloves, minced**
- 1 **can (8 oz.) tomato sauce**
- 2 **Tbsp. water**
- ½ **tsp. salt**
- ½ **to 1 tsp. ground cumin**
- ½ **tsp. dried oregano**
- ¼ **tsp. celery seed**
- ¼ **tsp. dill weed**
- ⅛ **to ¼ tsp. cayenne pepper**
- 2 **loaves (1 lb. each) sliced Italian bread**
  Grated Parmesan cheese

1. In a large skillet, cook beef, green pepper, onion and garlic over medium heat until meat is no longer pink; crumble meat; drain. Stir in the tomato sauce, water and seasonings. Bring to a boil over medium heat. Reduce heat; cover and simmer 30 minutes, stirring occasionally.
2. Meanwhile, cut circles from bread slices using a 2½-in. biscuit cutter. Press the circles into greased miniature muffin cups.
3. Bake at 400° for 5-6 minutes or until lightly toasted. Remove from tins and cool on wire racks. Fill each bread cup with about 1 Tbsp. chili mixture; sprinkle with Parmesan cheese. Broil for 2-3 minutes or until the cheese is golden brown.
1 appetizer: 57 cal., 1g fat (0 sat. fat), 5mg chol., 125mg sod., 8g carb. (1g sugars, 1g fiber), 3g pro.

> **TEST KITCHEN TIP**
> Add a savory layer of flavor to your beef dishes with a dash or two of ground cumin. Try it in chili, sloppy joes and tacos to start.

NO-GUILT BEEFY NACHOS

Nachos you can feel good about! This meaty topping has less fat and sodium than typical nacho beef because you use lean meat and make your own seasoning. The versatile dish is a tasty go-to for a party.
—*Carol Betz, Grand Rapids, MI*

PREP: 15 min. • **COOK:** 4 hours
MAKES: 20 servings (2½ qt.)

- 2 **lbs. lean ground beef (90% lean)**
- 1 **can Ranch Style beans (pinto beans in seasoned tomato sauce), undrained**
- 2 **Tbsp. chili powder**
- 1 **Tbsp. brown sugar**
- 2 **tsp. ground cumin**
- 2 **tsp. ground coriander**
- 1 **tsp. dried oregano**
- 1 **tsp. cayenne pepper**
- 1 **Tbsp. cider vinegar**
- ¾ **tsp. salt**
  Baked tortilla chips
  Optional: Shredded cheddar cheese, lettuce, sour cream and guacamole

Combine first 8 ingredients in a 4-qt. slow cooker. Cook, covered, on low until meat is crumbly, 4-6 hours. Stir in vinegar and salt. Serve with tortilla chips and, if desired, toppings.
Freeze option: Freeze cooled meat mixture in freezer containers. To use, partially thaw in refrigerator overnight. Heat through in a saucepan, stirring occasionally; add water if necessary. Serve with chips and toppings if desired.
½ cup: 99 cal., 4g fat (2g sat. fat), 28mg chol., 232mg sod., 5g carb. (1g sugars, 1g fiber), 10g pro.

TANGY MEATBALLS

A family favorite, these tender meatballs make a popular hors d'oeuvre at parties. The easy homemade barbecue sauce boasts terrific smoky-sweet flavor.
—*Jane Barta, St. Thomas, ND*

PREP: 20 min. • **BAKE:** 50 min.
MAKES: 4 dozen

- 2   large eggs
- 2   cups quick-cooking or rolled oats
- 1   can (12 oz.) evaporated milk
- 1   cup chopped onion
- 2   tsp. salt
- ½   tsp. pepper
- ½   tsp. garlic powder
- 3   lbs. lean ground beef (90% lean)

SAUCE
- 2   cups ketchup
- 1½   cups packed brown sugar
- ½   cup chopped onion
- 1   to 2 tsp. liquid smoke
- ½   tsp. garlic powder

1. In a large bowl, beat eggs. Add oats, milk, onion, salt, pepper and garlic powder. Add the ground beef; mix lightly but thoroughly. Shape into 1½-in. balls. Place meatballs on greased racks in shallow baking pans. Bake, uncovered, at 375° for 30 minutes; drain.
2. Place all of the meatballs in 1 of the pans. In a saucepan, bring all sauce ingredients to a boil. Pour over meatballs. Return to the oven and bake, uncovered, for 20 minutes or until meatballs are done.
4 meatballs: 423 cal., 12g fat (5g sat. fat), 100mg chol., 991mg sod., 51g carb. (35g sugars, 2g fiber), 27g pro.

READER REVIEW
"These are wonderful! If nothing else, make the sauce. It's delicious!"
MIKE FREEZN, TASTEOFHOME.COM

❄ 🍲
SLOW-COOKER PIZZA DIP

I created this dip for my daughter's pizza-themed birthday party. It was an instant hit and I've continued to bring this along to other gatherings. Everyone loves it!
—*Stephanie Gates, Waterloo, IA*

PREP: 15 min. • **COOK:** 2 hours
MAKES: 20 servings

- ½   lb. ground beef
- ½   lb. bulk pork sausage
- 1   can (28 oz.) crushed tomatoes
- ½   cup diced green pepper
- ¼   cup grated Parmesan cheese
- 2   Tbsp. tomato paste
- 2   tsp. Italian seasoning
- 1   garlic clove, minced
- ¾   tsp. crushed red pepper flakes
- ¼   tsp. salt
- ¼   tsp. pepper
       Hot garlic bread

1. In a large skillet, cook and crumble beef and sausage over medium heat until no longer pink, 5-7 minutes. Using a slotted spoon, transfer meat to a 3-qt. slow cooker. Stir in all remaining ingredients except garlic bread.
2. Cook, covered, on low 2-3 hours or until heated through. Serve with garlic bread.
Freeze option: Freeze cooled dip in freezer containers. To use the dip, partially thaw in refrigerator overnight. Heat through in a saucepan, stirring occasionally.
¼ cup dip: 68 cal., 4g fat (1g sat. fat), 14mg chol., 198mg sod., 4g carb. (2g sugars, 1g fiber), 4g pro.

POPPY SEED SQUARES

When I came across this unusual appetizer, I just knew I had to try it. Although I prepare these squares regularly, no one tires of them.
—*Jo Baden, Independence, KS*

PREP: 35 min. • **BAKE:** 25 min.
MAKES: about 8 dozen

- 1 lb. ground beef
- 1½ cups finely chopped fresh mushrooms
- 1 medium onion, finely chopped
- 1 can (10¾ oz.) condensed cream of celery or mushroom soup, undiluted
- 1 Tbsp. prepared horseradish
- 1 tsp. salt
- ½ tsp. pepper

CRUST
- 3 cups all-purpose flour
- 2 Tbsp. poppy seeds
- ¾ tsp. baking powder
- ¾ tsp. salt
- 1 cup shortening
- ½ cup cold water

1. In a large skillet, cook the beef, mushrooms and onion over medium heat until the meat is no longer pink; break into crumbles. Add the soup, horseradish, salt and pepper. Remove from the heat; set aside.

2. In a large bowl, combine the flour, poppy seeds, baking powder and salt. Cut in the shortening until the mixture resembles coarse crumbs. Gradually add water, tossing with a fork until a ball forms. Divide dough in half. Roll out 1 portion into a 15x10-in. rectangle; transfer the dough to an ungreased 15x10x1-in. baking pan.

3. Spoon the meat mixture over the crust. Roll out remaining dough into 15x10-in. rectangle; place over filling. Bake at 425° until golden brown, about 25 minutes. Cut into small squares.

1 piece: 43 cal., 3g fat (1g sat. fat), 3mg chol., 50mg sod., 3g carb. (0 sugars, 0 fiber), 1g pro.

POTLUCK ENCHILADA MEATBALLS

This is a twist on the ordinary potluck meatballs. It's easy, inexpensive and a hit at any occasion I serve them.
—*Terina Lewis, Decatur, IL*

- -

PREP: 1 hour + cooling • **COOK:** 3 hours
MAKES: 6 dozen

- 2 pkg. (8½ oz. each) cornbread/muffin mix
- 2 envelopes reduced-sodium taco seasoning, divided
- 2 large eggs, lightly beaten
- 3 cans (10 oz. each) enchilada sauce, divided
- 2 lbs. lean ground beef (90% lean)
- 1 jar (16 oz.) salsa
- 1 can (4 oz.) chopped green chiles
- 1 cup shredded Mexican cheese blend, divided

1. Preheat oven to 400°. Prepare and bake muffin mix according to package directions. Cool completely and crumble; transfer to a large bowl. Add 1 envelope taco seasoning, eggs, 1½ cups enchilada sauce and meat; mix lightly but thoroughly. Shape meat mixture into 1½-in. balls; bake on greased racks in 15x10x1-in. baking pans lined with foil until lightly browned, 10-12 minutes.
2. Place meatballs in a 5- or 6-qt. slow cooker. Combine remaining enchilada sauce, salsa, chiles, ½ cup cheese and remaining envelope taco seasoning; pour over meatballs. Sprinkle with remaining ½ cup cheese. Cook, covered, on low until the meatballs are cooked through, about 3 hours.

1 meatball: 68 cal., 3g fat (1g sat. fat), 20mg chol., 227mg sod., 7g carb. (2g sugars, 0 fiber), 4g pro.

> **TEST KITCHEN TIP**
> Slice up the leftover meatballs for change-of-pace nachos or use them for a zesty pizza topper.

CINDI DECLUE
Anchorage, AK

SLOW-COOKER CHEESEBURGER DIP

This fun dip recipe uses ingredients I always have in the fridge, so it's easy to throw together on short notice.
—*Cindi DeClue, Anchorage, AK*

- -

PREP: 25 min. • **COOK:** 1¾ hours
MAKES: 16 servings

- 1 lb. lean ground beef (90% lean)
- 1 medium onion, chopped
- 1 pkg. (8 oz.) cream cheese, cubed
- 2 cups shredded cheddar cheese, divided
- 1 Tbsp. Worcestershire sauce
- 2 tsp. prepared mustard
- ¼ tsp. salt
- ⅛ tsp. pepper
- 1 medium tomato, chopped
- ¼ cup chopped dill pickles
  Tortilla chips or crackers

1. In a large skillet, cook beef and onion over medium-high heat until beef is no longer pink, and onion is tender, 6-8 minutes; break up beef into crumbles; drain. Transfer to a greased 1½- or 3-qt. slow cooker. Stir in cream cheese, 1½ cups cheddar cheese, Worcestershire, mustard, salt and pepper. Sprinkle with the remaining ½ cup cheese.
2. Cook, covered, on low 1¾-2¼ hours or until mixture is heated through and the cheese is melted. Top with tomatoes and pickles. Serve with tortilla chips or crackers.

¼ cup: 157 cal., 12g fat (6g sat. fat), 46mg chol., 225mg sod., 2g carb. (1g sugars, 0 fiber), 10g pro.

HEARTY BROCCOLI DIP

You'll need just a few ingredients to stir up my no-fuss spring appetizer. People often ask me to bring the creamy dip to potlucks and parties. I never leave with leftovers.
—*Sue Call, Beech Grove, IN*

- -

PREP: 15 min. • **COOK:** 2 hours
MAKES: 5½ cups

1 lb. ground beef
1 lb. Velveeta, cubed
1 can (10¾ oz.) condensed cream of mushroom soup, undiluted
3 cups frozen chopped broccoli, thawed
2 Tbsp. salsa
   Tortilla chips

1. In a large skillet, cook beef over medium heat until no longer pink; drain. Transfer to a 3-qt. slow cooker. Add cheese, soup, broccoli and salsa; mix well.
2. Cover and cook on low for 2-3 hours or until heated through, stirring after 1 hour. Serve with chips.
2 Tbsp.: 61 cal., 4g fat (2g sat. fat), 17mg chol., 194mg sod., 2g carb. (1g sugars, 0 fiber), 4g pro.

TEST KITCHEN TIP
Double the amount of ground beef in this recipe, and use the cooked mixture as a filling for enchiladas.

FARMHOUSE BARBECUE MUFFINS

Tangy barbecue sauce, fluffy biscuits and cheddar cheese combine to make these hand-held delights. Try them with ground turkey or other shredded cheeses to vary the flavor if you'd like.
—*Karen Kenney, Harvard, IL*

- -

PREP: 20 min. • **BAKE:** 20 min.
MAKES: 10 servings

1 tube (12 oz.) refrigerated buttermilk biscuits
1 lb. ground beef
½ cup ketchup
3 Tbsp. brown sugar
1 Tbsp. cider vinegar
½ tsp. chili powder
1 cup shredded cheddar cheese

1. Separate dough into 10 biscuits; flatten into 5-in. circles. Press each onto the bottom and up the sides of a greased muffin cup; set aside.
2. In a skillet, cook beef over medium heat until no longer pink, 5-7 minutes; crumble meat; drain. In a small bowl, combine the ketchup, brown sugar, vinegar and chili powder; add to beef and mix well.
3. Divide the meat mixture among biscuit-lined muffin cups, using about ¼ cup for each. Sprinkle mixture with the cheese. Bake at 375° for 18-20 minutes or until golden brown. Cool for 5 minutes before serving.
1 muffin: 226 cal., 9 g fat (5 g sat. fat), 42 mg chol., 477 mg sod., 21 g carb., trace fiber, 14 g pro.

JALAPENO BEAN DIP

This is the snack my family often requests. We especially like to take this zippy dip on camping trips because it travels so well.
—*Lorene Goodwin, Belle Fourche, SD*

PREP: 15 min. • **COOK:** 30 min.
MAKES: 12 servings

- 2 lbs. ground beef
- 1 medium onion, chopped
- 1 garlic clove, minced
- 2 cans (8 oz. each) tomato sauce
- 1 can (16 oz.) chili beans, undrained
- 1 can (16 oz.) kidney beans, rinsed and drained
- 2 medium jalapeno peppers, seeded and chopped
- ½ tsp. salt
- ⅛ tsp. cayenne pepper
- 1 pkg. (9¼ oz.) corn chips
- 1 cup shredded cheddar cheese
- 1 cup sour cream

1. In a large skillet, cook beef and onion over medium heat until meat is no longer pink. Add garlic; cook 1 minute longer. Drain.
2. Stir in the tomato sauce, beans and jalapeno peppers. Bring to a boil. Add the salt and cayenne. Reduce heat; cover and simmer for 20 minutes.
3. To serve, spoon beef mixture over chips; sprinkle with cheese. Garnish with sour cream.
Note: Wear disposable gloves when cutting hot peppers; the oils can burn skin. Avoid touching your face.
1 serving: 407 cal., 22g fat (8g sat. fat), 60mg chol., 559mg sod., 29g carb. (3g sugars, 5g fiber), 23g pro.

❄ 🍲 HOISIN MEATBALLS

These meatballs are braised in hoisin sauce and cabernet sauvignon for a delicious, rich sauce. If you prefer not to use wine, simply substitute it with beef broth.
—*Lisa de Perio, Dallas, TX*

PREP: 15 min. • **COOK:** 2½ hours
MAKES: about 2 dozen

- 1 cup dry red wine or beef broth
- 3 Tbsp. hoisin sauce
- 2 Tbsp. soy sauce
- 1 large egg
- 4 green onions, chopped
- ¼ cup finely chopped onion
- ¼ cup minced fresh cilantro
- 2 garlic cloves, minced
- ½ tsp. salt
- ½ tsp. pepper
- 1 lb. ground beef
- 1 lb. ground pork
  Sesame seeds

1. Preheat broiler. In a 3-qt. slow cooker, whisk together wine, hoisin sauce and soy sauce. Cook mixture, covered, on high 30 minutes. Meanwhile, combine next 7 ingredients. Add the beef and pork; mix lightly but thoroughly. Shape into 1½-in. meatballs; place on a rack in a broiler pan. Broil 3-4 in. from heat until browned, 3-4 minutes.
2. Add meatballs to slow cooker. Cook, covered, on low, stirring halfway through, until meatballs are cooked through, 2-3 hours. Sprinkle with sesame seeds.
Freeze option: Freeze the cooled meatball mixture in freezer containers. To use, partially thaw in refrigerator overnight. Microwave, covered, on high until heated through, about 8 minutes, gently stirring halfway through.
1 meatball: 73 cal., 5g fat (2g sat. fat), 28mg chol., 156mg sod., 1g carb. (1g sugars, 0 fiber), 6g pro.

🍎 WONTON RAVIOLI

I created this recipe as a quick yet elegant meal. But it works well as an appetizer, too. You can substitute ingredients to your liking.
—*Jenny Johnson, White Bear Lake, MN*

PREP: 30 min. • **BAKE:** 10 min./batch
MAKES: 44 appetizers

- 1 lb. ground beef
- ⅓ cup chopped onion
- ½ tsp. minced garlic
- ½ tsp. dried oregano
- ½ tsp. dried basil
- 88 wonton wrappers
- 2¾ cups shredded part-skim mozzarella cheese
- 2 Tbsp. butter, melted
  Grated Parmesan cheese, optional
  Spaghetti sauce, warmed

1. In a large skillet, cook the beef, onion and garlic over medium heat until the meat is no longer pink, 5-7 minutes; crumble beef; drain. Stir in oregano and basil.

2. Preheat oven to 350°. Place 8 wonton wrappers on a greased baking sheet; top each with 1 Tbsp. meat mixture and 1 Tbsp. mozzarella cheese. Moisten edges with water; top with another wonton wrapper. Press edges with a fork to seal. Repeat with the remaining wrappers, meat mixture and cheese.

3. Brush the wontons with butter. Sprinkle with Parmesan cheese if desired. Bake until golden brown, 10-12 minutes. Serve with spaghetti sauce.

1 piece: 86 cal., 3g fat (1g sat. fat), 12mg chol., 135mg sod., 10g carb. (0 sugars, 0 fiber), 5g pro. **Diabetic exchanges:** ½ starch, ½ lean meat.

TEST KITCHEN TIP
Get creative with the filling in these savory appetizers. Replace the beef with ground pork or chicken or add a bit of grated Parmesan cheese.

PIZZA FONDUE

It's time to rethink the way your family does pizza night. I heard about this recipe on a talk show and then personalized it by using home-canned sauce.
—*Susan Carlson, Perry, NY*

TAKES: 25 min. • **MAKES:** 12 servings

- ½ lb. ground beef
- 1 medium onion, chopped
- 3 cans (8 oz. each) pizza sauce, divided
- 1½ tsp. fennel seed
- 1½ tsp. dried oregano
- ¼ tsp. garlic powder
- 1 Tbsp. cornstarch
- 1 cup shredded cheddar cheese
- 1 cup shredded part-skim mozzarella cheese
  Cubed French bread

1. In a large saucepan, cook beef and onion over medium heat until meat is no longer pink, 5-7 minutes; crumble meat; drain. Stir in 2 cans pizza sauce and seasonings. In a small bowl, combine cornstarch and remaining pizza sauce until blended; stir into beef mixture. Add the cheddar cheese, ½ cup at a time, stirring after each addition until the cheese is completely melted.

2. Transfer to a fondue pot. Stir in mozzarella cheese until melted. Serve with bread cubes.

1 serving: 134 cal., 7g fat (4g sat. fat), 25mg chol., 335mg sod., 7g carb. (3g sugars, 1g fiber), 9g pro.

Ground Beef

SOUPS, STEWS & CHILIS

From a pot of spicy chili to feed a game-day crowd to a bowl of warm and cheesy soup to share during a quiet weekend at home, ground beef is the hearty key element in every bowl in this chapter. Dig in!

BEEF TACO CHILI

This is one of my husband's absolute favorite dishes. It was also voted the Best Chili in our county's autumn Harvest Festival! If you like your chili with less broth, use just 1¾ cups water and 1½ tsp. bouillon.
—*Dana Beery, Ione, WA*

- -

PREP: 25 min. • **COOK:** 7 hours
MAKES: 6 servings (2¼ qt.)

- 1 lb. ground beef
- 1 medium onion, chopped
- 2½ cups water
- 2 cans (15 oz. each) pinto beans, rinsed and drained
- 1 can (14½ oz.) diced tomatoes, undrained
- 2 cans (8 oz. each) tomato sauce
- 2½ tsp. beef bouillon granules
- 2 garlic cloves, minced
- 1 envelope taco seasoning
- 2 Tbsp. chili powder
- 2 tsp. dried oregano
- 2 tsp. baking cocoa
- 1½ tsp. ground cumin
- 1 tsp. Louisiana-style hot sauce
- ½ tsp. pepper
  Optional: Sour cream, tortilla strips and sliced jalapenos

1. Cook the beef and onion in a large skillet over medium heat until meat is no longer pink, 5-7 minutes; crumble beef; drain. Transfer to a 4-qt. slow cooker. Stir in the remaining ingredients.
2. Cover and cook the chili on low for 7-9 hours or until heated through. Serve with optional toppings if desired.
1½ cups: 337 cal., 11g fat (3g sat. fat), 47mg chol., 1657mg sod., 39g carb. (7g sugars, 10g fiber), 23g pro.

BEEF & LENTIL CHILI

Lentils were one of the crops on my dad's farm when we were growing up, and they're the best-kept secret in this delicious chili recipe. This dish is great for a large family meal and also freezes well. Everyone who asks for this recipe is amazed at how simple it is.
—*Cindy Agee, Lewiston, ID*

- -

PREP: 10 min. • **COOK:** 1 hour
MAKES: 8 servings (2½ qt.)

- 2 lbs. ground beef
- 1 medium onion, chopped
- 1 garlic clove, minced
- 2 cans (14½ oz. each) stewed tomatoes, chopped
- 1 can (15 oz.) tomato sauce
- 3 Tbsp. chili powder
- 1 oz. semisweet chocolate
- ¼ tsp. salt
- 1 cup dried lentils, rinsed
- 2 cups water

In a Dutch oven, cook ground beef and onion over medium-high heat until the beef is no longer pink, 6-8 minutes; crumble meat. Add garlic; cook 1 minute longer. Drain. Add the next 5 ingredients; bring to a boil. Add lentils and water. Reduce heat; simmer, covered, until lentils are soft, about 1 hour, stirring often. Add water if mixture seems too dry.
1¼ cups: 367 cal., 16g fat (6g sat. fat), 70mg chol., 655mg sod., 29g carb. (8g sugars, 6g fiber), 29g pro.

DID YOU KNOW?
The chocolate here adds depth to the dominant tomatoes and chili powder—much like coffee adds depth to chocolate in baked goods. The chili will have a rich flavor, but you won't taste the chocolate itself.

CHEESEBURGER BROCCOLI CHOWDER

I invented this soup accidentally when I was new to cooking and didn't know that chowder was a kind of soup. So I made potatoes to go with my chowder and we ended up treating the soup as gravy and dunking the spuds into it. It may have been unusual, but it was delicious!
—*Karen Davies, Wanipigow, MB*

- -

PREP: 10 min. • **COOK:** 40 min.
MAKES: 4 servings

- ½ lb. ground beef
- ½ cup chopped onion
- ¼ cup chopped green pepper
- 1 can (10¾ oz.) condensed cheddar cheese soup, undiluted
- ¾ cup whole milk
- 1 tsp. Worcestershire sauce
- 1 cup chopped broccoli
- 1 to 2 potatoes, peeled and diced

In a large saucepan, cook beef with onion and green pepper until the meat is no longer pink, 5-7 minutes; crumble beef; drain. Stir in soup, milk and Worcestershire sauce. Add broccoli and potatoes. Bring to a boil, reduce heat and simmer, covered, until potatoes are tender, about 30 minutes.
1 cup: 243 cal., 11g fat (5g sat. fat), 42mg chol., 602mg sod., 22g carb. (7g sugars, 3g fiber), 14g pro.

CHRISTINA ADDISON
Blanchester, OH

GREEN CHILE STEW

Roasted Anaheim chiles add plenty of spark to this ground beef and pork stew. The savory blend of herbs provides even more flavor.
—*Mary Spill, Tierra Amarilla, NM*

- -

PREP: 10 min. • **COOK:** 50 min.
MAKES: 10 servings (3¾ qt.)

  1 lb. ground beef
  1 lb. ground pork
  8 to 10 Anaheim chiles, roasted, peeled and chopped or 3 cans (4 oz. each) chopped green chiles, drained
  4 medium potatoes, peeled and diced
  1 can (28 oz.) diced tomatoes, undrained
  2 cups water
  1 garlic clove, minced
  1 tsp. salt, optional
  ½ tsp. dried oregano
  ¼ tsp. pepper
  ¼ tsp. dried coriander

In a large stockpot or Dutch oven, brown beef and pork; drain. Add the remaining ingredients. Cover and simmer for 45 minutes.

Note: Wear disposable gloves when cutting hot peppers; the oils can burn skin. Avoid touching your face.

1½ cups: 276 cal., 12g fat (5g sat. fat), 58mg chol., 188mg sod., 22g carb. (4g sugars, 5g fiber), 20g pro.

BIG BATCH CHEESEBURGER SOUP

My mother-in-law gave me her recipe for cheeseburger soup and I changed it a bit to make it my own. It's the perfect comfort food to enjoy on a cold winter evening.
—*Christina Addison, Blanchester, OH*

- -

PREP: 20 min. • **COOK:** 7 hours
MAKES: 6 servings (2¼ qt.)

  1 lb. lean ground beef (90% lean)
  1 small onion, chopped
  1¾ lbs. potatoes (about 3-4 medium), peeled and cut into ½-in. pieces
  3 cups chicken broth
  1½ cups whole milk
  2 medium carrots, shredded
  1 celery rib, finely chopped
  1 Tbsp. dried parsley flakes
  ½ tsp. salt
  ½ tsp. dried basil
  ¼ tsp. pepper
  1 pkg. (8 oz.) Velveeta, cubed
  ¼ cup sour cream
     Chopped fresh parsley, optional

1. In a large skillet, cook beef and onion over medium heat until the meat is no longer pink, 6-8 minutes; crumble beef; drain. Transfer to a 4- or 5-qt. slow cooker. Add potatoes, broth, milk, carrots, celery and seasonings. Cook, covered, on low until vegetables are tender, 7-9 hours.
2. Stir in cheese until melted. Stir in sour cream. If desired, sprinkle with parsley.

1½ cups: 300 cal., 15g fat (8g sat. fat), 75mg chol., 949mg sod., 21g carb. (7g sugars, 2g fiber), 19g pro.

CHILI FOR A CROWD

My aunt gave me the basis for this recipe, which combines ground beef with kielbasa. It's a crowd-pleasing chili for a Super Bowl party or any other special event.
—*Lisa Humphreys, Wasilla, AK*

PREP: 25 min. • **COOK:** 1 hour
MAKES: 24 servings (6 qt.)

- 3 lbs. ground beef
- 2 cans (28 oz. each) diced tomatoes, undrained
- 4 cans (16 oz. each) kidney beans or 4 cans (15 oz. each) pinto beans or black beans, rinsed and drained
- 1 lb. smoked kielbasa, sliced and halved
- 2 large onions, halved and thinly sliced
- 2 cans (8 oz. each) tomato sauce
- ⅔ cup hickory-flavored barbecue sauce
- 1½ cups water
- ½ cup packed brown sugar
- 5 fresh banana peppers, seeded and sliced
- 2 Tbsp. chili powder
- 2 tsp. ground mustard
- 2 tsp. instant coffee granules
- 1 tsp. each dried oregano, thyme and sage
- ½ to 1 tsp. cayenne pepper
- ½ to 1 tsp. crushed red pepper flakes
- 2 garlic cloves, minced

In an 8-qt. stockpot or Dutch oven, cook the beef over medium heat until no longer pink; 5-7 minutes; crumble beef; drain. Stir in the remaining ingredients; bring to a boil. Reduce heat; cover and simmer for 1 hour, stirring occasionally.

1 cup: 207 cal., 11g fat (4g sat. fat), 40mg chol., 422mg sod., 13g carb. (8g sugars, 3g fiber), 15g pro.

READER REVIEW

"I've been trying so many chili recipes to find one that we love. This one finally did it. I halved the recipe and it's perfect for two full meals for two men. Serve with garlic toast. It's awesome."

DEVAN, TASTEOFHOME.COM

ABC SOUP

Instead of opening a can of alphabet soup, why not make some from scratch? Kids of all ages love this traditional soup with a tomato base, ground beef and alphabet pasta.
—*Sharon Brockman, Appleton, WI*

TAKES: 30 min.
MAKES: 11 servings (2¾ qt.)

- 1 lb. ground beef
- 1 medium onion, chopped
- 2 qt. tomato juice
- 1 can (15 oz.) mixed vegetables, undrained
- 1 cup water
- 2 beef bouillon cubes
- 1 cup uncooked alphabet pasta
     Salt and pepper to taste

In a large saucepan, cook beef and onion over medium heat until the meat is no longer pink, 5-7 minutes; crumble beef; drain. Add tomato juice, vegetables, water and bouillon; bring to a boil. Add pasta. Cook, uncovered, until pasta is tender, 6-8 minutes, stirring frequently. Add salt and pepper.

1 cup: 148 cal., 4g fat (2g sat. fat), 19mg chol., 858mg sod., 19g carb. (7g sugars, 2g fiber), 10g pro.

BEEFY BACON CHOWDER

Rave reviews are sure to follow when this creamy chowder appears on the table. The bacon makes it rich and hearty. It's a favorite with my whole family.
—*Nancy Schmidt, Center, CO*

TAKES: 30 min. • **MAKES:** 12 servings (3 qt.)

- 1 lb. ground beef
- 2 cups chopped celery
- ½ cup chopped onion
- 4 cups whole milk
- 3 cups cubed peeled potatoes, cooked
- 2 cans (10¾ oz. each) condensed cream of mushroom soup, undiluted
- 2 cups chopped carrots, cooked
     Salt and pepper to taste
- 12 bacon strips, cooked and crumbled

In a Dutch oven, cook the beef, celery and onion over medium heat until the meat is no longer pink; 5-7 minutes; crumble meat; drain. Add the milk, potatoes, soup, carrots, salt and pepper; heat through. Stir in the bacon just before serving.

1 cup: 214 cal., 11g fat (5g sat. fat), 36mg chol., 371mg sod., 17g carb. (6g sugars, 2g fiber), 13g pro.

GROUND BEEF CHILI

Everyone who tastes my chili comments that it is restaurant quality. It's especially good with homemade cornbread. I've always loved to cook, and I enjoy sharing my original recipes.
—*Shannon Wright, Erie, PA*

- -

PREP: 10 min. • **COOK:** 40 min.
MAKES: 16 servings (4 qt.)

- 3   lbs. ground beef
- 1   large onion, chopped
- 1   medium green pepper, chopped
- 2   celery ribs, chopped
- 2   cans (16 oz. each) kidney beans, rinsed and drained
- 1   can (29 oz.) tomato puree
- 1   jar (16 oz.) salsa
- 1   can (10½ oz.) condensed beef broth, undiluted
- 1   can (14½ oz.) diced tomatoes, undrained
- ¼ cup chili powder
- 2   Tbsp. Worcestershire sauce
- 1   to 2 cups water
- 1   Tbsp. dried basil
- 2   tsp. ground cumin
- 2   tsp. steak sauce
- 1   tsp. garlic powder
- 1   tsp. salt
- 1   tsp. coarsely ground pepper
- 1½ tsp. browning sauce, optional
     Optional: Additional chopped onion and shredded cheese

1. In a stockpot, cook the beef, onion, green pepper and celery over medium heat until meat is no longer pink and vegetables are tender; crumble the beef; drain.
2. Stir in beans, tomato puree, salsa, broth, tomatoes, chili powder, Worcestershire sauce, water, seasonings and, if desired, browning sauce. Bring to a boil. Reduce heat; simmer, uncovered, for 30 minutes or until the chili reaches the desired thickness.
3. If desired, garnish individual servings with chopped onion and shredded cheese.
1 cup: 242 cal., 11g fat (4g sat. fat), 57mg chol., 611mg sod., 13g carb. (4g sugars, 4g fiber), 21g pro.

CHICKEN ESCAROLE SOUP WITH MEATBALLS

This is an old recipe from southern Italy. My mother gave it to me when I was first married. It started out as a holidays-only dish...but my children and grandchildren love it so much that we have it every chance we get!
—*Norma Manna, Hobe Sound, FL*

- -

PREP: 20 min. • **COOK:** 1 hour 30 min.
MAKES: 24 servings (6 qt.)

- 15   chicken wings
- 4   medium carrots, cut into ½-in. pieces
- 1   large potato, cut into ½-in. cubes
- 4   celery ribs, sliced
- 1   large tomato, seeded and diced
- 1   large onion, diced
- 3½ tsp. salt, divided
- 1   tsp. pepper
- 4   qt. water
- 1   large egg, lightly beaten
- ½   cup dry bread crumbs
- 1   Tbsp. minced fresh parsley
- 1   garlic clove, minced
- 1   tsp. grated Parmesan cheese
- ½   lb. ground beef
- 1   small head (about 5 to 6 oz.) escarole, cored and separated

1. In a stockpot, combine wings, carrots, potato, celery, tomato, onion, 1 Tbsp. salt, pepper and water. Bring to a boil. Reduce heat; cover and simmer for 1 hour or until chicken and vegetables are tender.
2. Meanwhile, for the meatballs, combine egg, bread crumbs, parsley, garlic, cheese and the remaining ½ tsp. salt in a large bowl. Crumble the beef into the mixture and mix lightly but thoroughly. Shape into marble-sized balls.
3. Remove chicken meat from bones and cut into bite-sized pieces. Discard bones. Return chicken to the pot. Add meatballs and escarole; cook until meatballs are no longer pink, about 10 minutes longer.
1 cup: 115 cal., 6g fat (2g sat. fat), 33mg chol., 402mg sod., 7g carb. (2g sugars, 1g fiber), 9g pro.

HEARTY PASTA FAGIOLI

Here's a convenient spin on a classic Italian favorite. Spaghetti sauce and canned broth form the flavorful base.
—*Cindy Garland, Limestone, TN*

- -

PREP: 40 min. • **COOK:** 40 min.
MAKES: 24 servings (7½ qt.)

- 2 lbs. ground beef
- 6 cans (14½ oz. each) beef broth
- 2 cans (28 oz. each) diced tomatoes, undrained
- 2 jars (26 oz. each) spaghetti sauce
- 3 large onions, chopped
- 8 celery ribs, diced
- 3 medium carrots, sliced
- 1 can (16 oz.) kidney beans, rinsed and drained
- 1 can (15 oz.) cannellini beans, rinsed and drained
- 3 tsp. minced fresh oregano or 1 tsp. dried oregano
- 2½ tsp. pepper
- 1½ tsp. hot pepper sauce
- 8 oz. uncooked medium pasta shells
- 5 tsp. minced fresh parsley

1. In a large stockpot, cook beef over medium heat until no longer pink; 5-7 minutes; crumble beef; drain. Add broth, tomatoes, spaghetti sauce, onions, celery, carrots, beans, oregano, pepper and pepper sauce. Bring to a boil. Reduce heat; simmer, covered, 30 minutes.
2. Add pasta and parsley; simmer, covered, until pasta is tender, 10-14 minutes.
1¼ cups: 212 cal., 6g fat (2g sat. fat), 20mg chol., 958mg sod., 25g carb. (8g sugars, 5g fiber), 14g pro.

BACON CHEESEBURGER SOUP

This creamy recipe brings two of my absolute favorite foods together in one! The tomato, lettuce and crisp bacon toppings make this soup taste just like a burger!
—*Geoff Bales, Hemet, CA*

- -

PREP: 20 min. • **COOK:** 4 hours
MAKES: 6 servings (1½ qt.)

- 1½ lbs. lean ground beef (90% lean)
- 1 large onion, chopped
- ⅓ cup all-purpose flour
- ½ tsp. pepper
- 2½ cups chicken broth
- 1 can (12 oz.) evaporated milk
- 1½ cups shredded cheddar cheese
- 8 slices American cheese, chopped
- 1½ cups shredded lettuce
- 2 medium tomatoes, chopped
- 6 bacon strips, cooked and crumbled

1. In a large skillet, cook beef and onion over medium-high heat until no longer pink, 6-8 minutes; crumble beef; drain. Stir in flour and pepper; transfer to a 5-qt. slow cooker.
2. Stir in broth and milk. Cook, covered, on low for 4-5 hours or until flavors are blended. Stir in cheeses until melted. Top servings with remaining ingredients.
1 cup: 557 cal., 32g fat (17g sat. fat), 135mg chol., 1160mg sod., 18g carb. (10g sugars, 1g fiber), 42g pro.

SPICY TOUCHDOWN CHILI

Football, cool weather and chili just seem to go together. Whether I'm cheering on the local team on a Friday night or enjoying a Saturday afternoon of Oklahoma Sooner football with some friends, I enjoy serving this chili on game day.

—Chris Neal, Quapaw, OK

PREP: 30 min. • **COOK:** 4 hours
MAKES: 12 servings (3 qt.)

- 1   lb. ground beef
- 1   lb. bulk pork sausage
- 2   cans (16 oz. each) kidney beans, rinsed and drained
- 2   cans (15 oz. each) pinto beans, rinsed and drained
- 2   cans (14½ oz. each) diced tomatoes with mild green chiles, undrained
- 1   can (14½ oz.) diced tomatoes with onions, undrained
- 1   can (12 oz.) beer
- 6   bacon strips, cooked and crumbled
- 1   small onion, chopped
- ¼   cup chili powder
- ¼   cup chopped pickled jalapeno slices
- 2   tsp. ground cumin
- 2   garlic cloves, minced
- 1   tsp. dried basil
- ¾   tsp. cayenne pepper
    Optional: Shredded cheddar cheese, sour cream and chopped green onions

1. In a large skillet, cook beef over medium heat until no longer pink, 6-8 minutes; crumble meat; drain. Transfer to a 6-qt. slow cooker. Repeat with sausage.
2. Stir in the next 13 ingredients. Cook, covered, on low 4-5 hours or until heated through. If desired, top individual servings with shredded cheddar cheese, sour cream and chopped green onions.

1 cup: 365 cal., 15g fat (5g sat. fat), 48mg chol., 901mg sod., 34g carb. (7g sugars, 9g fiber), 22g pro.

READER REVIEW

"Dude! I will be making this chili for the rest of my natural life."

GREENRAINDROP, TASTEOFHOME.COM

CHEESY MEATBALL SOUP

With meat, potatoes and other vegetables, this rich-tasting soup is a meal in itself. The cheese sauce makes it taste just like a cheeseburger. I serve this soup with a nice crusty loaf of French bread.

—Ione Sander, Carlton, MN

PREP: 15 min. • **COOK:** 45 min.
MAKES: 6 servings (2 qt.)

- 1   large egg
- ¼   cup dry bread crumbs
- ½   tsp. salt
- 1   lb. ground beef
- 2   cups water
- 1   cup diced celery
- 1   cup whole kernel corn, drained
- 1   cup cubed peeled potatoes
- ½   cup sliced carrot
- ½   cup chopped onion
- 2   beef bouillon cubes
- ½   tsp. hot pepper sauce
- 1   jar (16 oz.) cheese dip

1. In a large bowl, combine egg, bread crumbs and salt. Crumble the beef over the mixture and mix lightly but thoroughly. Shape into 1-in. balls.
2. In a large saucepan, brown meatballs; drain. Add the water, celery, corn, potatoes, carrot, onion, bouillon and hot pepper sauce; bring to a boil.
3. Reduce heat; cover and simmer until the meat is no longer pink and the potatoes are tender, about 25 minutes. Stir in the cheese dip; heat through.

1⅓ cups: 421 cal., 24g fat (15g sat. fat), 118mg chol., 1959mg sod., 23g carb. (6g sugars, 2g fiber), 26g pro.

EASY CARROT-BEEF SOUP

My husband's grandmother passed this recipe along to us, and it's just wonderful—especially with a basket of warm bread on the side. This soup also freezes well.

—*Wendy Wilkins, Prattville, AL*

- -

PREP: 20 min. • **COOK:** 1 hour
MAKES: 10 servings (2½ qt.)

1	lb. ground beef, browned and drained
½	cup chopped celery
½	cup chopped onion
1	cup chopped green pepper
2½	cups grated carrots
1	can (32 oz.) tomato juice
2	cans (10¾ oz. each) condensed cream of celery soup, undiluted
1½	cups water
½	tsp. garlic salt
½	tsp. dried marjoram
1	tsp. sugar
½	tsp. salt
	Shredded Monterey Jack cheese

In a Dutch oven, combine all the ingredients except the cheese. Bring to a boil; reduce heat and simmer, uncovered, 1 hour or until the vegetables are tender. Sprinkle each serving with cheese.

1 cup: 130 cal., 5g fat (2g sat. fat), 23mg chol., 803mg sod., 11g carb. (6g sugars, 2g fiber), 10g pro.

❄️
MEATBALL SOUP

This soup is just like a meal in a bowl...or for heartier appetites, serve it with a sandwich. It's great for chilly days.

—*Sue Miller, Walworth, WI*

- -

PREP: 15 min. • **COOK:** 35 min.
MAKES: 5 servings

1	large egg, lightly beaten
¼	cup dry bread crumbs
¼	cup minced fresh parsley
2	Tbsp. grated Parmesan cheese
¼	tsp. garlic salt, optional
⅛	tsp. pepper
½	lb. lean ground beef (90% lean)
4	cups reduced-sodium beef broth
1	can (16 oz.) kidney beans, rinsed and drained
1	can (14½ oz.) stewed tomatoes
1	medium carrot, thinly sliced
1	tsp. Italian seasoning
¼	cup uncooked tiny shell pasta
	Minced fresh parsley, optional

1. Combine the first 6 ingredients. Crumble beef over the mixture and mix lightly but thoroughly. Shape into 1-in. balls. Brown meatballs in a large saucepan; drain. Add broth, beans, tomatoes, carrot and Italian seasoning. Bring to a boil. Reduce heat; cover and simmer for 10 minutes.

2. Add pasta; simmer until meat is no longer pink and pasta is tender, 10 minutes longer. If desired, top with minced fresh parsley and additional grated Parmesan cheese.

Freeze option: Divide cooled soup into individual portions; freeze up to 3 months.

1½ cups: 248 cal., 5g fat (2g sat. fat), 70mg chol., 778mg sod., 30g carb. (8g sugars, 6g fiber), 20g pro.

EASY CHILI

This quick and delicious recipe is handy when you want a fast and filling meal. It's a go-to for busy weeknights.

—Betty-Jean Molyneaux, Geneva, OH

- -

PREP: 5 min. • **COOK:** 40 min.
MAKES: 6 servings (2 qt.)

- 1 lb. ground beef
- 1 large onion, chopped
- 2 cans (16 oz. each) kidney beans, rinsed and drained
- 2 cans (14½ oz. each) diced tomatoes, undrained
- 1 celery rib, diced
- 1 tsp. salt
- 1 tsp. pepper
- ½ tsp. chili powder
- ¼ to ½ tsp. crushed red pepper flakes
  Optional: Shredded cheddar cheese, sour cream and green onions

In a large saucepan, cook beef and onion over medium heat until meat is no longer pink; 5-7 minutes; crumble beef; drain. Stir in the kidney beans, tomatoes, celery, salt, pepper, chili powder and red pepper flakes. Bring to a boil. Reduce heat; cover and simmer until flavors are blended, about 30 minutes. Top individual servings with shredded cheese, sour cream, and green onions if desired.

1⅓ cups: 308 cal., 9g fat (3g sat. fat), 47mg chol., 908mg sod., 33g carb. (8g sugars, 10g fiber), 24g pro.

SLOW-COOKER QUINOA CHILI

This is the recipe that turned my husband into a quinoa lover. I made it the day he got good news about a new job, and we'll always remember how excited we were as we ate this beautiful meal.
—*Claire Gallam, Alexandria, VA*

- -

PREP: 25 min. • **COOK:** 4 hours
MAKES: 10 servings (3¾ qt.)

- 1 lb. lean ground beef (90% lean)
- 1 medium onion, chopped
- 2 garlic cloves, minced
- 1 can (28 oz.) diced tomatoes with mild green chiles, undrained
- 1 can (14 oz.) fire-roasted diced tomatoes, undrained
- 1 can (15 oz.) garbanzo beans or chickpeas, rinsed and drained
- 1 can (15 oz.) black beans, rinsed and drained
- 2 cups reduced-sodium beef broth
- 1 cup quinoa, rinsed
- 2 tsp. onion soup mix
- 1 to 2 tsp. crushed red pepper flakes
- 1 tsp. garlic powder
- ¼ to ½ tsp. cayenne pepper
- ¼ tsp. salt
     Optional: Shredded cheddar cheese, chopped avocado, chopped red onion, sliced jalapeno, sour cream and cilantro

1. In a large skillet, cook beef, onion and garlic over medium-high heat 6-8 minutes or until meat is no longer pink; crumble meat; drain.
2. Transfer mixture to a 5- or 6-qt. slow cooker. Add the next 11 ingredients; stir to combine. Cook, covered, on low 4-5 hours, until the quinoa is tender. Serve with optional toppings as desired.
1½ cups: 318 cal., 7g fat (2g sat. fat), 37mg chol., 805mg sod., 41g carb. (7g sugars, 8g fiber), 21g pro. **Diabetic exchanges:** 2½ starch, 2 lean meat.

DID YOU KNOW?
The ancient Incas called quinoa "the mother grain," as it was a staple in their diet. Quinoa contains more protein than any other grain.

ITALIAN BEEF VEGETABLE SOUP

This hearty beef vegetable soup features a ton of fresh vegetables, making it the perfect dish to use up all that summer produce. It's also great during cooler weather! Make sure you serve this Italian soup with some breadsticks, rolls or flaky biscuits.
—*Courtney Stultz, Weir, KS*

- -

PREP: 20 min. • **COOK:** 5 hours
MAKES: 6 servings (1½ qt.)

- ½ lb. lean ground beef (90% lean)
- ¼ cup chopped onion
- 2 cups chopped cabbage
- 2 medium carrots, chopped
- 1 cup fresh Brussels sprouts, quartered
- 1 cup chopped fresh kale
- 1 celery rib, chopped
- 1 Tbsp. minced fresh parsley
- ½ tsp. pepper
- ½ tsp. dried basil
- ¼ tsp. salt
- 3 cups beef stock
- 1 can (14½ oz.) Italian diced tomatoes, undrained

1. In a large skillet, cook beef and onion over medium-high heat, until meat is browned, 4-5 minutes; crumble the meat. Transfer the mixture to a 3- or 4-qt. slow cooker.
2. Stir in remaining ingredients. Cook, covered, on low 5-6 hours or until carrots are tender.
Freeze option: Freeze cooled soup in freezer containers. To use, partially thaw in refrigerator overnight. Heat through in a saucepan, stirring occasionally.
1 cup: 127 cal., 3g fat (1g sat. fat), 24mg chol., 617mg sod., 14g carb. (9g sugars, 3g fiber), 11g pro. **Diabetic exchanges:** 1 starch, 1 lean meat.

ITALIAN WEDDING SOUP

Even in our hot Florida weather, this soup always satisfies! I add the cooked pasta at the end of the simmering time to keep it from getting mushy.
—Nancy Ducharme, Deltona, FL

- -

PREP: 20 min. • **COOK:** 15 min.
MAKES: 12 servings (3 qt.)

- 1   large egg, beaten
- ¾   cup grated Parmesan cheese
- ½   cup dry bread crumbs
- 1   small onion, chopped
- ¾   tsp. salt, divided
- 1¼ tsp. pepper, divided
- 1¼ tsp. garlic powder, divided
- 2   lbs. ground beef
- 2   qt. chicken broth
- ⅓   cup chopped fresh spinach
- 1   tsp. onion powder
- 1   tsp. dried parsley flakes
- 1¼ cups cooked medium pasta shells

1. In a large bowl, combine the egg, cheese, bread crumbs, onion, ¼ tsp. salt, ¼ tsp. pepper and ¼ tsp. garlic powder. Crumble beef over mixture and mix lightly but thoroughly. Shape into 1-in. balls.
2. In a Dutch oven, brown meatballs in small batches; drain. Add the broth, spinach, onion powder, parsley and remaining ½ tsp. salt, 1 tsp. pepper and 1 tsp. garlic powder; bring to a boil. Reduce heat; simmer, uncovered, for 5 minutes. Stir in pasta; heat through.
1 cup: 226 cal., 12g fat (5g sat. fat), 72mg chol., 942mg sod., 9g carb. (2g sugars, 0 fiber), 20g pro.

SWEDISH MEATBALL SOUP

To me, this is a very comforting, filling, homey soup. I especially like cooking it during the winter months and serving it with hot rolls, bread or muffins.
—Deborah Taylor, Inkom, ID

- -

PREP: 25 min. • **COOK:** 30 min.
MAKES: 8 servings (2 qt.)

- 1   large egg
- 2   cups half-and-half cream, divided
- 1   cup soft bread crumbs
- 1   small onion, finely chopped
- 1¾ tsp. salt, divided
- 1½ lbs. ground beef
- 1   Tbsp. butter
- 3   Tbsp. all-purpose flour
- ¾   tsp. beef bouillon granules
- ½   tsp. pepper
- ⅛   to ¼ tsp. garlic salt
- 3   cups water
- 1   lb. red potatoes, cubed
- 1   pkg. (10 oz.) frozen peas, thawed

1. In a large bowl, beat egg; add ⅓ cup cream, the bread crumbs, onion and 1 tsp. salt. Crumble beef over the mixture and mix lightly but thoroughly. Shape into ½-in. balls.
2. In a Dutch oven, brown meatballs in butter in batches. Remove from the pan; set aside. Drain fat.
3. Add flour, bouillon, pepper, garlic salt and remaining ¾ tsp. salt to pan; stir until smooth. Gradually stir in water; bring to a boil. Reduce heat; cook and stir for 2 minutes or until thickened. Add potatoes and meatballs.
4. Reduce heat; cover and simmer 25 minutes or until potatoes are tender. Stir in peas and the remaining 1⅔ cups cream; heat through.
Note: To make soft bread crumbs, tear bread into pieces and place in a food processor or blender. Cover and pulse until crumbs form. A slice of bread yields ½-¾ cup crumbs.
1 cup: 366 cal., 19g fat (9g sat. fat), 117mg chol., 785mg sod., 22g carb. (5g sugars, 3g fiber), 23g pro. fiber), 15g pro. **Diabetic exchanges:** 2 vegetable, 2 lean meat, 1½ starch.

ONE-POT SPINACH BEEF SOUP

My idea of a winning weeknight meal is this beefy soup simmering in one big pot. Grate some Parmesan and pass the saltines!
—*Julie Davis, Jacksonville, FL*

TAKES: 30 min.
MAKES: 8 servings (about 2½ qt.)

- 1 lb. ground beef
- 3 garlic cloves, minced
- 2 cartons (32 oz. each) reduced-sodium beef broth
- 2 cans (14½ oz. each) diced tomatoes with green pepper, celery and onion, undrained
- 1 tsp. dried basil
- ½ tsp. pepper
- ½ tsp. dried oregano
- ¼ tsp. salt
- 3 cups uncooked bow tie pasta
- 4 cups fresh spinach, coarsely chopped
   Grated Parmesan cheese

1. In a 6-qt. stockpot, cook beef and garlic over medium heat until the beef is no longer pink, 6-8 minutes; crumble beef; drain. Stir in broth, tomatoes and seasonings; bring to a boil. Stir in pasta; return to a boil. Cook, uncovered, until the pasta is tender, 7-9 minutes.
2. Stir in spinach until wilted. Sprinkle servings with cheese.
1⅓ cups: 258 cal., 7g fat (3g sat. fat), 40mg chol., 909mg sod., 30g carb. (8g sugars, 3g fiber), 17g pro.

BEEF NOODLE SOUP

This soup takes just minutes to make—but tastes like it simmered all day
—*Margery Bryan, Moses Lake, WA*

TAKES: 25 min. • **MAKES:** 8 servings (2 qt.)

- 1 lb. ground beef
- ½ cup chopped onion
- 2 cans (14½ oz. each) Italian stewed tomatoes
- 2 cans (10½ oz. each) beef broth
- 2 cups frozen mixed vegetables or 1 can (15 oz.) mixed vegetables
- 1 tsp. salt
- ¼ tsp. pepper
- 1 cup uncooked medium egg noodles

1. In a Dutch oven, cook beef and onion over medium heat until meat is no longer pink, 5-7 minutes; crumble beef; drain.
2. Add the tomatoes, broth, vegetables and seasonings. Bring to a boil; add noodles. Reduce heat to medium-low; cover and cook until noodles are tender, 10-15 minutes.
1 cup: 144 cal., 5g fat (2g sat. fat), 32mg chol., 804mg sod., 11g carb. (5g sugars, 2g fiber), 12g pro.

ITALIAN VEGGIE BEEF SOUP

My sweet father-in-law, Pop Pop, would bring this chunky soup to our house when we were under the weather. We like it so well, we take it to our own friends who need comfort. It always does the trick.

—*Sue Webb, Reisterstown, MD*

- -

TAKES: 30 min. • **MAKES:** 12 servings (4 qt.)

1½ lbs. lean ground beef (90% lean)
2 medium onions, chopped
4 cups chopped cabbage
1 pkg. (16 oz.) frozen mixed vegetables
1 can (28 oz.) crushed tomatoes
1 bay leaf
3 tsp. Italian seasoning
1 tsp. salt
½ tsp. pepper
2 cartons (32 oz. each) reduced-sodium beef broth

1. In a 6-qt. stockpot, cook ground beef and onions over medium-high heat until beef is no longer pink, breaking up beef into crumbles, 6-8 minutes; drain.
2. Add cabbage, mixed vegetables, tomatoes, seasonings and broth; bring to a boil. Reduce heat; simmer, uncovered, until cabbage is crisp-tender, 10-15 minutes. Remove bay leaf.
Freeze option: Freeze cooled soup in freezer containers. To use, partially thaw in refrigerator overnight. Heat through in a saucepan, stirring occasionally; add a little broth if necessary.
1⅓ cups: 159 cal., 5g fat (2g sat. fat), 38mg chol., 646mg sod., 14g carb. (6g sugars, 4g fiber), 15g pro. **Diabetic exchanges:** 2 lean meat, 1 vegetable, ½ starch.

ONE-POT BEEF & PEPPER STEW

I love most things made with green peppers, tomatoes or green chiles. One evening, I wanted to prepare a quick and satisfying dish and came up with this recipe with things I had on hand.
—*Sandra Clark, Sierra Vista, AZ*

- -

PREP: 10 min. • **COOK:** 30 min.
MAKES: 8 servings (3 qt.)

- 1 lb. lean ground beef (90% lean)
- 3 cans (14½ oz. each) diced tomatoes, undrained
- 4 large green peppers, coarsely chopped
- 1 large onion, chopped
- 2 cans (4 oz. each) chopped green chiles
- 3 tsp. garlic powder
- 1 tsp. pepper
- ¼ tsp. salt
- 2 cups uncooked instant rice
   Hot pepper sauce, optional

1. In a 6-qt. stockpot, cook beef over medium heat until no longer pink, 6-8 minutes; crumble beef; drain.

2. Add the tomatoes, green peppers, onion, chiles and seasonings; bring to a boil. Reduce heat; simmer, covered, 20-25 minutes or until the vegetables are tender.

3. Prepare rice according to the package directions. Serve with stew. If desired, add hot pepper sauce.

1½ cups: 244 cal., 5g fat (2g sat. fat), 35mg chol., 467mg sod., 35g carb. (8g sugars, 5g fiber), 15g pro. **Diabetic exchanges:** 2 vegetable, 2 lean meat, 1½ starch.

MEATY MUSHROOM CHILI

Because our two daughters did not like beans in their chili, I adapted a recipe to suit our whole family's tastes. We all agreed that mushrooms are an appealing alternative.
—*Marjol Burr, Catawba, OH*

- -

PREP: 15 min. • **COOK:** 70 min.
MAKES: 8 servings (2 qt.)

- 1 lb. bulk Italian sausage
- 1 lb. ground beef
- 1 cup chopped onion
- 1 lb. fresh mushrooms, sliced
- 1 can (46 oz.) V8 juice
- 1 can (6 oz.) tomato paste
- 1 tsp. sugar
- 1 tsp. Worcestershire sauce
- 1 tsp. salt
- 1 tsp. garlic powder
- 1 tsp. dried oregano
- ½ tsp. dried basil
- ½ tsp. pepper
   Optional: Sour cream and thinly sliced green onions

1. In a Dutch oven, cook the sausage, beef and onion over medium heat until the meat is no longer pink; crumble beef; drain.

2. Stir in mushrooms, V8 juice, tomato paste, sugar, Worcestershire sauce and seasonings. Bring to a boil.

3. Reduce the heat; cover and simmer for 1 hour. If desired, top with sour cream and green onions.

1 cup: 364 cal., 23g fat (9g sat. fat), 71mg chol., 1189mg sod., 17g carb. (11g sugars, 3g fiber), 21g pro.

RAVIOLI SOUP

We adore pasta, so I used it as the inspiration for this soup. The meaty tomato base pairs perfectly with the cheesy ravioli pillows.
—*Shelley Way, Cheyenne, WY*

PREP: 20 min. • **COOK:** 45 min.
MAKES: 10 servings (2½ qt.)

- 1 lb. ground beef
- 2 cups water
- 2 cans (one 28 oz., one 14½ oz.) crushed tomatoes
- 1 can (6 oz.) tomato paste
- 1½ cups chopped onions
- ¼ cup minced fresh parsley
- 2 garlic cloves, minced
- ¾ tsp. dried basil
- ½ tsp. sugar
- ½ tsp. dried oregano
- ½ tsp. onion salt
- ½ tsp. salt
- ¼ tsp. pepper
- ¼ tsp. dried thyme
- 1 pkg. (9 oz.) refrigerated cheese ravioli
- ¼ cup grated Parmesan cheese
  Additional minced fresh parsley, optional

1. In a Dutch oven, cook beef over medium heat until no longer pink, 5-7 minutes; crumble meat; drain. Add the water, tomatoes, tomato paste, onions, parsley, garlic, basil, sugar, oregano, onion salt, salt, pepper and thyme; bring to a boil. Reduce heat; cover and simmer for 30 minutes.
2. Cook ravioli according to the package directions; drain. Add to soup and heat through. Stir in Parmesan cheese. Sprinkle with additional parsley if desired.
1 cup: 235 cal., 8g fat (4g sat. fat), 42mg chol., 542mg sod., 25g carb. (5g sugars, 4g fiber), 17g pro.

> **TEST KITCHEN TIP**
> If you don't have tomato paste in your pantry, strain a can of diced tomatoes and add them to the soup instead for extra tomato flavor.

GROUND BEEF BARLEY SOUP

I first tasted this soup when a friend shared it with us one Sunday after church. It's now a favorite with our family, especially our three children.
—*Maggie Norman, Gaithersburg, MD*

PREP: 5 min. + chilling • **COOK:** 2 hours 40 min.
MAKES: 8 servings (2 qt.)

- 2 qt. water
- 2 meaty beef soup bones
- 2 beef bouillon cubes or 2 tsp. beef bouillon granules
- 1 lb. ground beef
- ¼ to ½ cup medium pearl barley
- 1 large carrot, diced
- 1 small onion, chopped
- 3 to 4 medium potatoes, peeled and diced
- 2 tsp. garlic salt
- 1 tsp. onion powder
- 2 tsp. dried parsley
- 1 tsp. salt
- 1 tsp. pepper

1. In a large Dutch oven, bring the water and soup bones to a rapid boil; add bouillon. Stir in ground beef in small amounts. Reduce heat; cover and simmer for 1½ hours or until the meat comes easily off the bones.
2. Remove bones. Strain broth; cool and chill. Skim off fat. Remove meat from bones; dice and return to broth along with remaining ingredients. Bring to a boil. Reduce heat; cover and simmer 1 hour or until vegetables are tender.
1 cup: 295 cal., 13g fat (5g sat. fat), 70mg chol., 1068mg sod., 18g carb. (2g sugars, 2g fiber), 25g pro.

SANDY'S SLOW-COOKED CHILI

I like to use my homemade stewed tomatoes and pizza sauce in this recipe. It's the perfect chili—not too spicy. It's a cinch to whip up.
—*Sandy McKenzie, Braham, MN*

PREP: 25 min. • **COOK:** 6 hours
MAKES: 14 servings (3½ qt.)

- 2 lbs. ground beef
- ½ cup chopped onion
- 2 garlic cloves, minced
- 2 cans (16 oz. each) dark red kidney beans, rinsed and drained
- 2 cans (16 oz. each) light red kidney beans, rinsed and drained
- 2 cans (14½ oz. each) stewed tomatoes, cut up
- 1 can (15 oz.) pizza sauce
- 1 can (4 oz.) chopped green chiles
- 4 tsp. chili powder
- 1 tsp. dried basil
- ½ tsp. salt
- ⅛ tsp. pepper

In a Dutch oven, cook beef, onion and garlic over medium heat until meat is no longer pink; 5-7 minutes; crumble beef; drain. Transfer to a 5-qt. slow cooker; stir in remaining ingredients. Cover and cook on low for 6 hours.

1 cup: 183 cal., 6g fat (3g sat. fat), 32mg chol., 409mg sod., 16g carb. (4g sugars, 4g fiber), 16g pro.

❄ MEATBALL & PASTA SOUP

This power-packed soup is the perfect way to get my son to eat his spinach and actually like it! We add French bread or dinner rolls.
—*Laura Greenberg, Lake Balboa, CA*

TAKES: 30 min. • **MAKES:** 8 servings (3 qt.)

- 8 cups vegetable stock
- 1 garlic clove, minced
- 1 tsp. salt, divided
- 1 large egg
- ½ cup dry bread crumbs
- ¼ cup 2% milk
- 2 Tbsp. ketchup
- 2 tsp. Worcestershire sauce
- 1 tsp. onion powder
- ½ tsp. pepper
- 1 lb. lean ground beef (90% lean)
- 4 medium carrots, chopped
- 1 cup uncooked orzo pasta
- 1 pkg. (6 oz.) fresh baby spinach

1. In a 6-qt. stockpot, bring the stock, garlic and ¾ tsp. salt to a boil. Meanwhile, in a large bowl, mix egg, bread crumbs, milk, ketchup, Worcestershire sauce, onion powder, pepper and the remaining ¼ tsp. salt. Add beef; mix lightly but thoroughly. Shape into 1-in. balls.

2. Add carrots, pasta and meatballs to boiling stock. Reduce heat; simmer, uncovered, for 10-12 minutes or until the meatballs are cooked through and pasta is tender, stirring occasionally. Stir in spinach until wilted.

Freeze option: Freeze cooled soup in freezer containers. To use, partially thaw in refrigerator overnight. Heat through in a saucepan, stirring occasionally, add water if necessary.

1½ cups: 254 cal., 6g fat (2g sat. fat), 59mg chol., 1058mg sod., 31g carb. (4g sugars, 2g fiber), 17g pro.

SMOKY PEANUT BUTTER CHILI

I eliminated beans from my standard chili recipe and added peanut butter and peanuts just for fun. Wow, it was amazing! Tried it on my family and they all loved it.
—*Nancy Heishman, Las Vegas, NV*

- -

PREP: 25 min. • **COOK:** 4 hours
MAKES: 12 servings (3 qt.)

- 1 Tbsp. peanut oil or canola oil
- 2½ lbs. lean ground beef (90% lean)
- 1 large green pepper, chopped
- 1 large red onion, chopped
- 1 large carrot, peeled and chopped
- 2 garlic cloves, minced
- 2 cans (15 oz. each) tomato sauce
- 2 cans (14½ oz. each) diced tomatoes with basil, oregano and garlic, undrained
- 2 cans (4 oz. each) chopped green chiles
- ½ cup creamy peanut butter
- 1 to 2 Tbsp. ground ancho chili pepper
- 1 tsp. kosher salt
- 1 tsp. smoked paprika
  Optional: Shredded smoked cheddar cheese and chopped peanuts

1. In a large skillet, heat oil over medium-high heat; add the beef and cook in batches until no longer pink, 7-10 minutes; crumble beef. Remove with a slotted spoon; drain.
2. Add the green pepper, onion and carrot to skillet; cook and stir until vegetables are slightly browned, about 2 minutes. Add garlic; cook 1 minute longer.
3. Transfer meat, vegetables and drippings to a 5- or 6-qt. slow cooker. Stir in the next 7 ingredients until combined. Cook, covered, on low 4 hours, or until vegetables are tender. If desired, sprinkle servings with shredded cheese and peanuts.
1 cup: 279 cal., 15g fat (4g sat. fat), 59mg chol., 878mg sod., 13g carb. (6g sugars, 4g fiber), 23g pro.

SLOW-COOKER SOUTHWEST BEEF STEW

I made this stew for my ladies' group at church, and everyone loved it! Best of all, I could start the soup before I left for work in the morning and have it ready to go when I got home.
—*Anita Roberson, Williamston, NC*

- -

PREP: 30 min. • **COOK:** 6 hours
MAKES: 11 servings (2¾ qt.)

- 1½ lbs. lean ground beef (90% lean)
- 1 large onion, chopped
- 2 cans (14½ oz. each) diced tomatoes, undrained
- 1 pkg. (16 oz.) frozen corn
- 1 can (15 oz.) black beans, rinsed and drained
- 1 can (14½ oz.) chicken broth
- 1 can (10 oz.) diced tomatoes and green chiles, undrained
- 1 tsp. garlic powder
- 1½ tsp. salt-free Southwest chipotle seasoning blend
- 1½ cups cooked rice
- ¼ cup shredded cheddar cheese

1. In a large skillet, cook the beef and onion over medium heat until the meat is no longer pink, 5-7 minutes; crumble beef; drain.
2. Transfer to a 5-qt. slow cooker. Stir in the next 7 ingredients. Cover and cook on low 6-8 hours or until heated through.
3. Stir in rice; heat through. Sprinkle each serving with cheese.
1 cup: 228 cal., 6g fat (3g sat. fat), 42mg chol., 482mg sod., 26g carb. (4g sugars, 4g fiber), 17g pro. **Diabetic exchanges:** 2 lean meat, 1½ starch, 1 vegetable.

NANCY HEISHMAN
Las Vegas, NV

SLOW-COOKED BEEF VEGETABLE SOUP

Convenient frozen veggies and hash browns make this meaty soup a snap to mix up. Simply brown the ground beef, then stir everything together to simmer all day. It's wonderful served with bread and a salad.

—*Carol Calhoun, Sioux Falls, SD*

PREP: 10 min. • **COOK:** 8 hours
MAKES: 10 servings (2½ qt.)

1 lb. ground beef
1 can (46 oz.) tomato juice
1 pkg. (16 oz.) frozen mixed vegetables, thawed
2 cups frozen cubed hash brown potatoes, thawed
1 envelope onion soup mix

1. In a large skillet, cook beef over medium heat until no longer pink, 5-7 minutes; crumble meat; drain. Transfer to a 5-qt. slow cooker. Stir in juice, vegetables, potatoes and soup mix.
2. Cover and cook on low for 8-10 hours.
1 cup: 139 cal., 4g fat (2g sat. fat), 22mg chol., 766mg sod., 16g carb. (6g sugars, 3g fiber), 11g pro.

DID YOU KNOW?
Slow cookers depend on the trapped heat and moisture to do their job, so avoid frequent peeking to check on your soup—it could extend cooking time by as much as 15 minutes per peek!

TEXAS STEW

I love to experiment with many different types of recipes. But as a mother of young children, I rely on family-friendly ones more and more. Everyone enjoys this stew.

—*Kim Balstad, Lewisville, TX*

PREP: 15 min. • **COOK:** 6 hours
MAKES: 12 servings (3 qt.)

1½ lbs. ground beef
1 medium onion, chopped
1 can (15½ oz.) hominy, drained
1 can (15¼ oz.) whole kernel corn, drained
1 can (15 oz.) sliced carrots, drained
1 can (15 oz.) sliced potatoes, drained
1 can (16 oz.) Ranch Style beans (pinto beans in seasoned tomato sauce)
1 can (14½ oz.) diced tomatoes, undrained
1 cup water
1 tsp. beef bouillon granules
½ tsp. garlic powder
   Chili powder to taste
   Dash Worcestershire sauce
   Dash hot pepper sauce

1. In a large skillet, cook beef and onion over medium heat until meat is no longer pink, 5-7 minutes; crumble beef; drain.
2. Transfer mixture to a 5-qt. slow cooker. Stir in the remaining ingredients. Cover and cook on low until heated through, 6-8 hours.
1 cup: 223 cal., 8g fat (3g sat. fat), 38mg chol., 710mg sod., 21g carb. (5g sugars, 5g fiber), 15g pro.

THE SOUTH IN A POT SOUP

With black-eyed peas, sweet potatoes, ground beef and comforting spices, this soup has every wonderful memory from my childhood simmered together in one tasty pot.
—*Stephanie Rabbitt-Schapp, Cincinnati, OH*

PREP: 15 min. • **COOK:** 45 min.
MAKES: 8 servings (2½ qt.)

1 Tbsp. canola oil
1½ lbs. lean ground beef (90% lean)
1 large sweet onion, diced
1 large sweet potato, peeled and diced
1 medium sweet pepper (any color), diced
1 can (15½ oz.) black-eyed peas, rinsed and drained
1 Tbsp. ground cumin
1 Tbsp. curry powder
¾ tsp. salt
½ tsp. coarsely ground pepper
2 cans (14½ oz. each) reduced-sodium beef broth
4 cups chopped collard greens or chopped fresh spinach

1. In a Dutch oven, heat oil over medium heat. Cook and stir ground beef until no longer pink, 8-10 minutes; crumble meat. Add the onion, sweet potato and pepper; saute until onion and pepper are slightly softened, 4-5 minutes.
2. Add black-eyed peas, cumin, curry, salt and pepper; stir in broth and bring to a boil. Reduce heat; simmer until the sweet potato is almost tender, 15-18 minutes.
3. Add the greens; cook 15-18 minutes, or until tender. If desired, add more cumin and curry.
1¼ cups: 267 cal., 9g fat (3g sat. fat), 55mg chol., 544mg sod., 23g carb. (8g sugars, 5g fiber), 22g pro. **Diabetic exchanges:** 2 lean meat, 1 starch, 1 vegetable, ½ fat.
For slow cooker: In a 4- to 5-qt. slow cooker, crumble ground beef; add next 8 ingredients (You don't need canola oil.). Pour in enough broth to reach desired consistency. Cook, covered, on low 6-8 hours. A half-hour before serving, skim off any fat; add greens.

SPICY MONTANA CHILI

This thick and chunky chili has some kick to it. I like to top it with shredded cheddar and then serve it with a side of cornbread.
—*Donna Evaro, Casper, WY*

- -

PREP: 30 min. • **COOK:** 5 hours
MAKES: 8 servings (about 2½ qt.)

 2 lbs. ground beef
 1 large sweet onion, chopped
 1 medium sweet red pepper, finely chopped
 1 medium sweet yellow pepper, finely chopped
 2 cans (16 oz. each) chili beans, undrained
 2 cans (14½ oz. each) stewed tomatoes, drained
 ½ cup tomato juice
 2 jalapeno peppers, seeded and minced
 2 garlic cloves, minced
 2 tsp. ground cumin
 2 tsp. chili powder
 1 tsp. salt
 1 tsp. cayenne pepper
    Shredded cheddar cheese, optional

1. In a large skillet, cook the beef, onion and peppers over medium heat until the meat is no longer pink, 5-7 minute; crumble beef; drain.

2. Transfer to a 4- or 5-qt. slow cooker. Stir in the beans, tomatoes, tomato juice, jalapenos, garlic, cumin, chili powder, salt and cayenne. Cover and cook on low for 5-6 hours or until heated through. If desired, top with shredded cheddar cheese.

Note: Wear disposable gloves when cutting hot peppers; the oils can burn skin. Avoid touching your face.

1⅓ cups: 365 cal., 15g fat (6g sat. fat), 70mg chol., 920mg sod., 36g carb. (11g sugars, 9g fiber), 28g pro.

GROUND BEEF VEGGIE STEW

This is a wonderful hearty stew to help use up all the late-summer veggies in your garden. I like that it's filling enough to make a meal, and it's good for you, too!
—*Courtney Stultz, Weir, KS*

- -

TAKES: 30 min. • **MAKES:** 6 servings

 1 lb. lean ground beef (90% lean)
 1 Tbsp. olive oil
 1 small yellow summer squash, chopped
 1 small zucchini, chopped
 1 small sweet red pepper, chopped
 2 cans (15 oz. each) diced tomatoes
 1 cup water
 1 tsp. salt
 ¼ tsp. pepper
 3 Tbsp. minced fresh cilantro
    Reduced-fat sour cream, optional

1. In a large saucepan, cook the beef over medium-high heat, until no longer pink, 5-7 minutes; crumble meat; drain. Remove from pan; set aside.

2. In the same saucepan, add oil, squash, zucchini and red pepper; cook and stir until vegetables are crisp-tender, 5-7 minutes. Add the beef, tomatoes, water, salt and pepper; bring to a boil. Reduce to a simmer; cook, stirring occasionally, until the vegetables are tender, 5-8 minutes. Stir in cilantro just before serving. If desired, top with sour cream.

1¼ cups: 180 cal., 9g fat (3g sat. fat), 47mg chol., 663mg sod., 9g carb. (6g sugars, 3g fiber), 16g pro. **Diabetic exchanges:** 2 lean meat, 1 vegetable, ½ fat.

CHILI CON CARNE

At chili suppers, this one always disappears first! It's nice at home, too, since the longer it sits in the refrigerator, the better the flavor seems to get.

—*Janie Turner, Tuttle, OK*

PREP: 20 min. • **COOK:** 1½ hours
MAKES: 10 servings (2½ qt.)

- 2 lbs. ground beef
- 2 Tbsp. olive oil
- 2 medium onions, chopped
- 2 garlic cloves, minced
- 1 medium green pepper, chopped
- 1½ tsp. salt
- 2 Tbsp. chili powder
- 3 tsp. beef bouillon granules
- ⅛ tsp. cayenne pepper
- ¼ tsp. ground cinnamon
- 1 tsp. ground cumin
- 1 tsp. dried oregano
- 2 cans (14½ oz. each) diced tomatoes, undrained
- 1 cup water
- 1 can (16 oz.) kidney beans, rinsed and drained
   Optional: Sour cream and jalapeno slices

1. In a Dutch oven, cook beef over medium heat until no longer pink; 5-7 minutes; crumble beef. Drain and set aside.
2. In the same pot, heat oil; saute onions until tender. Add garlic; cook 1 minute longer. Stir in the green pepper, salt, chili powder, bouillon, cayenne, cinnamon, cumin and oregano. Cook for 2 minutes, stirring until combined.
3. Add tomatoes and browned beef. Stir in water. Bring to a boil. Reduce heat; cover and simmer for about 1 hour.
4. Add beans and heat through. If desired, top with sour cream and jalapeno slices.
1 cup: 264 cal., 14g fat (4g sat. fat), 56mg chol., 892mg sod., 15g carb. (5g sugars, 5g fiber), 20g pro.

VEGETABLE SOUP WITH HAMBURGER

I work full time, but my family sits down to a home-cooked meal just about every night. I rely on simple recipes like this .

—*Theresa Jackson, Cicero, NY*

PREP: 15 min. • **COOK:** 8 hours
MAKES: 10 servings (2½ qt.)

- 1 lb. lean ground beef (90% lean)
- 1 medium onion, chopped
- 2 garlic cloves, minced
- 4 cups V8 juice
- 1 can (14½ oz.) stewed tomatoes
- 2 cups coleslaw mix
- 2 cups frozen green beans
- 2 cups frozen corn
- 2 Tbsp. Worcestershire sauce
- 1 tsp. dried basil
- ½ tsp. salt
- ¼ tsp. pepper

1. In a large saucepan, cook beef and onion over medium heat until meat is no longer pink, 5-7 minutes; crumble meat. Add garlic; cook 1 minute longer. Drain.
2. In a 5-qt. slow cooker, combine remaining ingredients. Stir in the beef mixture. Cover and cook on low until vegetables are tender, 8-10 hours.
1 cup: 145 cal., 4g fat (2g sat. fat), 28mg chol., 507mg sod., 17g carb. (7g sugars, 3g fiber), 11g pro. **Diabetic exchanges:** 1 vegetable, 1 lean meat, ½ starch.

SLOPPY JOE STEW

This old-fashioned stew has a slightly sweet taste from the addition of canned corn. You can make the stew ahead of time and reheat it for a quick meal later on.
—*Clair Long, Destrehan, LA*

PREP: 10 min. • **COOK:** 1¼ hours
MAKES: 6 servings

   2   lbs. ground beef
   1   green pepper, chopped
   1   medium onion small, chopped
 2½   cups water
   1   can (11 oz.) whole kernel corn, drained
   2   cans (10¾ oz. each) condensed
         tomato soup, undiluted
   1   to 2 Tbsp. sugar
   1   Tbsp. Worcestershire sauce
   1   tsp. hot pepper sauce
         Salt and pepper to taste

1. In a Dutch oven, cook beef, green pepper and onion over medium heat until meat is no longer pink, 5-7 minutes; crumble meat; drain.
2. Add the remaining ingredients to the beef mixture; bring to a boil. Reduce heat; cover and simmer until the vegetables are tender and the flavors have blended, about 1 hour.
1½ cups: 353 cal., 15g fat (6g sat. fat), 74mg chol., 666mg sod., 25g carb. (15g sugars, 3g fiber), 29g pro.

❄
CHEESY CHILI

My six grandchildren enjoy feasting on big bowls of this zesty chili. It's so creamy and tasty, you can even serve it as a dip at parties.
—*Codie Ray, Tallulah, LA*

TAKES: 25 min.
MAKES: 12 servings (3 qt.)

   2   lbs. ground beef
   2   medium onions, chopped
   2   garlic cloves, minced
   3   cans (10 oz. each) diced tomatoes
         and green chiles, undrained
   1   can (28 oz.) diced tomatoes,
         undrained
   2   cans (4 oz. each) chopped green chiles
  ½   tsp. pepper
   2   lbs. Velveeta, cubed
         Optional: Sour cream, sliced jalapeno
         pepper, chopped tomato and minced
         fresh cilantro

1. In a large saucepan, cook the beef, onions and garlic until the meat is no longer pink, 5-7 minutes; crumble meat; drain. Stir in the tomatoes, chiles and pepper; bring to a boil.
2. Reduce heat; simmer, uncovered, for 10-15 minutes. Stir in cheese until melted. Serve immediately. If desired, top with sour cream, jalapenos, tomatoes and cilantro.
Freeze option: Freeze cooled chili in freezer containers for up to 3 months. To use, partially thaw in refrigerator overnight. Heat through in a saucepan, stirring occasionally; add broth or water if necessary.
1 cup: 396 cal., 25g fat (15g sat. fat), 85mg chol., 1166mg sod., 13g carb. (9g sugars, 2g fiber), 29g pro.

SOUTHWESTERN BEEF BARLEY STEW

Hearty and easy to fix, this thick stew has a comforting, chili-like flavor. It's my best barley recipe. I'm sure you'll agree it's a tasty dish.
—*Lisa Kolenich, Regina, SK*

- -

TAKES: 30 min. • **MAKES:** 3 servings

½ lb. lean ground beef (90% lean)
½ cup sliced celery
⅓ cup chopped onion
1¾ cups water
2 tsp. reduced-sodium beef bouillon granules
1½ tsp. chili powder
¼ tsp. pepper
½ cup quick-cooking barley
1 can (14½ oz.) diced tomatoes, undrained

1. In a large saucepan, cook the beef, celery and onion over medium heat until the meat is no longer pink and vegetables are tender; crumble beef; drain.
2. Stir in the water, bouillon, chili powder and pepper. Bring to a boil. Stir in barley. Reduce heat; cover and simmer for 10-12 minutes or until the barley is tender. Stir in tomatoes; heat through.

1⅓ cups: 269 cal., 7g fat (3g sat. fat), 37mg chol., 456mg sod., 33g carb. (6g sugars, 9g fiber), 20g pro. **Diabetic exchanges:** 2 lean meat, 1½ starch, 1 vegetable.

READER REVIEW

"This was so delicious! I couldn't find quick-cooking barley so we used some leftover cooked quinoa and that was a tasty substitution."

CURLYLIS85, TASTEOFHOME.COM

BEEF LENTIL SOUP

You may make this soup as the main course in a hearty lunch or dinner. On cold evenings here in New England, I've often enjoyed sipping a steaming mug in front of our fireplace.
—*Guy Turnbull, Arlington, MA*

PREP: 15 min. • **COOK:** 70 min.
MAKES: 6 servings

- 1 lb. lean ground beef (90% lean)
- 1 can (46 oz.) tomato or V8 juice
- 4 cups water
- 1 cup dried lentils, rinsed
- 2 cups chopped cabbage
- 1 cup sliced carrots
- 1 cup sliced celery
- 1 cup chopped onion
- ½ cup diced green pepper
- ½ tsp. pepper
- ½ tsp. dried thyme
- 1 bay leaf
- 1 pkg. (10 oz.) frozen chopped spinach, thawed

1. In a large stockpot, cook beef over medium heat until no longer pink, 5-7 minutes; crumble meat; drain.

2. Add tomato juice, water, lentils, cabbage, carrots, celery, onion, green pepper, pepper, thyme and bay leaf. Bring to a boil. Reduce heat; simmer, uncovered, for 1-1½ hours or until the lentils and vegetables are tender.

3. Add spinach and heat through. Remove bay leaf.

1 cup: 314 cal., 8g fat (3g sat. fat), 47mg chol., 661mg sod., 37g carb. (10g sugars, 8g fiber), 27g pro. **Diabetic exchanges:** 2 vegetable, 2 lean meat, 1½ starch.

❄ TACO STEW

These ingredients are simple, but together they make an awesome stew. If you want a little added crunch, crush a few tortilla chips on top of each bowl.
—*Suzanne Francis, Marysville, WA*

TAKES: 30 min. • **MAKES:** 6 servings (2 qt.)

- 1 lb. ground beef
- 2 cans (15 oz. each) black beans, rinsed and drained
- 2 cans (10 oz. each) diced tomatoes and green chiles
- 1 can (15 oz.) tomato sauce
- 1½ cups frozen corn (about 7 oz.)
- 2 tsp. chili powder
- ½ tsp. ground cumin
  Crushed tortilla chips, optional

1. In a large saucepan, cook beef over medium heat until no longer pink, 6-8 minutes; crumble beef; drain.

2. Stir in beans, tomatoes, tomato sauce, corn, chili powder and cumin. Bring to a boil. Reduce heat; simmer 5-10 minutes to allow flavors to blend. If desired, top individual servings with tortilla chips.

Freeze option: Freeze the cooled stew in freezer containers. To use, partially thaw in refrigerator overnight. Heat through in a saucepan, stirring occasionally, add water if necessary.

1⅓ cups: 313 cal., 10g fat (3g sat. fat), 47mg chol., 1041mg sod., 35g carb. (3g sugars, 9g fiber), 23g pro.

Ground Beef

SANDWICHES & BURGERS

Dress 'em up, dress 'em down—burgers are a staple of modern cooking. With all their variations, there's a sandwich just right for family weeknight dinners in or weekend cookouts for a crowd.

5i
EASY GRILLED HAMBURGERS

These easy hamburgers come together in a snap. Just grill and then add your favorite toppings. If it's too cold to grill out, you can use one of the other suggested cooking methods, instead.
—*James Schend, Pleasant Prairie, WI*

PREP: 20 min. • **GRILL:** 15 min.
MAKES: 4 servings

- 1⅓ **lbs. ground beef**
- ¾ **tsp. salt**
- ¼ **tsp. pepper**
- 4 **hamburger buns, split and toasted**
  Optional: Lettuce leaves, sliced tomato, sliced onion, bacon and mayonnaise

Shape ground beef into four ¾-in.-thick patties. Just before grilling, sprinkle with salt and pepper. Grill burgers, covered, over medium heat until a thermometer reads 160°, 5-7 minutes on each side. Top bun bottoms with burgers. If desired, serve with lettuce, tomato, onion, bacon and mayonnaise.

1 burger: 265 cal., 13g fat (5g sat. fat), 62mg chol., 495mg sod., 15g carb. (2g sugars, 1g fiber), 21g pro.

Pan-Fried Burgers: In a large skillet, heat 1 Tbsp. butter or oil over medium heat. Add burgers; cook until a thermometer reads 160°, 6-8 minutes on each side.

Oven-Baked Burgers: Place beef patties on a lightly greased baking sheet. Bake them at 350° until thermometer reads 160°, 15-20 minutes, turning once.

Air-Fried Burgers: Place burgers in a single layer on tray in air-fryer basket. Air-fry at 350° until a thermometer reads 160°, 8-10 minutes, turning halfway through cooking.

ITALIAN BURRITOS

My family is very picky, so I created this Italian burrito loaded with beef, cheese and sauce to satisfy everyone. It turned out great! The dish is quick, easy and delicious.
—*Donna Holter, Centennial, CO*

- -

PREP: 20 min. • **BAKE:** 20 min.
MAKES: 8 servings

    1   lb. lean ground beef (90% lean)
    1   cup marinara sauce
    ½   cup shredded part-skim mozzarella
        cheese
    ¼   cup grated Parmesan cheese
    ¼   tsp. garlic powder
    8   whole wheat tortillas (8 in.)

1. Preheat oven to 375°. In a large skillet, cook beef over medium heat until no longer pink, 6-8 minutes; crumble meat; drain. Stir in marinara sauce, cheeses and garlic powder.
2. Spoon ⅓ cup filling in the center of each tortilla. Fold bottom and sides of tortilla over the filling and roll up. Place on a baking sheet coated with cooking spray. Bake 18-20 minutes or until bottoms are light brown.
1 burrito: 275 cal., 10g fat (3g sat. fat), 42mg chol., 326mg sod., 26g carb. (4g sugars, 3g fiber), 18g pro. **Diabetic exchanges:** 2 starch, 2 lean meat.

TEST KITCHEN TIP
If your tortillas don't fold easily, wrap them in a damp paper towel and microwave for 20 seconds—then they'll fold like a dream!

❄ 🍎 WEST COAST SNAPPY JOES

Meet my California-inspired sloppy joe! Load it up with whatever taco toppings you like. The meat filling is also incredible served over mac and cheese.
—*Devon Delaney, Westport, CT*

- -

TAKES: 30 min. • **MAKES:** 6 servings

    1   lb. lean ground beef (90% lean)
    1   medium onion, chopped
    1   garlic clove, minced
    1   can (8 oz.) tomato sauce
    ⅓   cup soft sun-dried tomato halves
         (not packed in oil), chopped
    ⅓   cup chopped roasted sweet
         red peppers
    2   Tbsp. chopped pickled
         jalapeno peppers
    2   Tbsp. tomato paste
    1   Tbsp. brown sugar
    1   Tbsp. balsamic vinegar
    ½   tsp. Montreal steak seasoning
    ½   tsp. pepper
    6   hamburger buns, split
         Optional: Chopped avocado,
         sour cream, shredded cheddar
         cheese and chopped green onions

1. In a large skillet, cook beef, onion and garlic over medium heat until the beef is no longer pink, 6-8 minutes; crumble beef; drain.
2. Stir in tomato sauce, sun-dried tomatoes, roasted peppers, jalapenos, tomato paste, brown sugar, vinegar, steak seasoning and pepper. Bring to a boil. Reduce heat; simmer, uncovered, until thickened, 4-6 minutes, stirring occasionally. Serve on buns with toppings as desired.
Freeze option: Freeze cooled meat mixture in freezer containers. To use, partially thaw in refrigerator overnight. Heat through in a saucepan, stirring occasionally; add water if necessary.
1 sandwich: 288 cal., 8g fat (3g sat. fat), 47mg chol., 575mg sod., 32g carb. (10g sugars, 3g fiber), 20g pro. **Diabetic exchanges:** 2 starch, 2 lean meat.

SPINACH TOMATO BURGERS

Every Friday night is burger night at our house. The tomatoes add fresh flavor and the cool spinach dip brings it all together. We often skip the buns and serve these over a bed of grilled cabbage.
—*Courtney Stultz, Weir, KS*

- -

TAKES: 20 min. • **MAKES:** 4 servings

 1   **large egg, lightly beaten**
 2   **Tbsp. fat-free milk**
 ½   **cup soft bread crumbs**
 1   **tsp. dried basil**
 ½   **tsp. salt**
 ¼   **tsp. pepper**
 1   **lb. lean ground beef (90% lean)**
 4   **whole wheat hamburger buns, split**
 ¼   **cup spinach dip**
 ¼   **cup julienned soft sun-dried tomatoes (not packed in oil)**
    Lettuce leaves

1. Combine the first 6 ingredients. Add beef; mix lightly but thoroughly. Shape into four ½-in.-thick patties.
2. Place the burgers on an oiled grill rack or in a greased 15x10x1-in. pan. Grill, covered, over medium heat or broil 4-5 in. from heat until a thermometer reads 160°, 4-5 minutes per side.
3. Grill buns, cut side down, over medium heat until toasted. Serve burgers on buns; top with spinach dip, tomatoes and lettuce.

1 burger: 389 cal., 17g fat (6g sat. fat), 125mg chol., 737mg sod., 29g carb. (7g sugars, 4g fiber), 29g pro. **Diabetic exchanges:** 3 lean meat, 2 starch, 1½ fat.

PRESTO PIZZA PATTIES

Let me share my busy-day secret weapon: pizza burgers! I make the patties ahead of time so they're ready when I need a meal fast.
—*Barbara Schindler, Napoleon, OH*

- -

TAKES: 30 min. • **MAKES:** 6 servings

 1   **can (8 oz.) pizza sauce, divided**
 ½   **cup seasoned bread crumbs**
 ½   **cup finely chopped green pepper**
 ¼   **cup finely chopped onion**
 2   **large egg whites**
 1   **garlic clove, minced**
 1   **lb. lean ground beef (90% lean)**
 6   **slices Italian bread (½ in. thick)**
 2   **tsp. olive oil**
 1½   **tsp. Italian seasoning**
 ½   **cup shredded part-skim mozzarella cheese**

1. In a large bowl, combine ⅓ cup pizza sauce, bread crumbs, pepper, onion, egg whites and garlic. Add beef; mix lightly but thoroughly. Shape into 6 oval patties.
2. In a large nonstick skillet, cook patties over medium heat for 4-5 minutes on each side or until a thermometer reads 160°.
3. Meanwhile, place bread on an ungreased baking sheet. Brush tops with oil; sprinkle with Italian seasoning. Broil 3-4 in. from the heat for 1-2 minutes or until golden brown.
4. Place the remaining pizza sauce in a microwave-safe bowl. Microwave, covered, on high for 10-20 seconds or until heated through. Place patties on toast; top with sauce and cheese.

Freeze option: Place patties on waxed paper-lined baking sheet; wrap and freeze until firm. Remove from pan and transfer to a freezer container; return to freezer. Freeze remaining pizza sauce in an airtight container. To use, cook the frozen patties and pizza sauce as directed, increasing time as necessary for a thermometer to read 160° for patties and for sauce to be heated through.

1 serving: 299 cal., 11g fat (4g sat. fat), 53mg chol., 527mg sod., 26g carb. (3g sugars, 2g fiber), 23g pro. **Diabetic exchanges:** 3 lean meat, 1½ starch.

SLOPPY JOE DOGS

There are so many different ways to top a hot dog, but this tasty sloppy joe version beats them all!

—*Kimberly Wallace, Dennison, OH*

- -

PREP: 20 min. • **COOK:** 15 min.
MAKES: 16 servings

SLOPPY JOE TOPPING
- 2 lbs. ground beef
- 2 celery ribs, chopped
- 1 small green pepper, finely chopped
- 1 small onion, chopped
- 1 can (10¾ oz.) condensed tomato soup, undiluted
- ¼ cup packed brown sugar
- ¼ cup ketchup
- 1 Tbsp. cider vinegar
- 1 Tbsp. prepared mustard
- 1½ tsp. Worcestershire sauce
- 1 tsp. pepper
- ½ tsp. salt
- ¼ tsp. garlic powder

DOGS
- 16 hot dogs
- 16 hot dog buns, split
     Optional: Warmed cheese dip and grilled onions

1. In a Dutch oven, cook the beef, celery, green pepper and onion over medium heat until meat is no longer pink, 5-7 minutes; crumble beef; drain. Stir in the remaining topping ingredients; heat through.

2. Grill hot dogs, covered, over medium heat until heated through, 6-10 minutes, turning occasionally. Serve on buns. Top each with ¼ cup beef mixture. If desired, top with warmed cheese dip and grilled onions.

1 serving: 422 cal., 23g fat (9g sat. fat), 68mg chol., 959mg sod., 31g carb. (10g sugars, 1g fiber), 22g pro.

READER REVIEW

"I made this delicious sauce for dinner last night and it was a huge success! My husband *really* liked it.... the salty hot dog with the slightly sweet sauce made for an excellent meal."

BICKTASW, TASTEOFHOME.COM

KIMBERLY WALLACE
Dennison, OH

BACON & DATE GOAT CHEESE BURGERS

Every bite of this burger is a rich and decadent combination of sweet and savory. If you can't find maple bacon in your local grocery store, use regular bacon and add 1½ tablespoons maple syrup to the spinach-goat cheese mixture in the food processor.
—*Sharon Michelle Anglin, Livingston, MT*

PREP: 30 min. • **GRILL:** 10 min.
MAKES: 6 servings

- 2¾ cups fresh baby spinach, divided
- 1 pkg. (8 oz.) pistachios, shelled
- 2 Tbsp. lemon juice
- 2 garlic cloves, halved
- ½ to 1½ tsp. crushed red pepper flakes
- ¼ tsp. salt
- ¼ tsp. pepper
- 1 pkg. (5.3 oz.) fresh goat cheese, crumbled
- ¼ cup olive oil
- 1½ lbs. ground beef
- 1 pkg. (8 oz.) pitted dates, chopped
- 6 brioche hamburger buns, split
- 1 medium red onion, sliced
- ½ lb. maple-flavored bacon, cooked

1. Place 2 cups spinach, pistachios, lemon juice, garlic, pepper flakes, salt and pepper in a food processor; pulse until chopped. Add goat cheese; process until blended. Continue processing while gradually adding the oil in a steady stream to reach a spreadable consistency. Refrigerate until serving.
2. In a large bowl, combine beef and dates; mix lightly but thoroughly. Shape them into six ½-in.-thick patties. Place burgers on an oiled grill rack or in a greased 15x10x1-in. pan. Grill burgers, covered, over medium heat or broil 4-5 in. from heat until a thermometer reads 160°, 4-5 minutes per side. Grill buns until they're toasted.
3. Top the bun bottoms with the remaining ¾ cups spinach, the burgers, red onion and bacon. Spread 4 tsp. goat cheese mixture over the cut side of each bun top; place on burger. Cover and refrigerate any remaining goat cheese mixture; save for another use.
1 burger: 804 cal., 45g fat (11g sat. fat), 118mg chol., 788mg sod., 67g carb. (34g sugars, 9g fiber), 39g pro.

BEEF-STUFFED FRENCH BREAD

My husband, David, loves this tasty sandwich. The meaty, cheesy filling comes together in a jiffy.
—*Julie Scott, Pratt, KS*

TAKES: 25 min. • **MAKES:** 4 servings

- 1 unsliced loaf French bread (1 lb.)
- 1 lb. ground beef
- 1 can (10¾ oz.) condensed cheddar cheese soup, undiluted
- 1 Tbsp. Worcestershire sauce
- 1 medium green pepper, chopped
- 1 celery rib, chopped
- ¼ tsp. salt
- ½ tsp. pepper
- 4 slices American cheese, halved

1. Preheat oven to 350°. Cut off top of bread. Carefully hollow out bottom of loaf, leaving a ½-in. shell. Cut removed bread into small cubes; set aside.
2. In a skillet, cook beef until no longer pink, 5-7 minutes; crumble meat; drain. Add soup, Worcestershire sauce, green pepper, celery, salt, pepper. Cook and stir 3-4 minutes. Stir in the reserved bread cubes.
3. Spread into bread shell; top with cheese. Replace bread top. Place on an ungreased baking sheet. Bake for 6-8 minutes or until the cheese is melted.
1 sandwich: 658 cal., 24g fat (11g sat. fat), 77mg chol., 1691mg sod., 71g carb. (10g sugars, 5g fiber), 37g pro.

GROUND BEEF GYROS

If your family likes gyros as much as mine, they'll love this version—it's made with ground beef instead of lamb. I found the recipe in a newspaper and adapted it to our tastes. These are much like the ones served at restaurants—the sauce adds an authentic touch.
—*Ruth Stahl, Shepherd, MT*

TAKES: 30 min. • **MAKES:** 4 servings

SAUCE
- 1 cup plain yogurt
- ⅓ cup chopped seeded cucumber
- 2 Tbsp. finely chopped onion
- 1 garlic clove, minced
- 1 tsp. sugar

GYROS
- 1½ tsp. dried oregano
- 1 tsp. garlic powder
- 1 tsp. onion powder
- 1 tsp. salt, optional
- ¾ tsp. pepper
- 1 lb. ground beef
- 4 pita pocket halves
- 3 cups shredded lettuce
- 1 large tomato, chopped
- 1 small onion, sliced

1. Combine the sauce ingredients. Chill.
2. In a large bowl, combine the seasonings; crumble beef over mixture and mix lightly but thoroughly. Shape into 4 patties.
3. Grill, covered, over medium heat or broil 4 in. from the heat for 6-7 minutes on each side or until a thermometer reads 160°.
4. Cut patties into thin slices; stuff into pita halves. Add lettuce, tomato and onion. Serve with the yogurt sauce.
1 gyro: 357 cal., 16g fat (6g sat. fat), 78mg chol., 257mg sod., 27g carb. (7g sugars, 3g fiber), 26g pro.

> **TEST KITCHEN TIP**
> To save time, you can use pre-made tzatziki from your local market's deli case—even better if you're near a Greek deli!

BUFFALO BEEF BURGERS

This tangy, amped-up burger puts a new twist on ever-popular Buffalo wings. The zippy mayo topping gives these sandwiches their kick.
—*Michael Cohen, Los Angeles, CA*

TAKES: 30 min. • **MAKES:** 6 servings

- 2 Tbsp. butter, softened
- 2 Tbsp. brown sugar
- ¾ cup mayonnaise
- ¼ cup Louisiana-style hot sauce
- 2 lbs. ground beef
- 1 tsp. salt
- ½ tsp. coarsely ground pepper
- 6 kaiser rolls, split
- 1 celery rib, finely chopped
- 6 Tbsp. crumbled blue cheese

1. In a small bowl, beat the butter and brown sugar until light and fluffy. Add mayonnaise and hot sauce; beat until smooth. Set aside.
2. Crumble beef into a large bowl; sprinkle with the salt and pepper and mix lightly but thoroughly. Shape into 6 patties.
3. Grill the burgers, covered, over medium heat for 5-7 minutes on each side until a thermometer reads 160° and juices run clear.
4. Place the burgers on rolls. Top each with 2 Tbsp. Buffalo mayonnaise and 1 Tbsp. each of celery and cheese.
1 burger: 769 cal., 51g fat (15g sat. fat), 141mg chol., 1109mg sod., 35g carb. (6g sugars, 1g fiber), 40g pro.

⑤ BURGER AMERICANA

Go on a burger road trip in your own backyard. Grill the patties and load them sky-high. Start with classic cheddar cheese, lettuce and tomato, then start experimenting!
—*Susan Mahaney, New Hartford, NY*

- -

TAKES: 25 min. • **MAKES:** 4 servings

- ½ cup seasoned bread crumbs
- 1 large egg, lightly beaten
- ½ tsp. salt
- ½ tsp. pepper
- 1 lb. ground beef
- 1 Tbsp. olive oil
- 4 sesame seed hamburger buns, split
  Toppings of your choice

1. In a large bowl, combine bread crumbs, egg, salt and pepper. Add beef; mix lightly but thoroughly. Shape into four ½-in.-thick patties. Press a shallow indentation in the center of each patty with your thumb. Brush both sides of patties with oil.
2. Grill burgers, covered, over medium heat or broil 4 in. from heat 4-5 minutes on each side or until a thermometer reads 160°. Serve on buns with toppings.
1 burger: 429 cal., 20g fat (6g sat. fat), 123mg chol., 796mg sod., 32g carb. (3g sugars, 1g fiber), 28g pro.

PICADILLO SLIDERS

When I'm pressed for time, these beefy sliders are my go-to. Any leftover picadillo will make fabulous nachos or a tasty queso dip. It freezes well, too!
—*Patterson Watkins, Philadelphia, PA*

- -

PREP: 15 min. • **COOK:** 25 min.
MAKES: 1½ dozen

- 1 Tbsp. canola oil
- 1 medium yellow onion, diced
- 2 garlic cloves, minced
- 2 lbs. ground beef
- ½ cup pimiento-stuffed olives, halved
- 2 cans (14½ oz. each) diced tomatoes, drained
- 1 cup beef broth
- ¼ cup red wine vinegar
- ¼ cup raisins
- 2 Tbsp. tomato paste
- 1 Tbsp. chili powder
- 2 tsp. ground cumin
- 1 tsp. ground cinnamon
- 1½ tsp. salt
- 18 potato dinner rolls

1. In a large skillet, heat oil over medium heat. Saute onion until translucent, 6-8 minutes; add garlic and cook 1 minute more. Add ground beef; cook until no longer pink, 6-8 minutes; crumble meat. With a slotted spoon, remove meat; drain excess fat.
2. Return the meat to skillet. Add the next 10 ingredients. Stir over medium heat until well blended. Reduce heat; simmer until sauce has thickened, 10-15 minutes.
3. Toast rolls. Spoon beef mixture on each roll (they may be juicy). Serve immediately.
1 slider: 249 cal., 9g fat (2g sat. fat), 31mg chol., 631mg sod., 29g carb. (6g sugars, 2g fiber), 14g pro.

READER REVIEW
"I usually serve picadillo over rice. I really like the creativity of putting the mixture on sliders!"
RLLEWIS7, TASTEOFHOME.COM

BANH MI BURGER

I love burgers cooked in a cast-iron pan, and banh mi sandwiches are delicious, so why not combine the two? You can make your own banh mi burger sauce with Sriracha, mayonnaise, lime juice, fish sauce and sugar.
—Jessica Thompson, Manor, TX

- -

PREP: 15 min. • **COOK:** 20 min.
MAKES: 4 servings

- ½ cup water
- ½ cup white vinegar
- ¼ cup sugar
- 1 tsp. salt, divided
- 1 large carrot, julienned
- ½ medium daikon radish, julienned
- 1 lb. ground beef
- ⅛ tsp. pepper
- 4 kaiser rolls, split
- ½ cup Sriracha mayonnaise
- ½ medium cucumber, thinly sliced
- 8 sprigs fresh cilantro

1. In a small saucepan, combine water, vinegar, sugar and ½ tsp. salt. Bring to a boil; whisk until sugar is dissolved. Remove from heat. Add the carrots and radish; let them stand until serving.
2. Shape beef into four ¾-in.-thick patties. Sprinkle with pepper and remaining ½ tsp. salt. In a 12-in. cast-iron or another heavy skillet, cook the burgers over medium heat until a thermometer reads 160°, 8-10 minutes on each side. Remove and keep warm. Wipe the pan clean.
3. In the same pan, toast rolls over medium heat, cut side down, 30-60 seconds. Spread rolls with mayonnaise. Drain the pickled vegetables. Serve the burgers on rolls with pickled vegetables, cucumber and cilantro.
1 burger: 576 cal., 36g fat (8g sat. fat), 72mg chol., 858mg sod., 36g carb. (5g sugars, 3g fiber), 27g pro.

❄ STROGANOFF SANDWICHES

This recipe is perfect for a game day, either at a tailgate party or at home. I often make the meat mixture ahead of time and add the sour cream just before serving.
—Susan Graham, Cherokee, IA

- -

PREP: 10 min. • **COOK:** 30 min.
MAKES: 8 servings

- 1½ lbs. ground beef
- 1 medium onion, chopped
- ½ cup sliced fresh mushrooms
- 6 to 8 bacon strips, cooked and crumbled
- 2 garlic cloves, minced
- 2 Tbsp. all-purpose flour
- ½ tsp. salt
- ½ tsp. paprika
- ⅛ tsp. ground nutmeg
- 1 can (10¾ oz.) condensed cream of mushroom soup, undiluted
- 1 cup sour cream
- 8 hamburger buns, split

1. In a large cast-iron or heavy skillet, cook beef, onion and mushrooms over medium heat until meat is no longer pink, 5-7 minutes; crumble meat; drain. Add bacon and garlic.
2. Combine the flour, salt, paprika and nutmeg; gradually stir into beef mixture until blended. Stir in soup (mixture will be thick) and heat through. Add sour cream. Cook until heated through, stirring occasionally (do not boil), 3-4 minutes longer. Serve on buns.
Freeze option: Freeze cooled meat mixture in freezer containers. To use, partially thaw in refrigerator overnight. Heat through in a saucepan, stirring occasionally; add water if necessary. Serve on buns.
1 sandwich: 392 cal., 19g fat (9g sat. fat), 67mg chol., 845mg sod., 30g carb. (6g sugars, 2g fiber), 22g pro.

BURGERS WITH SPICY DILL SALSA

When I make burgers or hot dogs for barbecues or boating, I do a take-along topping that tastes like relish meets salsa.
—*Valonda Seward, Coarsegold, CA*

- -

PREP: 20 min. • **GRILL:** 10 min./batch
MAKES: 12 servings (3 cups salsa)

SALSA
- 1 jar (10 oz.) dill pickle relish
- 3 plum tomatoes, seeded and finely chopped
- 1 small white onion, finely chopped
- ½ cup finely chopped red onion
- ½ cup minced fresh cilantro
- 1 Tbsp. olive oil
- 1 to 2 serrano peppers, seeded and chopped

BURGERS
- 3 lbs. ground beef
- 2 tsp. salt
- 1 tsp. pepper
- 12 hamburger buns, split

1. In a bowl, mix the first 7 ingredients.
2. In another bowl, combine beef, salt and pepper; mix lightly but thoroughly. Shape into twelve ½-in.-thick patties.
3. In 2 batches, grill the burgers, covered, over medium heat or broil 4 in. from heat for 4-5 minutes on each side or until a thermometer reads 160°. Serve with salsa.
Note: Wear disposable gloves when cutting hot peppers; the oils can burn skin. Avoid touching your face.
1 burger with ¼ cup salsa: 371 cal., 16g fat (6g sat. fat), 70mg chol., 926mg sod., 31g carb. (4g sugars, 2g fiber), 25g pro.

❆
KUNG PAO SLOPPY JOES

What happens when you combine two favorites into one easy dish? Clean plates, that's what! My family loves Chinese food, but takeout can be expensive and not always the healthiest. This colorful stovetop sloppy joe recipe will please everyone at dinnertime, including the kids. My husband prefers to skip the bun and eat it over brown rice or rolled in lettuce wrap.
—*Julie Peterson, Crofton, MD*

- -

TAKES: 30 min. • **MAKES:** 6 servings

- 1 lb. lean ground beef (90% lean)
- 1 small sweet red pepper, chopped
- 4 green onions, chopped, divided
- 2 garlic cloves, minced
- 2 tsp. minced fresh gingerroot
- 1 to 1½ tsp. Sriracha chili sauce
- ½ cup reduced-sodium soy sauce
- 6 Tbsp. rice vinegar, divided
- ¼ cup water
- 3 Tbsp. sesame oil, divided
- 2 Tbsp. cornstarch
- 2 Tbsp. brown sugar
- 1 pkg. (12 oz.) broccoli coleslaw mix
- ½ cup chopped unsalted peanuts
- 6 hamburger buns, split, or flour tortillas (8 in.)
  Fresh cilantro leaves, optional

1. In a large cast-iron or other heavy skillet, cook beef, red pepper and 2 green onions over medium-high heat until the beef is no longer pink and the vegetables are tender, 6-8 minutes; crumble meat; drain. Add garlic, ginger and chili sauce; cook 1 minute longer.
2. In a small bowl, mix soy sauce, 4 Tbsp. vinegar, water, 1 Tbsp. oil, cornstarch and brown sugar until smooth; stir into beef mixture. Bring to a boil, stirring constantly; cook and stir until thickened, 1-2 minutes.
3. For the slaw, in a large bowl, combine coleslaw mix, remaining 2 green onions, 2 Tbsp. vinegar and 2 Tbsp. oil; toss to coat.
4. Spoon ½ cup of the beef mixture onto the bun bottoms. Top with ½ cup slaw and peanuts. If desired, top with cilantro leaves. Serve remaining slaw on the side.
Freeze option: Freeze cooled meat mixture in freezer containers. To use, partially thaw in refrigerator overnight. Heat through in a saucepan, stirring occasionally; add water if necessary.
1 sandwich: 461 cal., 21g fat (5g sat. fat), 47mg chol., 1299mg sod., 44g carb. (16g sugars, 4g fiber), 25g pro.

51

GREEN CHILE CHEESEBURGERS

A diner outside of Albuquerque, New Mexico, served the most amazing burgers topped with freshly roasted green chiles. They have a smoky flavor and a bit of a bite—perfect after a long day of driving.
—*James Schend, Pleasant Prairie, WI*

- -

PREP: 20 min. • **GRILL:** 15 min.
MAKES: 6 servings

- 3 whole green chiles, such as Anaheim or Hatch
- 2 lbs. ground beef
- 1 tsp. salt
- ½ tsp. pepper
- 6 slices sharp cheddar cheese
- 6 hamburger buns, split and toasted
  Optional: Lettuce leaves, sliced tomato, sliced onion, bacon and mayonnaise

1. Grill the peppers, covered, over high heat until they are blistered and blackened all over, 8-10 minutes, turning as needed. Immediately place peppers in a small bowl; let them stand, covered, 20 minutes. Reduce grill temperature to medium heat.
2. Meanwhile, in a large bowl, combine beef, salt and pepper; mix lightly but thoroughly. Shape into six ¾-in.-thick patties.
3. Peel off and discard charred skin from peppers. Cut peppers lengthwise in half; carefully remove stems and seeds. Cut into slices or coarsely chop.
4. Grill burgers, covered, over medium heat until a thermometer reads 160°, 5-7 minutes on each side. Top with cheese and chiles; grill, covered, until cheese is melted, 1-2 minutes longer. Top bun bottoms with the burgers. If desired, serve with lettuce, tomato, onion, bacon and mayonnaise.
1 burger: 482 cal., 26g fat (11g sat. fat), 116mg chol., 552mg sod., 23g carb. (4g sugars, 1g fiber), 36g pro.

ORANGE BEEF LETTUCE WRAPS

This is a lighter version of a restaurant favorite. I also recommend trying these healthy wraps with ground chicken or turkey.
—*Robin Haas, Cranston, RI*

- -

PREP: 20 min. • **COOK:** 15 min.
MAKES: 8 servings

SAUCE
- ¼ cup rice vinegar
- 3 Tbsp. water
- 3 Tbsp. orange marmalade
- 1 Tbsp. sugar
- 1 Tbsp. reduced-sodium soy sauce
- 2 garlic cloves, minced
- 1 tsp. Sriracha chili sauce

WRAPS
- 1½ lbs. lean ground beef (90% lean)
- 2 garlic cloves, minced
- 2 tsp. minced fresh gingerroot
- ¼ cup reduced-sodium soy sauce
- 2 Tbsp. orange juice
- 1 Tbsp. sugar
- 1 Tbsp. orange marmalade
- ¼ tsp. crushed red pepper flakes
- 2 tsp. cornstarch
- ¼ cup cold water
- 8 Bibb or Boston lettuce leaves
- 2 cups cooked brown rice
- 1 cup shredded carrots
- 3 green onions, thinly sliced

1. In a small bowl, combine sauce ingredients.
2. In a large skillet, cook beef, garlic and ginger over medium heat 8-10 minutes or until meat is no longer pink, crumble beef; drain.
3. Stir in soy sauce, orange juice, sugar, marmalade and pepper flakes. In a small bowl, mix cornstarch and water; stir into pan. Cook and stir 1-2 minutes or until sauce is thickened.
4. To serve, fill lettuce leaves with rice; cover with beef mixture. Top with carrots and green onions; drizzle with sauce.
1 wrap: 250 cal., 8g fat (3g sat. fat), 53mg chol., 462mg sod., 26g carb. (11g sugars, 2g fiber), 19g pro. **Diabetic exchanges:** 2 starch, 2 lean meat.

STUFFED SOURDOUGH SANDWICHES

Easy and freezer-ready, these stuffed sandwiches are delicious to boot. Sometimes I use cubed sharp cheddar cheese instead of shredded cheese when preparing.
—*Shannon Hansen, Oxnard, CA*

- -

TAKES: 30 min. • **MAKES:** 8 servings

- 1½ lbs. ground beef
- ½ cup chopped onion
- 1 can (15 oz.) tomato sauce
- 1 can (4 oz.) chopped green chiles
- 2 Tbsp. chili powder
- ½ cup chopped fresh mushrooms
- 2 Tbsp. sliced ripe olives
- ¼ tsp. garlic salt
- 1 cup shredded cheddar cheese
- 8 sourdough rolls

1. In a large skillet, cook beef and onion over medium heat until the meat is no longer pink, 5-7 minutes; crumble meat; drain.
2. Add the tomato sauce, chiles, chili powder, mushrooms, olives and garlic salt. Bring to a boil. Reduce the heat; simmer, uncovered, for 10 minutes or until heated through. Add the cheese; cook and stir until melted.
3. Cut ¼ in. off the top of each roll; set aside. Carefully hollow out the bottom of each roll, leaving a ¼-in. shell (discard removed bread or save for another use). Fill each roll with about ½ cup meat mixture. Replace bread tops.
4. Place filled sandwiches on a baking sheet. Bake at 350° for 10-15 minutes or until heated through.
Freeze option: Wrap individual sandwiches tightly in foil; freeze for up to 3 months. To use, thaw in the refrigerator overnight. Place foil-wrapped sandwiches on baking sheets. Bake at 350° for 20-25 minutes or until heated through.
1 sandwich: 336 cal., 14g fat (7g sat. fat), 57mg chol., 811mg sod., 29g carb. (2g sugars, 3g fiber), 23g pro.

MANGO JALAPENO SLOPPY JOE SLIDERS

I've loved sloppy joes since I can remember. In an attempt to give them a makeover, I thought of this idea, which was a big hit with my family, friends and co-workers! If you can't find a mango, chopped pineapple would work just as well.
—*Shea Goldstein, Royal Palm Beach, FL*

- -

PREP: 10 min. • **COOK:** 25 min.
MAKES: 12 servings

1	lb. ground beef
½	cup water
1	envelope taco seasoning
2	Tbsp. hot pepper sauce
2	Tbsp. steak sauce
2	Tbsp. olive oil
1	small onion, halved and sliced
1	small green pepper, sliced
1	medium mango, peeled and chopped
1	tsp. sugar
1	jalapeno pepper, sliced
¼	tsp. salt
12	dinner or slider rolls, split
¼	cup butter, melted
1	cup mayonnaise
½	cup salsa verde
1½	cups shredded sharp white cheddar cheese

1. In a large cast-iron or other heavy skillet, cook beef over medium heat until no longer pink, 8-10 minutes; crumble meat; drain. Add water, taco seasoning, pepper sauce and steak sauce; cook and stir until sauce thickens, 2-4 minutes. Remove and keep warm.
2. In another skillet, heat oil over medium-high heat. Add onion, green pepper, mango, sugar, jalapeno and salt; cook and stir until lightly browned, 8-10 minutes.
3. Meanwhile, place the rolls, cut side up, on an ungreased baking sheet. Broil 3-4 in. from heat until golden brown, 2-3 minutes.
4. Spread rolls with melted butter. Combine mayonnaise and salsa verde; spread over roll bottoms. Top with beef mixture, pepper mixture and cheese; replace tops. Serve with the extra sauce .
1 slider: 443 cal., 31g fat (10g sat. fat), 66mg chol., 870mg sod., 28g carb. (7g sugars, 2g fiber), 14g pro.

❄ 🍎 GREEK SLOPPY JOES

Feta is one of my favorite kinds of cheese. It's delish in a burger, but it truly shines in this Mediterranean-style sloppy joe.
—*Sonya Labbe, West Hollywood, CA*

TAKES: 25 min. • **MAKES:** 6 servings

- 1 lb. lean ground beef (90% lean)
- 1 small red onion, chopped
- 2 garlic cloves, minced
- 1 can (15 oz.) tomato sauce
- 1 tsp. dried oregano
  Romaine leaves
- 6 kaiser rolls, split and toasted
- ½ cup crumbled feta cheese

1. In a large skillet, cook beef, onion and garlic over medium heat until beef is no longer pink, 6-8 minutes; crumble beef; drain. Stir in tomato sauce and oregano. Bring to a boil. Reduce heat; simmer, uncovered, until the sauce is slightly thickened, 8-10 minutes, stirring occasionally.

2. Place romaine on roll bottoms; top with meat mixture. Sprinkle with feta cheese; replace tops.

Freeze option: Freeze cooled meat mixture in freezer containers. To use, partially thaw in refrigerator overnight. Heat through in a saucepan, stirring occasionally; add water if necessary.

1 sandwich: 337 cal., 10g fat (4g sat. fat), 52mg chol., 767mg sod., 36g carb. (3g sugars, 3g fiber), 24g pro. **Diabetic exchanges:** 3 lean meat, 2 starch, 1 vegetable.

GREEK BEEF PITAS

A local restaurant that's famous for pitas inspired me to make my own Greek-style sandwiches at home. Feel free to add olives if you'd like.
—*Nancy Sousley, Lafayette, IN*

TAKES: 25 min. • **MAKES:** 4 servings

- 1 lb. lean ground beef (90% lean)
- 1 small onion, chopped
- 3 garlic cloves, minced
- 1 tsp. dried oregano
- ¾ tsp. salt, divided
- 1 cup reduced-fat plain Greek yogurt
- 1 medium tomato, chopped
- ½ cup chopped peeled cucumber
- 1 tsp. dill weed
- 4 whole pita breads, warmed
  Optional: Additional chopped tomatoes and cucumber

1. In a large skillet, cook beef, onion and garlic over medium heat 8-10 minutes or until the beef is no longer pink and vegetables are tender; crumble beef; drain. Stir in oregano and ½ tsp. salt.

2. In a small bowl, mix the yogurt, tomato, cucumber, dill and remaining ¼ tsp. salt. Spoon ¾ cup of the beef mixture over each pita bread; top with 3 Tbsp. yogurt sauce. If desired, top with additional tomatoes and cucumbers. Serve with the remaining yogurt sauce.

1 serving: 407 cal., 11g fat (4g sat. fat), 74mg chol., 851mg sod., 40g carb. (5g sugars, 2g fiber), 34g pro.

FALL VEGETABLE SLOPPY JOES

I make this dish in the fall and sneak grated vegetables into the sloppy joe mixture. It's especially handy when children don't like to eat their vegetables! Just walk away until the end of the day and let the slow cooker do all the work. Also delicious: Top the filling with a little shredded cheese before serving.
—Nancy Heishman, Las Vegas, NV

PREP: 30 min. • **COOK:** 4 hours
MAKES: 18 servings

- 8 bacon strips, cut into 1-in. pieces
- 2 lbs. lean ground beef (90% lean)
- 1 medium onion, chopped
- 2 garlic cloves, minced
- 2 cups shredded peeled butternut squash
- 2 medium parsnips, peeled and shredded
- 2 medium carrots, peeled and shredded
- 1 can (12 oz.) cola
- 1 can (8 oz.) tomato paste
- 1 cup water
- ⅓ cup honey mustard
- 1½ tsp. ground cumin
- 1¼ tsp. salt
- 1 tsp. ground allspice
- ½ tsp. pepper
- 18 hamburger buns, split

1. In a large skillet, cook bacon over medium heat until crisp, stirring occasionally. Remove with a slotted spoon; drain on paper towels. Discard drippings.

2. In the same skillet, cook beef, onion and garlic over medium heat until beef is no longer pink and the onion is tender, 10-12 minutes; crumble beef; drain.

3. Transfer beef mixture to a 5- or 6-qt. slow cooker. Stir in squash, parsnips, carrots, cola, tomato paste, water, mustard and seasonings. Cook, covered, on low until vegetables are tender, 4-5 hours. Stir in bacon. Serve on buns.

Freeze option: Freeze cooled meat mixture in freezer containers. To use, partially thaw in refrigerator overnight. Heat through in a saucepan, stirring occasionally; add water if necessary.

1 sandwich: 275 cal., 8g fat (3g sat. fat), 35mg chol., 526mg sod., 35g carb. (9g sugars, 3g fiber), 17g pro. **Diabetic exchanges:** 2 starch, 2 lean meat.

STUFFED CHORIZO BURGERS WITH TOMATILLO SALSA

I created this chorizo burger for the first time I was meeting my new boyfriend's family. Needless to say, they loved the recipe—and fell in love with me, too! These burgers are perfect with plantain chips or a spicy potato salad from the grocer.
—Vivi Taylor, Middleburg, FL

PREP: 35 min. + chilling • **GRILL:** 15 min.
MAKES: 6 servings

- 5 oz. fresh chorizo
- 1⅓ cups crumbled Cotija or feta cheese
- 2 Tbsp. chopped fresh cilantro
- 2 garlic cloves, minced
- 1 tsp. minced seeded jalapeno pepper
- 2 lbs. ground beef
- ¾ tsp. coarsely ground pepper
- ¼ tsp. salt
- 6 hamburger buns, split
- 1½ cups tomatillo salsa (about 12 oz.), warmed

Optional: Sliced red onions, heirloom tomatoes, hot pepper sauce and fresh cilantro leaves

1. In a small skillet, cook chorizo over medium heat until it is cooked through, 4-6 minutes; crumble the meat. Drain and cool slightly. Combine chorizo with cheese, cilantro, garlic and jalapeno.

2. Shape ground beef into twelve ¼-in.-thick patties. Spread chorizo mixture over 6 patties to within ½ in. of edges; top with the remaining patties, pinching edges to seal. Refrigerate for 30 minutes.

3. Sprinkle burgers with pepper and salt; grill them covered, on a greased rack over medium direct heat 6-8 minutes per side, or until a thermometer reads 160°. Remove from heat; tent with foil and let them stand 4-5 minutes.

4. Meanwhile, grill buns until golden brown. Serve burgers on buns with salsa and toppings as desired.

1 burger: 594 cal., 34g fat (14g sat. fat), 141mg chol., 1418mg sod., 27g carb. (5g sugars, 1g fiber), 42g pro.

JUICY & DELICIOUS MIXED-SPICE BURGERS

We like trying to make street foods at home, perfecting recipes for dishes like gyros and these spiced burgers, known as kofta.
—*Anne Henry, Toronto, ON*

TAKES: 30 min. • **MAKES:** 6 servings

- 1 medium onion, finely chopped
- 3 Tbsp. minced fresh parsley
- 2 Tbsp. minced fresh mint
- 1 garlic clove, minced
- ¾ tsp. ground allspice
- ¾ tsp. pepper
- ½ tsp. ground cinnamon
- ½ tsp. salt
- ¼ tsp. ground nutmeg
- 1½ lbs. lean ground beef (90% lean)
  Optional: Lettuce leaves and refrigerated tzatziki sauce

1. Combine the first 9 ingredients. Add beef, mix lightly but thoroughly. Shape meat into six 4x2-in. oblong patties.
2. Grill patties, covered, over medium heat or broil 4 in. from heat, 4-6 minutes on each side or until a thermometer reads 160°. If desired, place on lettuce leaves and serve with sauce.
1 burger: 192 cal., 9g fat (4g sat. fat), 71mg chol., 259mg sod., 3g carb. (2g sugars, 1g fiber), 22g pro. **Diabetic exchanges:** 3 lean meat.

❄ 5i BARBECUE SLIDERS

When surprise company dropped by, all I had defrosted was sausage and ground beef. We combined the two for juicy burgers on the grill.
—*B.J. Larsen, Erie, CO*

TAKES: 25 min. • **MAKES:** 8 servings

- 1 lb. ground beef
- 1 lb. bulk pork sausage
- 1 cup barbecue sauce, divided
- 16 Hawaiian sweet rolls, split
  Optional: Lettuce leaves, sliced plum tomatoes and red onion

1. In a large bowl, mix beef and sausage lightly but thoroughly. Shape mixture into sixteen ½-in.-thick patties.
2. Grill patties, covered, over medium heat or broil 4-5 in. from heat until a thermometer reads 160°, 3-4 minutes on each side. Brush with ¼ cup sauce during the last 2 minutes of cooking. Serve on rolls with remaining barbecue sauce; top as desired.
Freeze option: Place patties on a waxed-paper-lined baking sheet; cover and freeze until firm. Remove from pan and transfer to an airtight container; return to freezer. To use, grill frozen patties as directed, increasing time as necessary.
2 sliders: 499 cal., 24g fat (9g sat. fat), 96mg chol., 885mg sod., 47g carb. (23g sugars, 2g fiber), 24g pro.

TEST KITCHEN TIP
For a healthier option, make these with 90% lean ground beef and turkey breakfast sausage—you'll save nearly 100 calories and more than half the fat per serving.

FAJITA BURGER WRAPS

This combo gives you a tender burger, crisp veggies and a crunchy shell, plus fajita flavor. Kids love it.
—*Antonio Smith, Canal Winchester, OH*

TAKES: 30 min. • **MAKES:** 4 servings

- 1 lb. lean ground beef (90% lean)
- 2 Tbsp. fajita seasoning mix
- 2 tsp. canola oil
- 1 medium onion, halved and sliced
- 1 medium green pepper, cut into thin strips
- 1 medium red sweet pepper, cut into thin strips
- 4 flour tortillas (10 in.)
- ¾ cup shredded cheddar cheese

1. In a large bowl, combine the beef and fajita seasoning, mixing lightly but thoroughly. Shape into four ½-in.-thick patties.

2. In a large skillet, heat oil over medium heat. Add burgers; cook 4 minutes on each side. Remove from pan. In same skillet, add onion and peppers; cook and stir for 5-7 minutes or until lightly browned and tender.

3. On the center of each tortilla, place ½ cup pepper mixture, 1 burger and 3 Tbsp. cheese. Fold sides of tortilla over the burger; fold top and bottom to close, forming a square.

4. Wipe skillet clean. Place wraps in skillet, seam side down. Cook on medium heat for 1-2 minutes on each side or until the tortillas are golden brown and a thermometer inserted in beef reads 160°.

1 wrap: 533 cal., 23g fat (9g sat. fat), 92mg chol., 1190mg sod., 45g carb. (5g sugars, 3g fiber), 34g pro.

MOM'S FAVORITE OLIVE BURGERS

When she was in her 80s, my mom would reminisce about the olive burgers she loved at Coney Island. I used her instructions to make them and ended up pleasing both of us.
—*Lorraine Hickman, Lansing, MI*

TAKES: 25 min. • **MAKES:** 4 servings

- 1 lb. ground beef
- 2 tsp. reduced-sodium soy sauce
- 2 tsp. Worcestershire sauce
- ¼ tsp. garlic powder
- ¼ tsp. onion powder
- 1 Tbsp. butter
- ½ cup sliced green olives with pimientos, drained
- ¼ cup Miracle Whip
- 1 Tbsp. stone-ground mustard
- 4 hamburger buns, toasted
- ¼ cup crumbled feta cheese, optional
  Bibb lettuce leaves, optional

1. In a large bowl, combine beef, soy sauce, Worcestershire, garlic powder and onion powder, mixing lightly but thoroughly. Shape into four ½-in.-thick patties, indenting the center slightly.

2. Melt butter in a large nonstick skillet; cook the burgers over medium heat until a thermometer reads 160°, 4-6 minutes on each side.

3. Meanwhile, in a small bowl, combine olives, Miracle Whip and mustard. Serve burgers on buns with olive mixture. If desired, top with feta cheese and lettuce.

1 burger with 2 Tbsp. olive mixture: 425 cal., 24g fat (8g sat. fat), 79mg chol., 837mg sod., 25g carb. (5g sugars, 1g fiber), 25g pro.

SO-EASY SLOPPY JOES

Everybody in the family will love the zesty flavor of this yummy comfort food. Try it spooned over warmed cornbread if you don't have buns.
—*Karen Anderson, Cuyahoga Falls, OH*

TAKES: 30 min. • **MAKES:** 6 servings

1½ lbs. ground beef
1 can (10 oz.) diced tomatoes
    and green chiles, undrained
1 can (6 oz.) tomato paste
¼ cup ketchup
2 Tbsp. brown sugar
1 Tbsp. spicy brown mustard
¼ tsp. salt
6 sandwich buns, split
    Fresh arugula, optional

In a large skillet, cook beef over medium heat until no longer pink, 5-7 minutes; crumble the meat; drain. Stir in the tomatoes, tomato paste, ketchup, brown sugar, mustard and salt. Bring to a boil. Reduce the heat; simmer, uncovered, for 5 minutes. Top meat with arugula. Serve on buns.
Freeze option: Freeze cooled meat mixture in freezer containers. To use, partially thaw in refrigerator overnight. Heat through in a saucepan, stirring occasionally and adding a little water if necessary. Serve on buns with arugula if desired.
1 sandwich: 478 cal., 18g fat (6g sat. fat), 70mg chol., 918mg sod., 49g carb. (15g sugars, 2g fiber), 30g pro.

🍎

HAWAIIAN BEEF SLIDERS

Sweet and savory with just a hint of heat, these dynamite burgers are packed with flavor. The combination of pineapple and bacon may sound unusual, but you'll find they're a perfect match.
—*Mary Relyea, Canastota, NY*

PREP: 30 min. + marinating • **GRILL:** 10 min.
MAKES: 1½ dozen

1 can (20 oz.) unsweetened
    crushed pineapple
1 tsp. pepper
¼ tsp. salt
1½ lbs. lean ground beef (90% lean)
¼ cup reduced-sodium soy sauce
2 Tbsp. ketchup
1 Tbsp. white vinegar
2 garlic cloves, minced
¼ tsp. crushed red pepper flakes
18 miniature whole wheat buns
    Baby spinach leaves
3 center-cut bacon strips,
    cooked and crumbled
    Sliced jalapeno peppers, optional

1. Drain pineapple, reserving juice and 1½ cups pineapple (save the extra pineapple for another use). In a large bowl, combine ¾ cup reserved crushed pineapple, the pepper and salt. Crumble the beef over the mixture and mix lightly but thoroughly. Shape into 18 patties; place in two 11x7-in. dishes.
2. In a small bowl, combine the soy sauce, ketchup, vinegar, garlic, pepper flakes and the reserved pineapple juice. Pour half the marinade into each dish with the patties; cover and refrigerate 1 hour, turning once.
3. Drain burgers and discard marinade. On a lightly oiled grill, cook patties, covered, over medium heat or broil 4 in. from heat on each side. Grill or broil until a thermometer reads 160° and juices run clear, 4-5 minutes.
4. Grill the buns, uncovered, until toasted, 1-2 minutes. Serve burgers on buns with spinach, remaining ¾ cup reserved pineapple, bacon and, if desired, jalapeno peppers.
3 sliders: 350 cal., 12g fat (4g sat. fat), 74mg chol., 444mg sod., 34g carb. (13g sugars, 4g fiber), 27g pro. **Diabetic exchanges:** 3 lean meat, 2 starch, ½ fat.

OPEN-FACED PIZZA BURGERS

I'm not sure where I first saw this recipe, but I'm glad I did! My family requests these burgers often. A dash of oregano livens up canned pizza sauce.
—*Sharon Schwartz, Burlington, WI*

TAKES: 30 min. • **MAKES:** 12 servings

1½ lbs. ground beef
¼ cup chopped onion
1 can (15 oz.) pizza sauce
1 can (4 oz.) mushroom stems and pieces, drained
1 Tbsp. sugar
½ tsp. dried oregano
6 hamburger buns, split and toasted
1½ cups shredded part-skim mozzarella cheese

1. In a large skillet, cook beef and onion over medium heat until the meat is no longer pink, 3-5 minutes, breaking into crumbles. Drain. Stir in the pizza sauce, mushrooms, sugar and oregano; mix well. Spoon onto buns; sprinkle with mozzarella cheese.

2. Place on ungreased baking sheets. Broil 4 in. from the heat until the cheese is melted, 2 minutes.

Freeze option: Place the split and toasted buns on a baking sheet. Spoon the meat mixture onto buns; freeze for 1 hour. Transfer to freezer-safe airtight containers. To use, thaw completely in the refrigerator. Sprinkle with cheese. Broil as directed in the recipe.

1 serving: 205 cal., 8g fat (4g sat. fat), 36mg chol., 357mg sod., 15g carb. (4g sugars, 1g fiber), 16g pro.

READER REVIEW

"This was wonderful — quick, simple and delicious. My whole family enjoyed."

JENRUNN, TASTEOFHOME.COM

CHEESEBURGER QUESADILLAS

I created these fun cheeseburger-quesadilla mashups in honor of my family's two favorite foods. They are so yummy and easy to make!
—*Jennifer Stowell, Deep River, IA*

TAKES: 25 min. • **MAKES:** 4 servings

1	lb. ground beef
1	cup ketchup
⅓	cup prepared mustard
4	bacon strips, cooked and crumbled
2	Tbsp. Worcestershire sauce
⅔	cup mayonnaise
2	Tbsp. 2% milk
2	Tbsp. dill pickle relish
¼	tsp. pepper
8	flour tortillas (8 in.)
1	cup shredded cheddar cheese
	Optional: Shredded lettuce and chopped tomatoes

1. In a large skillet, cook beef over medium heat until no longer pink, 6-8 minutes, crumble meat; drain. Stir in ketchup, mustard, bacon and Worcestershire sauce; bring to a boil. Reduce heat; simmer, uncovered, until slightly thickened, 5-7 minutes, stirring occasionally.
2. Meanwhile, in a small bowl, combine the mayonnaise, milk, relish and pepper; set aside.
3. Preheat griddle over medium heat. Sprinkle 4 tortillas with cheese; top with beef mixture and remaining tortillas. Place on griddle; cook until golden brown and cheese is melted, 1-2 minutes on each side. Serve with sauce and, if desired, lettuce and tomatoes.

1 quesadilla with about ¼ cup sauce: 1002 cal., 60g fat (17g sat. fat), 110mg chol., 2115mg sod., 75g carb. (18g sugars, 4g fiber), 39g pro.

> **TEST KITCHEN TIP**
> The crossover nature of these quesadillas mean that you can serve them alongside traditional Tex-Mex sides, or pair them up as you would a burger—it's all good!

❄ KING BURGERS

My husband and I made up this recipe together. The sauce for this juicy burger tastes even better when it has been refrigerated overnight.
—*Mary Potter, Sterling Heights, MI*

TAKES: 30 min. • **MAKES:** 6 servings

5	Tbsp. butter, divided
¼	cup mayonnaise
2	Tbsp. prepared horseradish
2	Tbsp. Dijon mustard
⅛	tsp. salt
⅛	tsp. pepper
1½	lbs. ground beef
⅓	cup beef broth
2½	tsp. hamburger seasoning, divided
6	hamburger buns, split
	Optional: Shredded lettuce, sliced tomato and red onion

1. Cut 2 Tbsp. butter into 6 slices, let remaining butter soften. Place slices in a single layer on a small plate; freeze until firm. For sauce, in a small bowl, mix mayonnaise, horseradish, mustard, salt and pepper until blended.
2. In a large bowl, combine beef, broth and 1½ tsp. hamburger seasoning; mix lightly but thoroughly. Shape into 6 patties. Place a butter slice in the center of each; shape beef around the butter slices, forming ¾-in.-thick patties. Sprinkle the patties with the remaining 1 tsp. of hamburger seasoning.
3. Grill burgers, covered, over medium heat for 5-7 minutes on each side or until a thermometer reads 160°.
4. Spread buns with the softened butter. Grill them over medium heat, cut side down, for 30-60 seconds or until toasted. Serve burgers on buns with sauce and toppings.

Freeze option: Place patties on a foil-lined baking sheet; wrap and freeze until firm. Transfer to a freezer container; return to freezer. To use, cook frozen patties as directed, increasing time as necessary for a thermometer to read 160°.

1 burger: 482 cal., 32g fat (12g sat. fat), 99mg chol., 822mg sod., 23g carb. (3g sugars, 1g fiber), 25g pro.

STUFFED SMOKY BEEF & PORK BURGERS

These stuffed burgers are far from ordinary. The ground pork makes them juicy and extra flavorful. Stuffing them takes a bit of extra time, but it's well worth it!
—*Francine Lizotte, Surrey, BC*

PREP: 30 min. + chilling • **GRILL:** 15 min.
MAKES: 12 servings

- 2 lbs. ground beef
- 2 lbs. ground pork
- ½ cup panko bread crumbs
- ½ cup finely chopped red onion
- 3 Tbsp. minced fresh basil
- 2 tsp. smoked paprika
- ½ tsp. salt
- ½ tsp. pepper
- ¾ cup finely chopped fresh pineapple
- ¾ cup barbecue sauce
- 12 bacon strips, cooked and crumbled
     Sliced Jarlsberg cheese, optional
- 12 hamburger buns, split
     Optional: Additional barbecue sauce, chopped red onion and fresh basil.

1. Combine the first 8 ingredients, mixing lightly but thoroughly. Shape into 24 thin patties. Divide pineapple, barbecue sauce and bacon over the center of 12 patties; top with the remaining patties, pressing edges firmly to seal. Refrigerate, covered, for 1 hour.
2. Grill burgers, covered, over medium heat or broil 4 in. from heat until a thermometer reads 160°, 7-8 minutes on each side. Top with cheese if desired; grill, covered, until cheese is melted, 1-2 minutes longer. Serve on buns and, if desired, top with additional barbecue sauce, red onion and fresh basil.
1 burger: 508 cal., 25g fat (9g sat. fat), 105mg chol., 724mg sod., 33g carb. (10g sugars, 1g fiber), 35g pro.

SUN-DRIED TOMATO BISTRO BURGERS

This burger brings together many flavors my family enjoys, complete with a surprise in the center. You can use Gorgonzola, feta, smoked Gouda, blue cheese or another family favorite.
—*Aaron Shields, Hamburg, NY*

PREP: 40 min. • **GRILL:** 10 min.
MAKES: 8 servings

- 1 jar (7 oz.) oil-packed sun-dried tomatoes
- 3 medium onions, halved and thinly sliced
- 3 Tbsp. balsamic vinegar
- ½ cup finely chopped red onion
- 2 Tbsp. dried basil
- 2 tsp. ground cumin
- 2 tsp. ground chipotle pepper
- ½ tsp. salt
- ¼ tsp. pepper
- 3 lbs. lean ground beef (90% lean)
- 1 cup crumbled goat cheese
- 8 hamburger buns, split
     Mixed salad greens, optional

1. Drain tomatoes, reserving ⅓ cup oil; set aside. In a large skillet, saute sliced onions in 3 Tbsp. of the reserved oil until softened. Add vinegar. Reduce heat to medium-low; cook, stirring occasionally, until deep golden brown, 30-40 minutes.
2. Meanwhile, chop sun-dried tomatoes and transfer to a large bowl. Add the red onion, seasonings and remaining 7 tsp. of reserved oil. Crumble beef over mixture and mix lightly but thoroughly. Shape into 16 patties. Place 2 Tbsp. goat cheese on the center of each of 8 patties. Top with the remaining patties and press edges firmly to seal.
3. Grill burgers, covered, over medium heat until a thermometer reads 160° and juices run clear, 5-7 minutes on each side.
4. Place buns, cut side down, on grill until toasted, 1-2 minutes. If desired, top buns with mixed greens. Serve burgers on buns with onions.
1 burger with 2 Tbsp. onions: 596 cal., 32g fat (10g sat. fat), 123mg chol., 588mg sod., 36g carb. (7g sugars, 5g fiber), 42g pro.

CARAMELIZED-ONION BACON BURGERS

These juicy, flavorful burgers feature a nice tang with the barbecue sauce on top. They're always a hit at get-togethers.
—*Jordan Mason, Brookville, PA*

- -

PREP: 30 min. • **GRILL:** 15 min.
MAKES: 4 servings

⅓ cup plus ½ cup barbecue sauce, divided
1 lb. ground beef
4 bacon strips, halved
1 large sweet onion, sliced
4 Tbsp. butter, divided
4 hamburger buns, split
4 slices cheddar cheese

1. Place ⅓ cup barbecue sauce in a small bowl. Crumble beef over barbecue sauce and mix lightly but thoroughly. Shape into 4 patties.
2. In a small skillet, cook bacon over medium heat until crisp. Remove to paper towels; drain.
3. In another skillet, saute sliced onion in 2 Tbsp. butter until softened. Reduce heat to medium-low; cook, stirring occasionally, for 20-25 minutes or until golden brown.
4. Spread buns with remaining 2 Tbsp. butter; set aside. Grill burgers, covered, over medium heat or broil 4 in. from the heat for 5-7 minutes on each side or until a thermometer reads 160° and juices run clear. Top with cheese. Grill 1 minute longer or until cheese is melted.
5. Place buns, cut side down, on grill for 1-2 minutes or until toasted. Spread buns with remaining ½ cup barbecue sauce. Serve burgers on buns with onion and bacon.
1 burger: 645 cal., 40g fat (20g sat. fat), 137mg chol., 1153mg sod., 35g carb. (14g sugars, 2g fiber), 35g pro.

❄ PIZZA SLOPPY JOES

If you're tired of the same old sloppy joes, here's a tasty twist! These messy, kid-friendly sandwiches have a definite pizza flavor that families will love...but be sure to serve them with a fork!
—*Connie Pettit, Logan, OH*

- -

TAKES: 30 min. • **MAKES:** 6 servings

1 lb. lean ground beef (90% lean)
1 medium onion, chopped
¼ cup chopped green pepper
1 jar (14 oz.) pizza sauce
3 oz. sliced turkey pepperoni (about 50 slices), chopped
½ tsp. dried basil
¼ tsp. dried oregano
6 hamburger buns, split
6 Tbsp. shredded part-skim mozzarella cheese

1. In a large nonstick skillet, cook the beef, onion and pepper over medium heat until meat is no longer pink, 5-7 minutes; crumble beef. Drain if necessary. Stir in the pizza sauce, pepperoni and herbs. Bring to a boil. Reduce heat; cover and simmer for 10 minutes.
2. Spoon ⅔ cup of the beef mixture onto each bun; sprinkle with cheese. Place on a baking sheet. Broil 3-4 in. from the heat for 1 minute or until cheese is melted. Replace tops of buns.
Freeze option: Freeze cooled meat mixture in freezer containers. To use, partially thaw in refrigerator overnight. Heat through in a saucepan, stirring occasionally; add water if necessary. Serve on buns.
1 sandwich: 329 cal., 11g fat (4g sat. fat), 59mg chol., 825mg sod., 29g carb. (8g sugars, 3g fiber), 26g pro.

FETA MUSHROOM BURGERS

I got this recipe from my son-in-law and tweaked it to make it healthier. The burgers are so quick to whip up on the grill.
—Dolores Block, Frankenmuth, MI

TAKES: 25 min. • **MAKES:** 6 servings

- 1 lb. lean ground beef (90% lean)
- 3 Italian turkey sausage links (4 oz. each), casings removed
- 2 tsp. Worcestershire sauce
- ½ tsp. garlic powder
- 2 Tbsp. balsamic vinegar
- 1 Tbsp. olive oil
- 6 large portobello mushrooms, stems removed
- 1 large onion, cut into ½-in. slices
- 6 Tbsp. crumbled feta or blue cheese
- 6 whole wheat hamburger buns or sourdough rolls, split
- 10 fresh basil leaves, thinly sliced

1. Combine first 4 ingredients; mix lightly but thoroughly. Shape into six ½-in.-thick patties. Mix vinegar and oil; brush over mushrooms.
2. Place burgers, mushrooms and onion on an oiled grill rack over medium heat. Grill, covered, until a thermometer inserted in burgers reads 160° and mushrooms and onion are tender, 4-6 minutes per side.
3. Fill mushroom caps with cheese; grill, covered, until cheese is melted, 1-2 minutes. Grill buns, cut side down, until toasted, 30-60 seconds. Serve burgers on buns; top with mushrooms, basil and onion.
1 burger: 371 cal., 15g fat (5g sat. fat), 72mg chol., 590mg sod., 31g carb. (8g sugars, 5g fiber), 28g pro. **Diabetic exchanges:** 4 lean meat, 2 starch, 1 vegetable, ½ fat.

SLIDERS WITH SPICY BERRY SAUCE

For patriotic food, you can't beat a burger. My sliders have red tomatoes, white cheddar and blueberry sauce. For extra pop, I mix in ginger beer and chipotle.
—Crystal Schlueter, Northglenn, CO

- -

PREP: 40 min. • **GRILL:** 10 min./batch
MAKES: 2 dozen

- 2 cups fresh blueberries
- 1 cup ginger beer or ginger ale
- ½ cup balsamic ketchup
- 2 Tbsp. steak sauce
- 2 Tbsp. honey
- 1 to 2 Tbsp. finely chopped chipotle peppers in adobo sauce
- ¼ tsp. salt
- ¼ tsp. pepper
- SLIDERS
- 2 pkg. (12 oz. each) Hawaiian sweet rolls
- 3 Tbsp. butter, softened
- 3 lbs. ground beef
- 1½ tsp. salt
- ¾ tsp. pepper
- 6 slices sharp white cheddar or provolone cheese, quartered
- 1 medium red onion, halved and thinly sliced
- 3 plum tomatoes, thinly sliced

1. In a saucepan, combine the first 8 ingredients; bring to a boil. Reduce heat; simmer, uncovered, 15-20 minutes or until thickened, stirring occasionally. Cool slightly. Transfer to a food processor; process until pureed. Reserve ¼ cup sauce for brushing burgers (the rest is for serving).
2. Split rolls horizontally in half. Spread bottoms with butter. In a large bowl, combine the beef, salt and pepper, mixing lightly but thoroughly. Shape into twenty-four ½-in.-thick patties, pressing an indentation in the center of each.
3. In two batches, grill burgers, covered, over medium heat 3-4 minutes on each side or until a thermometer reads 160°; brush tops with the ¼ cup reserved sauce after turning. Top with cheese; grill, covered, 15-30 seconds longer or until melted. Serve on rolls with onion, tomatoes and the remaining sauce.

1 slider with about 2 tsp. sauce: 272 cal., 13g fat (6g sat. fat), 62mg chol., 422mg sod., 23g carb. (11g sugars, 2g fiber), 16g pro.

ITALIAN JOES ON TEXAS TOAST

This is toasty-good for a weeknight on the go. If you double the crushed tomatoes, meat and wine, you'll have enough sauce to freeze.
—Ashley Armstrong, Kingsland, GA

- -

TAKES: 30 min. • **MAKES:** 8 servings

- 1 lb. ground beef
- 1 small green pepper, finely chopped
- 1 medium onion, finely chopped
- 3 garlic cloves, minced
- ½ cup dry red wine or beef broth
- 1 can (14½ oz.) diced tomatoes, undrained
- ¼ cup tomato paste
- ¼ tsp. salt
- ⅛ tsp. pepper
- 1 pkg. (11¼ oz.) frozen garlic Texas toast
- 8 slices part-skim mozzarella cheese

1. Preheat oven to 425°. In a large skillet, cook beef with green pepper, onion and garlic over medium-high heat until meat is no longer pink, 5-7 minutes; crumble meat; drain. Stir in wine and bring to a boil; cook until wine is reduced by half, about 2 minutes. Stir in tomatoes, tomato paste, salt and pepper; return to a boil. Reduce heat; simmer, uncovered, until mixture is thickened, 2-3 minutes, stirring occasionally.
2. Meanwhile, place Texas toast on a foil-lined 15x10x1-in. pan; bake until lightly browned, 8-10 minutes.
3. Spoon beef mixture onto toast; top with cheese. Bake until cheese is melted, 3-4 minutes. Serve immediately.

1 open-faced sandwich: 353 cal., 19g fat (7g sat. fat), 58mg chol., 626mg sod., 25g carb. (5g sugars, 2g fiber), 22g pro.

5i
BROCCOLI-CHEDDAR BEEF ROLLS

My grandma's recipe for beef rolls is easy to change up. Load them with ham, veggies—even olives— however you like!
—*Kent Call, Riverside, UT*

- -

TAKES: 30 min. • **MAKES:** 6 servings

½	lb. lean ground beef (90% lean)
2	cups chopped fresh broccoli
1	small onion, chopped
½	tsp. salt
¼	tsp. pepper
6	hard rolls
2	cups shredded cheddar cheese, divided

1. Preheat to 325°. In a large skillet, cook beef with broccoli and onion over medium heat until meat is no longer pink, 4-6 minutes. Crumble beef and stir in salt and pepper.
2. Cut one-third off the top of each roll; discard or save for another use. Hollow out bottoms, leaving ½-in.-thick shells; place on a baking sheet.
3. Tear bread removed from centers into ½-in. pieces; place in a bowl. Stir in 1½ cups cheese and the beef mixture. Spoon into bread shells. Sprinkle with remaining ½ cup cheese. Bake until heated through and the cheese is melted, 10-15 minutes.
1 serving: 394 cal., 18g fat (9g sat. fat), 61mg chol., 783mg sod., 34g carb. (2g sugars, 2g fiber), 23g pro.

READER REVIEW
"My family really enjoyed this recipe! Since it's easy and relatively quick to make, it will definitely be on our 'make again' list."
KSMOLLYSMOM, TASTEOFHOME.COM

❄ WHISKEY CHEDDAR BURGERS

This juicy burger has big flavors to satisfy even the heartiest appetites. It always impresses at our cookouts.
—*Amber Nicholson, Winooski, VT*

- -

TAKES: 30 min. • **MAKES:** 8 servings

¼	cup whiskey
1	Tbsp. reduced-sodium soy sauce
1	Tbsp. Worcestershire sauce
1	cup shredded sharp cheddar cheese
¼	cup finely chopped onion
2	Tbsp. seasoned bread crumbs
3	garlic cloves, minced
½	tsp. salt
½	tsp. paprika
½	tsp. dried basil
½	tsp. pepper
1½	lbs. lean ground beef (90% lean)
8	onion rolls or hamburger buns, split
	Optional: Lettuce leaves, sliced tomato, cheddar cheese slices and barbecue sauce

1. Combine the first 11 ingredients. Add beef; mix lightly but thoroughly. Shape into eight ½-in.-thick patties.
2. On a greased grill, cook the burgers, covered, over medium heat or broil 4 in. from heat for 4-5 minutes on each side or until a thermometer reads 160°. Serve burgers on rolls with toppings as desired.
Freeze option: Place patties on a waxed paper-lined baking sheet; wrap and freeze until firm. Remove from pan and transfer to an airtight container; return to freezer. To use, grill frozen patties as directed, increasing time as necessary for a thermometer to read 160°.
1 burger: 370 cal., 14g fat (6g sat. fat), 67mg chol., 654mg sod., 28g carb. (4g sugars, 1g fiber), 26g pro.

ASHLEY ARMSTRONG
Kingsland, GA

Ground Beef

MEAT LOAVES & MEAT PIES

With this variety, meat loaf night will never be ho-hum. And meat pies— wrapped in a pastry crust, topped with potatoes, or in hand-held portions— are a delight. Talk about comfort food!

HOME-STYLE GLAZED MEAT LOAF

Grated carrots and cheese add a hint of color to this down-home glazed meat loaf. We look forward to meat loaf sandwiches the next day!
—*Sandra Etelamaki, Ishpeming, MI*

- -

PREP: 15 min. • **BAKE:** 1 hour + standing
MAKES: 12 servings

2	large eggs, beaten
⅔	cup 2% milk
1½	cups shredded cheddar cheese
1	cup crushed saltines (about 30 crackers)
1	cup finely shredded carrots
½	cup finely chopped onion
½	tsp. salt
¼	tsp. garlic powder
¼	tsp. pepper
2	lbs. lean ground beef
½	cup packed brown sugar
½	cup ketchup
2	Tbsp. Dijon mustard
	Minced fresh parsley, optional

1. Preheat the oven to 350°. In a large bowl, combine eggs, milk, cheese, saltines, carrots, onion, salt, garlic powder and pepper. Crumble the beef over the mixture and mix it lightly but thoroughly. Shape into a loaf. Place in a greased 13x9-in. baking dish. Bake, uncovered, for 50 minutes.

2. For glaze, in a small saucepan, bring brown sugar, ketchup and mustard to a boil. Reduce heat; simmer, uncovered, for 3-5 minutes or until heated through. Spoon over meat loaf.

3. Bake 10-15 minutes longer or until meat is no longer pink and a thermometer reads 160°. Drain; let stand for 10 minutes before slicing. If desired, top with minced fresh parsley.

1 piece: 266 cal., 12g fat (6g sat. fat), 100mg chol., 494mg sod., 18g carb. (12g sugars, 1g fiber), 20g pro.

UPSIDE-DOWN MEAT PIE

This recipe, which my sister gave me more than 30 years ago, is perfect whenever friends drop by. It mixes up in a jiffy, yet it's substantial and satisfying.

—*Cora Dowling, Toledo, OH*

PREP: 25 min. • **BAKE:** 20 min.
MAKES: 4 servings

- 1 lb. ground beef
- ½ cup chopped onion
- ½ tsp. salt
- 1 can (15 oz.) tomato sauce

BAKING POWDER BISCUITS

- 1 cup all-purpose flour
- 2 tsp. baking powder
- 1 tsp. celery salt
- 1 tsp. paprika
- ½ tsp. salt
- ¼ tsp. pepper
- 3 Tbsp. butter
- ½ cup 2% milk

1. In a large cast-iron or other ovenproof skillet, cook ground beef and onion until the beef is browned and the onion is tender; crumble meat; drain. Add salt and tomato sauce; simmer 10-15 minutes.

2. Meanwhile, combine flour, baking powder, celery salt, paprika, salt and pepper in a bowl. Cut in butter until mixture resembles coarse meal. Add the milk and stir until a soft dough forms. Drop dough by tablespoonfuls onto meat mixture.

3. Bake, uncovered, at 475° until biscuits are golden, about 20 minutes.

1 serving: 421 cal., 20g fat (11g sat. fat), 83mg chol., 1827mg sod., 33g carb. (5g sugars, 2g fiber), 26g pro.

MEXICAN-STYLE MEAT LOAVES

On a vacation to Arizona, I fell in love with a type of Latin American meatballs called *albondigas*. After playing with different spices, I created a version that is amazing as a meat loaf.

—*James Schend, Pleasant Prairie, WI*

PREP: 20 min. • **BAKE:** 50 min. + standing
MAKES: 2 loaves (8 servings each)

- 3 large eggs, lightly beaten
- ⅔ cup 2% milk
- ⅔ cup thick and zesty tomato sauce
- 2 Tbsp. Worcestershire sauce
- 1 large onion, finely chopped
- 2 cans (2¼ oz. each) sliced ripe olives, drained
- ¾ cup dry bread crumbs
- ⅓ cup minced fresh cilantro
- 2½ tsp. ground cumin
- 2½ tsp. chili powder
- 1 tsp. salt
- 1 tsp. pepper
- 3 lbs. lean ground beef (90% lean)
  Optional: Salsa and additional cilantro

1. Preheat the oven to 350°. In a large bowl, combine the first 12 ingredients. Add beef; mix lightly but thoroughly. Transfer mixture to 2 greased 9x5-in. loaf pans.

2. Bake 50-55 minutes or until a thermometer reads 160°. Let loaves stand 10 minutes before slicing. If desired, top with salsa and cilantro.

1 piece: 196 cal., 10g fat (3g sat. fat), 89mg chol., 453mg sod., 7g carb. (2g sugars, 1g fiber), 19g pro. **Diabetic exchanges:** 3 lean meat, ½ starch.

BARBECUED ONION MEAT LOAVES

Onion soup mix and stuffing are the surprise ingredients in these super-simple mini meat loaves. They're definite family-pleasers.
—*Nicole Russman, Lincoln, NE*

- -

TAKES: 25 min. • **MAKES:** 5 servings

- 1   large egg, lightly beaten
- ⅓   cup 2% milk
- 2   Tbsp. plus ¼ cup barbecue sauce, divided
- ½   cup crushed seasoned stuffing
- 1   Tbsp. onion soup mix
- 1¼ lbs. lean ground beef (90% lean)
       Minced fresh parsley, optional

1. In a large bowl, combine egg, milk, 2 Tbsp. barbecue sauce, stuffing and onion soup mix. Crumble beef over mixture and mix lightly but thoroughly. Shape into 5 loaves; arrange around the edge of a microwave-safe dish.
2. Microwave, uncovered, on high for 4½ - 5½ minutes or until no pink remains and a thermometer reads 160°. Cover and let stand for 5-10 minutes. Top with the remaining ¼ cup barbecue sauce. If desired, sprinkle with minced parsley.
1 serving: 234 cal., 10g fat (4g sat. fat), 100mg chol., 451mg sod., 9g carb. (3g sugars, 1g fiber), 25g pro. **Diabetic exchanges:** 3 lean meat, ½ starch.

JUDY BATSON
Tampa, FL

BEEF & BLUE CHEESE TART

This elegant, rustic recipe goes together in minutes and is so simple. It is perfect for when you're entertaining guests!
—*Judy Batson, Tampa, FL*

- -

PREP: 20 min. • **BAKE:** 15 min.
MAKES: 6 servings

- ½   lb. lean ground beef (90% lean)
- 1¾ cups sliced fresh mushrooms
- ½   medium red onion, thinly sliced
- ¼   tsp. salt
- ¼   tsp. pepper
- 1   tube (13.8 oz.) refrigerated pizza crust
- ½   cup reduced-fat sour cream
- 2   tsp. Italian seasoning
- ½   tsp. garlic powder
- ¾   cup crumbled blue cheese

1. Preheat oven to 425°. In a large skillet, cook beef, mushrooms and onion over medium heat until meat is no longer pink, 5-7 minutes; crumble meat; drain. Stir in salt and pepper; set aside.
2. On a lightly floured surface, roll the crust into a 15x12-in. rectangle. Transfer the crust to a parchment-lined baking sheet.
3. In a small bowl, combine the sour cream, Italian seasoning and garlic powder; spread over crust to within 2 in. of edges. Spoon beef mixture over top. Fold up edges of crust over filling, leaving center uncovered.
4. Bake for 15-18 minutes or until the crust is golden. Using the parchment, slide tart onto a wire rack. Sprinkle with blue cheese; let stand for 5 minutes before slicing.
1 piece: 328 cal., 12g fat (5g sat. fat), 43mg chol., 803mg sod., 35g carb. (6g sugars, 1g fiber), 19g pro. **Diabetic exchanges:** 2 starch, 2 lean meat, 2 fat.

READER REVIEW
"We've added this to our favorite-recipes list and have it regularly now. It is so easy to make and super satisfying. Great with a side salad."
NITCHALS, TASTEOFHOME.COM

SASSY SALSA MEAT LOAVES

Here's a twist on classic meat loaf that can be made ahead and will last for a few days. Make meat loaf sandwiches with the leftovers, buns and a little Monterey Jack cheese.
—*Tasha Tully, Owings Mills, MD*

PREP: 25 min. • **BAKE:** 65 min. + standing
MAKES: 2 loaves (6 servings each)

¾ cup uncooked instant brown rice
1 can (8 oz.) tomato sauce
1½ cups salsa, divided
1 large onion, chopped
1 large egg, lightly beaten
1 celery rib, finely chopped
¼ cup minced fresh parsley
2 Tbsp. minced fresh cilantro
2 garlic cloves, minced
1 Tbsp. chili powder
1½ tsp. salt
½ tsp. pepper
2 lbs. lean ground beef (90% lean)
1 lb. ground turkey
½ cup shredded reduced-fat Monterey Jack cheese or Mexican cheese blend

1. Preheat oven to 350°. Cook the rice according to package directions; cool slightly.
2. In a large bowl, combine the tomato sauce, ½ cup salsa, onion, egg, celery, parsley, garlic seasonings; stir in rice. Add beef and turkey; mix lightly but thoroughly.
3. Shape into two 8x4-in. loaves and place in a greased 15x10x1-in. baking pan. Bake until a thermometer inserted in center reads 160°, 1 to 1¼ hours.
4. Spread with the remaining 1 cup of salsa and sprinkle with cheese; bake until cheese is melted, about 5 minutes. Let stand 10 minutes before slicing.
Freeze option: Bake meat loaves without topping. Securely wrap cooled meat loaves in foil and freeze. To use, partially thaw in refrigerator overnight. Unwrap meat loaves; place in a greased 15x10x1-in. baking pan. Reheat in a preheated 350° oven until a thermometer inserted in center reads 165°, 40-45 minutes; top as directed.
1 piece: 237 cal., 11g fat (4g sat. fat), 91mg chol., 634mg sod., 9g carb. (2g sugars, 1g fiber), 25g pro. **Diabetic exchanges:** 3 lean meat, ½ starch, ½ fat.

BEEF POTPIE

For more than a dozen years, this has been the No. 1 dish to serve company at our house. So far, everyone has given it a thumbs-up rating.
—*Hannah McDowell, Penns Creek, PA*

PREP: 45 min. • **BAKE:** 35 min. + standing
MAKES: 6 servings

CRUST
- 1 cup all-purpose flour
- ½ cup whole wheat flour
- ½ tsp. salt
- 6 Tbsp. shortening
- 2 Tbsp. cold butter
- 1 cup shredded cheddar cheese
- ¼ cup cold water

FILLING
- 1 lb. ground beef
- 2 celery ribs, chopped
- 1 medium onion, chopped
- ¼ cup chopped green pepper
- 1 can (8 oz.) tomato sauce
- 1 can (7 oz.) whole kernel corn, drained
- 1 Tbsp. Worcestershire sauce
- ¼ tsp. salt
- ⅛ tsp. pepper

1. In a large bowl, combine flours and salt. Cut in shortening and butter until crumbly. Add cheese; toss to blend. Gradually add water, tossing with a fork until dough forms a ball. Divide dough in half. Cover and refrigerate.

2. For filling, in a large skillet, cook the beef, celery, onion and green pepper over medium heat until meat is no longer pink; 5-7 minutes; crumble the meat; drain. Stir in the remaining ingredients. Bring to a boil. Reduce heat; cover and simmer for 15 minutes.

3. On a lightly floured surface, roll out half of dough to fit the bottom of an ungreased 8-in. square baking dish. Transfer to the dish. Spoon filling over crust. Roll out the remaining dough to fit the top of the dish; cut slits or use cookie cutters to cut out shapes. Place crust over filling; trim and flute edges.

4. If desired, arrange cutouts over crusts. Bake at 375° until bubbly and crust is golden brown, 35-40 minutes. Let stand for 10-15 minutes before cutting.

1 serving: 487 cal., 29g fat (12g sat. fat), 67mg chol., 802mg sod., 33g carb. (4g sugars, 3g fiber), 23g pro.

ZIPPY SWEET & SOUR MEAT LOAF

Put a zippy twist on your meat loaf. It won't take long for it to become a most-requested meal.
—*Deb Thompson, Lincoln, NE*

TAKES: 25 min. + standing • **MAKES:** 4 servings

- 1 large egg, lightly beaten
- 5 Tbsp. ketchup, divided
- 2 Tbsp. prepared mustard
- ½ cup dry bread crumbs
- 2 Tbsp. onion soup mix
- ¼ tsp. salt
- ¼ tsp. pepper
- 1 lb. lean ground beef (90% lean)
- ¼ cup sugar
- 2 Tbsp. brown sugar
- 2 Tbsp. cider vinegar

1. In a large bowl, combine the egg, 2 Tbsp. ketchup, mustard, bread crumbs, dry soup mix, salt and pepper. Crumble beef over mixture and mix lightly but thoroughly. Shape into an oval loaf.

2. Place loaf in a shallow 1-qt. microwave-safe dish. Cover and microwave on high for 7-8 minutes; let rest 5 minutes. Microwave 1-3 minutes longer or until no pink remains and a thermometer reads 160°; drain.

3. In a small bowl, combine the sugars, vinegar and remaining ketchup; drizzle over meat loaf. Cover and microwave on high for 2-3 minutes longer or until heated through. Let stand for 10 minutes before slicing.

1 serving: 353 cal., 11g fat (4g sat. fat), 122mg chol., 944mg sod., 37g carb. (25g sugars, 1g fiber), 25g pro.

CHEDDAR-TOPPED BARBECUE MEAT LOAF

My family loves the bold barbecue flavor of this tender meat loaf. I love that it's such an easy recipe to prepare in the slow cooker.
—*David Snodgrass, Columbia, MO*

PREP: 20 min. • **COOK:** 3¼ hours
MAKES: 8 servings

- 3   large eggs, lightly beaten
- ¾   cup old-fashioned oats
- 1   large green or sweet red pepper, chopped (about 1½ cups)
- 1   small onion, finely chopped
- 1   envelope onion soup mix
- 3   garlic cloves, minced
- ½   tsp. salt
- ¼   tsp. pepper
- 2   lbs. lean ground beef (90% lean)
- 1   cup ketchup
- 2   Tbsp. brown sugar
- 1   Tbsp. barbecue seasoning
- 1   tsp. ground mustard
- 1   cup shredded cheddar cheese

1. Cut three 18x3-in. strips of heavy-duty foil; crisscross them so they resemble the spokes of a wheel. Place the strips on the bottom and up the sides of a 3-qt. slow cooker. Coat strips with cooking spray.
2. In a large bowl, combine eggs, oats, the chopped pepper, onion, soup mix, garlic, salt and pepper. Add beef; mix lightly but thoroughly. Shape into a 7-in. round loaf.
3. Place loaf in center of strips in slow cooker. Cook, covered, on low for 3-4 hours or until a thermometer reads at least 160°.
4. In a small bowl, mix ketchup, brown sugar, barbecue seasoning and mustard; pour over meat loaf and sprinkle with cheese. Cook, covered, on low until cheese is melted, about 15 minutes longer. Let stand 5 minutes. Using foil strips, remove meat loaf to a platter.
1 piece: 356 cal., 17g fat (7g sat. fat), 154mg chol., 1358mg sod., 22g carb. (13g sugars, 2g fiber), 29g pro.

> **TEST KITCHEN TIP**
> If you prefer, you can cook this in a regular oven instead—bake at 350° for 1 hour. Top with sauce and cheese; bake 5-10 minutes longer or until the cheese is melted.

FRENCH MEAT & VEGETABLE PIE

Some time ago, a co-worker brought a meat pie to lunch. The aroma was familiar—and after one taste, I was amazed to discover it was the same pie my grandmother used to serve when I was a youngster! My co-worker shared the recipe, and I have been enjoying it ever since.
—*Rita Winterberger, Huson, MT*

PREP: 20 min. • **BAKE:** 30 min.
MAKES: 8 servings

- 2   Tbsp. canola oil
- 1   large onion, thinly sliced
- 1   lb. ground beef
- 1   lb. ground pork
- 1   cup mashed potatoes (with added milk and butter)
- 1   can (8 oz.) mixed vegetables, drained
- 2   tsp. ground allspice
- 1   tsp. salt
- ¼   tsp. pepper
     Dough for double-crust pie
- 1   large egg, lightly beaten, optional

1. Preheat oven to 375°. In a skillet, heat oil over medium heat. Saute onion until tender, 1-2 minutes. Remove onion and set aside.
2. In the same skillet, brown the beef and pork together until no longer pink; crumble meat; drain. Combine onion, meat, potatoes, vegetables and seasonings.
3. On a lightly floured surface, roll half of the dough into an ⅛-in.- thick circle; transfer to a 9-in. pie plate. Trim even with rim. Roll the remaining dough to an ⅛-in.-thick circle. Fill bottom crust with meat mixture. Place second crust over filling; trim, seal and flute edge. Cut slits in top. If desired, brush with egg.
4. Bake until golden brown, 30-35 minutes.
Dough for double-crust pie: Combine 2½ cups all-purpose flour and ½ tsp. salt; cut in 1 cup cold butter until dough is crumbly. Gradually add ⅓ - ⅔ cup ice water, tossing with a fork until dough holds together when pressed. Divide dough in half. Shape each half into a disk; wrap and refrigerate 1 hour.
1 serving: 531 cal., 32g fat (12g sat. fat), 103mg chol., 724mg sod., 35g carb. (4g sugars, 1g fiber), 25g pro.

STOVETOP MEAT LOAVES

Who says meat loaf has to bake in the oven for hours? For this convenient recipe, all you need is your stovetop and 30 minutes. I appreciate that it's a quick, simple dish to make for one or two people, but tastes as if you were in the kitchen all day.

—*Emily Sund, Geneseo, IL*

TAKES: 30 min. • **MAKES:** 2 servings

- 3 Tbsp. 2% milk
- 2 Tbsp. quick-cooking oats
- 1 Tbsp. chopped onion
- ⅛ tsp. salt
- ½ lb. lean ground beef
- ½ tsp. cornstarch
- ½ cup Italian tomato sauce
- ¼ cup cold water

1. In a small bowl, combine milk, oats, onion and salt. Crumble beef over mixture and mix lightly but thoroughly. Shape into 2 loaves.
2. In a small nonstick skillet, brown loaves on all sides; drain. Combine the cornstarch, tomato sauce and water until smooth. Pour over meat loaves. Bring to a boil. Reduce heat to medium-low; cover and cook until meat is no longer pink, 15-20 minutes.
1 meat loaf: 292 cal., 13g fat (5g sat. fat), 99mg chol., 548mg sod., 10g carb. (2g sugars, 2g fiber), 33g pro. **Diabetic exchanges:** 3 lean meat, ½ starch.

ELAINE CLARK
Wellington, KS

HEARTY BEEF & CABBAGE POCKETS

When I found this recipe many years ago, the only ingredients listed were hamburger, salt, cabbage, onion and pepper. After a bit of experimenting, I decided this is one for the books. You can use a 48-ounce package of frozen whole wheat bread dough if you can't find the frozen rolls—just cut the bread into 24 pieces. Or, if you have the time, use a homemade dough.

—*Elaine Clark, Wellington, KS*

PREP: 1 hour + rising • **BAKE:** 15 min.
MAKES: 2 dozen

- 24 frozen Texas-size whole wheat dinner rolls (3 lbs. total), thawed
- 1½ lbs. lean ground beef (90% lean)
- ½ lb. reduced-fat bulk pork sausage
- 1 large onion, chopped
- 1 lb. carrots, grated
- 2 cans (4 oz. each) chopped green chiles
- 2 Tbsp. prepared mustard
- ½ tsp. salt
- ½ tsp. pepper
- 1 small head cabbage, shredded
- 2 large egg whites
- 2 tsp. water
  Caraway seeds

1. Let dough stand at room temperature 30-40 minutes or until softened. In a Dutch oven, cook beef, sausage and onion over medium heat until meat is no longer pink, 12-15 minutes; crumble meat; drain. Stir in carrots, chiles, mustard, salt and pepper. Add cabbage in batches; cook and stir until tender.
2. On a lightly floured surface, press or roll each dinner roll into a 5-in. circle. Top with a heaping ⅓ cup of filling; bring edges of dough up over filling and pinch to seal.
3. Place filled rolls, seam side down, on baking sheets coated with cooking spray. Cover with kitchen towels; let rise in a warm place until they almost double in size, about 45 minutes.
4. Whisk egg whites and water; brush over tops. Sprinkle with caraway seeds. Bake at 350° for 15-20 minutes or until golden brown.
Freeze option: Freeze baked and cooled pockets in an airtight container. To use, reheat pockets on a baking sheet coated with cooking spray at 350° for 30-35 minutes or until heated through; cover loosely with foil, if needed, to prevent overbrowning.
1 stuffed pocket: 239 cal., 7g fat (2g sat. fat), 24mg chol., 379mg sod., 33g carb. (5g sugars, 2g fiber), 12g pro. **Diabetic exchanges:** 2 starch, 1 lean meat.

ITALIAN MUSHROOM MEAT LOAF

Healthful oats and flaxseed amp up the nutrition in this tasty Italian meat loaf.
—*Kylie Werning, Candler, NC*

- -

PREP: 30 min. • **BAKE:** 1 hour
MAKES: 8 servings

1 large egg, lightly beaten
¼ lb. fresh mushrooms, chopped
½ cup old-fashioned oats
½ cup chopped red onion
¼ cup ground flaxseed
½ tsp. pepper
1 pkg. (19½ oz.) Italian turkey sausage links, casings removed, crumbled
1 lb. lean ground beef (90% lean)
1 cup marinara or spaghetti sauce
   Shredded Parmesan cheese, optional

1. Preheat oven to 350°. In a large bowl, combine the egg, mushrooms, oats, onion, flax and pepper. Crumble turkey and beef over mixture; mix lightly but thoroughly.
2. Shape into a 10x4-in. loaf. Place in a 13x9-in. baking dish coated with cooking spray. Bake, uncovered, for 50 minutes; drain.
3. Top with marinara sauce. Bake until no pink remains and a thermometer reads 160°, 10-15 minutes longer. If desired, top with Parmesan cheese.

1 piece: 261 cal., 14g fat (3g sat. fat), 103mg chol., 509mg sod., 10g carb. (3g sugars, 2g fiber), 25g pro. **Diabetic exchanges:** 3 lean meat, ½ starch.

TANGY BEEF TURNOVERS

My mom's recipe for these flavorful pockets called for dough to be made from scratch, but I streamlined it by using refrigerated crescent rolls. My children love the turnovers plain or dipped in ketchup—mustard works, too!
—*Claudia Bodeker, Ash Flat, AR*

- -

TAKES: 30 min. • **MAKES:** 1 dozen

1 lb. ground beef
1 medium onion, chopped
1 jar (16 oz.) sauerkraut, rinsed, drained and chopped
1 cup shredded Swiss cheese
3 tubes (8 oz. each) refrigerated crescent rolls

1. Preheat oven to 375°. In a large skillet, cook beef and onion over medium heat until meat is no longer pink, 5-7 minutes; crumble meat; drain. Add sauerkraut and cheese.
2. Unroll crescent roll dough and separate into rectangles. Place on greased baking sheets; pinch seams to seal. Place ½ cup beef mixture in the center of each rectangle. Bring corners to the center and pinch to seal.
3. Bake turnovers for 15-18 minutes or until crust is golden brown.

2 turnovers: 634 cal., 35g fat (7g sat. fat), 63mg chol., 1426mg sod., 54g carb. (14g sugars, 2g fiber), 27g pro.

MEAT SHELL POTATO PIE

Guests always comment on the presentation and flavor of this delightfully different dish.
—*Julie Sterchi, Campbellsville, KY*

- -

PREP: 20 min. • **BAKE:** 40 min.
MAKES: 6 servings

- 1 lb. ground chuck or lean ground beef (90% lean)
- 1 can (10¾ oz.) condensed cream of mushroom soup, undiluted, divided
- ¼ cup chopped onion
- 1 large egg
- ¼ cup dry bread crumbs
- 2 Tbsp. chopped fresh parsley
- ¼ tsp. salt
      Pinch pepper
- 2 cups mashed potatoes
- 4 bacon strips, cooked and crumbled
- ½ cup shredded cheddar cheese

1. Preheat the oven to 350°. In a large bowl, combine beef, ½ cup soup, the onion, egg, bread crumbs, parsley, salt and pepper; mix lightly but thoroughly. Press onto bottom and up sides of a 9-in. pie plate. Bake for 25 minutes; drain.
2. In a bowl, combine potatoes and remaining soup; mix until fluffy. Spread over meat crust. Sprinkle with bacon and cheese. Return to the oven and bake for 15 minutes. Let stand for a few minutes. Cut into wedges.
1 wedge: 326 cal., 16g fat (7g sat. fat), 102mg chol., 842mg sod., 21g carb. (1g sugars, 1g fiber), 22g pro.

MINI MEAT LOAF SHEET-PAN MEAL

I grew up with this classic meat loaf recipe, but I adapted it to mini meat loaves so they would bake more quickly. The sauce topping is always a hit. I added the potatoes and asparagus to make an easy complete meal.
—*Deanne Johnson, Reading, PA*

- -

PREP: 35 min. • **BAKE:** 40 min.
MAKES: 6 servings

- 2 large eggs, lightly beaten
- 1 cup tomato juice
- ¾ cup quick-cooking oats
- ¼ cup finely chopped onion
- ½ tsp. salt
- 1½ lbs. lean ground beef (90% lean)
- ¼ cup ketchup
- 3 Tbsp. brown sugar
- 1 tsp. prepared mustard
- ¼ tsp. ground nutmeg
- 3 large potatoes, peeled and cut into ½-in. pieces
- 3 Tbsp. olive oil, divided
- ½ tsp. garlic salt, divided
- ¼ tsp. pepper, divided
- 1 lb. fresh asparagus, trimmed and halved

1. Preheat the oven to 425°. In a large bowl, combine eggs, tomato juice, oats, onion and salt. Add beef; mix lightly but thoroughly. Shape into six 4x2½-in. loaves; place them on a sheet pan or in a large, shallow roasting pan. Combine ketchup, brown sugar, mustard and nutmeg; brush over loaves.
2. Toss the potatoes with 2 Tbsp. oil, ¼ tsp. garlic salt and ⅛ tsp. pepper. Add to pan in single layer. Bake 25 minutes.
3. Combine the asparagus with remaining 1 Tbsp. oil, ¼ tsp. garlic salt and ⅛ tsp. pepper; toss to coat. Add asparagus to pan. Bake until a thermometer inserted into meat loaves reads 160° and vegetables are tender, 15-20 minutes. Let stand 5-10 minutes before serving.
1 meat loaf with 1¼ cups vegetables: 460 cal., 19g fat (5g sat. fat), 133mg chol., 690mg sod., 45g carb. (13g sugars, 3g fiber), 29g pro.

READER REVIEW

"This was a great recipe. Making mini loaves allowed me to have onions in just half of them, pleasing everyone at the table."

KIM, TASTEOFHOME.COM

❄ JAMAICAN BEEF PATTIES

My mom was born in Jamaica and lived there until she moved to the United States during her university years. The dish I've loved the most my whole life is Jamaican Beef Patties. The savory flavor and spices are just right and the pastry is flaky and delicious.
—*Natasha Watson, Douglasville, GA*

PREP: 35 min. • **BAKE:** 25 min.
MAKES: 8 servings

FILLING
- 1 lb. ground beef
- 1 medium onion, chopped
- 1 tsp. curry powder
- 1 tsp. dried thyme
- 1 tsp. pepper
- ¾ tsp. salt

CRUST
- 2 cups all-purpose flour
- 1½ tsp. curry powder
  Dash salt
- ½ cup cold butter
- ⅓ cup ice water
- 1 large egg, lightly beaten

1. Preheat oven to 350°. In a large skillet, cook beef and onion over medium heat until the beef is no longer pink and onion is tender, 6-8 minutes; crumble meat; drain. Stir in curry powder, thyme, pepper and salt; set aside.

2. For crust, in a large bowl, whisk together flour, curry powder and salt. Cut in butter until mixture resembles coarse crumbs. Add water; stir until just moistened. Divide dough into 8 portions.

3. On a lightly floured surface, roll out each portion into a 6-in. circle. Place about ¼ cup filling on half of each circle. Fold crust over filling. Press edges with a fork to seal.

4. Transfer to parchment-lined baking sheets; brush with beaten egg. Bake until the crust is light brown, 22-25 minutes. Remove to wire racks. Serve warm.

Freeze option: Cover and freeze the unbaked patties on a parchment-lined baking sheet until firm. Transfer to freezer containers; return to freezer. To use, bake on a parchment-lined baking sheet at 350° until heated through, 25-30 minutes.

1 patty: 336 cal., 19g fat (10g sat. fat), 89mg chol., 373mg sod., 26g carb. (1g sugars, 2g fiber), 14g pro.

UPPER PENINSULA PASTIES

I grew up in Michigan's Upper Peninsula, where pasties—traditional meat pies often eaten by hand—are popular. There's a debate on whether they should be served with gravy or ketchup, but no matter what you dunk them in, they're super comforting.
—*Carole Derifield, Valdez, AK*

- -

PREP: 35 min. + chilling • **BAKE:** 1 hour
MAKES: 12 servings

CRUST
- 2 cups shortening
- 2 cups boiling water
- 5½ to 6 cups all-purpose flour
- 2 tsp. salt

FILLING
- 6 medium red potatoes (about 3 lbs.), peeled
- 2 small rutabagas (about 1½ lbs.), peeled
- 1 lb. ground beef
- ½ lb. ground pork
- 2 medium onions, chopped into ¼-in. pieces
- 3 tsp. salt
- 2 tsp. pepper
- 2 tsp. garlic powder
- ¼ cup butter
  Optional: Half-and-half cream or a large egg, lightly beaten

1. In a large bowl, stir shortening and water until the shortening is melted. Gradually stir in flour and salt until a very soft dough forms; cover and refrigerate for 1½ hours.
2. Cut the potatoes and rutabagas into ⅛- or ¼-in. cubes. Do not make cubes too large or they will not cook properly. Gently combine ground beef and pork; crumble meat. In a large bowl, combine potatoes, rutabagas, onions, meat mixture and seasonings.
3. Divide dough into 12 equal portions. On a floured surface, roll out 1 portion at a time into an 8-in. circle. Mound 1½ - 2 cups filling on half of each circle; dot with 1 tsp. butter. Moisten edges with water; carefully fold dough over filling and press edges with a fork to seal.
4. Place them on ungreased baking sheets. Cut several slits in top of pasties. If desired, brush with the cream or beaten egg. Bake at 350° until golden brown, about 1 hour. Cool on wire racks. Serve pasties hot or cold. Store in the refrigerator.

1 pasty: 757 cal., 44g fat (13g sat. fat), 46mg chol., 1060mg sod., 69g carb. (5g sugars, 5g fiber), 19g pro.

NANCY ZIMMERMAN
Cape May Court House, NJ

❄ 🍎 ZESTY HORSERADISH MEAT LOAF

You'll love the bit of heat in this tasty meat loaf. Make sandwiches out of the leftovers to get double duty out of the classic comfort food.
—*Nancy Zimmerman,*
Cape May Court House, NJ

- -

PREP: 15 min. • **BAKE:** 45 min. + standing
MAKES: 8 servings

- 4 slices whole wheat bread, crumbled
- ¼ cup fat-free milk
- ½ cup finely chopped celery
- ¼ cup finely chopped onion
- ¼ cup prepared horseradish
- 2 Tbsp. Dijon mustard
- 2 Tbsp. chili sauce
- 1 large egg, lightly beaten
- 1½ tsp. Worcestershire sauce
- ½ tsp. salt
- ¼ tsp. pepper
- 1½ lbs. lean ground beef (90% lean)
- ½ cup ketchup

1. Preheat oven to 350°. Soak bread in milk for 5 minutes. Drain and discard milk. Stir in the next 9 ingredients. Crumble beef over the mixture and mix lightly but thoroughly.
2. Shape into a loaf in a 15x10x1-in. baking pan coated with cooking spray. Spread top of loaf with the ketchup. Bake until a thermometer inserted in the center of the meat loaf reads 160°, 45-55 minutes. Let stand 10 minutes before cutting.

Freeze option: Omitting ketchup, bake as directed. Securely wrap cooled meat loaf in foil, then freeze. To use, partially thaw in refrigerator overnight. Unwrap and spread top with the ketchup. Reheat on a greased 15x10x1-in. baking pan in a preheated 350° oven until a thermometer inserted in the center reads 165°. Let stand 10 minutes before cutting.

1 piece: 207 cal., 8g fat (3g sat. fat), 79mg chol., 640mg sod., 14g carb. (7g sugars, 1g fiber), 19g pro. **Diabetic exchanges:** 2 lean meat, 1 starch.

SUPER CALZONES

A friend gave me this simple recipe at my wedding shower. My husband loves these little hand-held pizzas.
—*Laronda Warrick, Parker, KS*

- -

PREP: 30 min. • **BAKE:** 20 min.
MAKES: 4 servings

½ lb. ground beef
2 Tbsp. finely chopped onion
2 Tbsp. finely chopped green pepper
1 garlic clove, minced
1 can (15 oz.) tomato sauce
1 tsp. Italian seasoning
1 tube (13.8 oz.) refrigerated pizza crust
3 oz. cream cheese, softened
1 cup shredded part-skim mozzarella cheese
1 can (4 oz.) mushroom stems and pieces, drained
1 can (2¼ oz.) sliced ripe olives, drained

1. In a large skillet, cook the beef, onion, green pepper and garlic over medium heat until meat is no longer pink, 5-7 minutes; crumble beef. Drain and set aside.
2. In a small saucepan, bring tomato sauce and Italian seasoning to a boil. Reduce heat; cover and simmer for 5 minutes. Stir ½ cup into the meat mixture; keep remaining sauce warm.
3. Unroll pizza crust onto a floured surface. Roll into a 12-in. square; cut into quarters. Spread cream cheese over each to within ½ in. of edges. Top with meat mixture. Sprinkle with mozzarella cheese, mushrooms and olives.
4. Fold dough over filling, forming triangles; press edges with a fork to seal. Place triangles on a greased baking sheet.
5. Bake at 400° for 20-25 minutes or until golden brown. Serve with the remaining sauce.
1 calzone: 541 cal., 24g fat (11g sat. fat), 67mg chol., 1552mg sod., 58g carb. (10g sugars, 4g fiber), 28g pro.

❄

MEAT LOAF CORDON BLEU

I'm a school counselor and mother of one young child. Even with my busy schedule, I can make this in the morning and pop it into the oven when I get home.
—*Barb Jacobsen, Campbell, NE*

- -

PREP: 15 min. • **BAKE:** 1¼ hours
MAKES: 10 servings

1 large egg, beaten
1 envelope meat loaf seasoning mix
½ cup tomato sauce
2 cups soft bread crumbs
2 lbs. lean ground beef
8 thin slices fully cooked ham
8 thin slices Swiss cheese
1 can (4 oz.) sliced mushrooms

1. In a large bowl, mix together egg, meat loaf seasoning, tomato sauce and bread crumbs. Add ground beef; mix lightly but thoroughly.
2. On a piece of waxed paper, pat meat mixture into an 18x9-in. rectangle. Top with layers of ham, cheese and mushrooms. Roll rectangle, jelly-roll style, starting from short side. Pinch the edges to seal.
3. Place the loaf, seam side down, in a shallow baking pan. Bake at 350° until no pink remains, about 1¼ hours. Let stand several minutes before slicing.
Freeze option: Securely wrap cooled meat loaf in foil; freeze. To use, partially thaw in refrigerator overnight. Unwrap; reheat on a greased 15x10x1-in. baking pan in a preheated 350° oven until meat is heated through and a thermometer inserted in center reads 160°.
Note: To make soft bread crumbs, tear bread into pieces and place in a food processor or blender. Cover and pulse until crumbs form. A slice of bread yields ½ - ¾ cup crumbs.
1 piece: 287 cal., 14g fat (7g sat. fat), 105mg chol., 659mg sod., 10g carb. (1g sugars, 1g fiber), 28g pro.

½ cup half-and-half cream
1 large egg yolk
2 Tbsp. finely chopped onion
¼ tsp. salt
½ lb. ground beef
1 tube (4 oz.) refrigerated crescent rolls
  Large egg, lightly beaten, optional
1 tsp. dried parsley flakes

1. In a saucepan, saute mushrooms in butter until softened. Stir in flour and ⅛ tsp. pepper until blended. Gradually add the cream. Bring to a boil; cook and stir until thickened, about 2 minutes. Remove from heat and set aside.
2. In a bowl, combine the egg yolk, onion, salt, 2 Tbsp. mushroom sauce and the remaining ⅛ tsp. pepper. Crumble beef over mixture and mix lightly but thoroughly. Shape meat mixture into 2 loaves.
3. Separate crescent dough into 2 rectangles on a baking sheet. Seal perforations. Place a meat loaf on each rectangle; bring the dough edges together and pinch to seal. If desired, brush with egg wash.
4. Bake at 350° until golden brown and a thermometer inserted into meat loaf reads 160°, 24-28 minutes.
5. Meanwhile, warm the remaining sauce over low heat; stir in parsley. Serve sauce with the Wellingtons.
1 serving: 578 cal., 37g fat (16g sat. fat), 207mg chol., 909mg sod., 28g carb. (7g sugars, 1g fiber), 28g pro.

❄ MEAT LOAF MUFFINS

Serve these tangy meat loaf muffins for dinner or slice them up for a take-along sandwich lunch. They're just as flavorful after freezing.
—*Cheryl Norwood, Canton, GA*

- -

TAKES: 30 min. • **MAKES:** 6 servings

1 large egg, lightly beaten
½ cup dry bread crumbs
½ cup finely chopped onion
½ cup finely chopped green pepper
¼ cup barbecue sauce
1½ lbs. lean ground beef (90% lean)
3 Tbsp. ketchup
  Additional ketchup, optional

1. Preheat the oven to 375°. Combine first 5 ingredients. Add the beef; mix lightly but thoroughly. Press about ⅓ cup of mixture into each of 12 ungreased muffin cups.
2. Bake 15 minutes. Brush tops of loaves with the ketchup; bake until a thermometer reads 160°, 5-7 minutes. If desired, serve muffins with additional ketchup.
Freeze option: Bake muffins without ketchup; cover and freeze on a waxed paper-lined baking sheet until firm. Transfer muffins to an airtight freezer container; return to freezer. To use, partially thaw in refrigerator overnight. Place the meat loaf muffins on a greased shallow baking pan. Spread with ketchup. Bake in a preheated 350° oven until heated through.
2 meat loaf muffins: 260 cal., 11g fat (4g sat. fat), 102mg chol., 350mg sod., 15g carb. (7g sugars, 1g fiber), 24g pro.

GROUND-BEEF WELLINGTONS

Trying new recipes is one of my favorite hobbies. It's also the most gratifying. What could beat the smiles and compliments of the ones you love? This recipe is easy enough for weeknights yet fancy enough to serve for special occasions.
—*Julie Frankamp, Nicollet, MN*

- -

PREP: 30 min. • **BAKE:** 25 min.
MAKES: 2 servings

½ cup chopped fresh mushrooms
1 Tbsp. butter
2 tsp. all-purpose flour
¼ tsp. pepper, divided

❄ JERK-SEASONED MEAT LOAVES

I wanted meat loaf, but also something unique, so I decided to spice it up using Jamaican jerk seasoning. My family loved it!
—*Iris Cook, Batavia, IL*

- -

PREP: 10 min. • **BAKE:** 40 min. + standing
MAKES: 2 loaves (6 servings each)

- 2   large eggs, lightly beaten
- 1   medium onion, finely chopped
- ½   cup dry bread crumbs
- 2   Tbsp. green pepper, finely chopped
- 1   Tbsp. Caribbean jerk seasoning
- 2   garlic cloves, minced
- 2   tsp. garlic powder
- 2   tsp. dried cilantro flakes
- 1   tsp. dried basil
- 3   lbs. ground beef

GLAZE
- ½   cup packed brown sugar
- 2   Tbsp. peach nectar or juice
- 2   Tbsp. ketchup
- 2   tsp. barbecue sauce
-     Dash garlic powder
-     Dash pepper

1. Preheat oven to 350°. In a large bowl, combine the first 9 ingredients. Add beef; mix lightly but thoroughly. Transfer mixture to 2 ungreased 9x5-in. loaf pans.
2. Mix next 6 ingredients; spread over tops of loaves. Bake until a thermometer reads 160°, 40-50 minutes. Let stand 10 minutes before slicing.
Freeze option: Securely wrap cooled meat loaf in foil, then freeze. To use, partially thaw in refrigerator overnight. Unwrap; reheat on a greased 15x10x1-in. baking pan at 350° until heated through and a thermometer inserted in center reads 165°.

1 piece: 283 cal., 14g fat (5g sat. fat), 101mg chol., 223mg sod., 15g carb. (11g sugars, 1g fiber), 22g pro.

DID YOU KNOW?
The specific ingredients often vary, but jerk seasoning usually contains chiles, thyme, garlic, onion and spices such as cinnamon, ginger, allspice and cloves.

FESTIVE MEAT LOAF PINWHEEL

This crowd-size pinwheel is special enough for holiday dinner and features ham, Swiss cheese and a delicious homemade tomato sauce.
—*Vera Sullivan, Amity, OR*

- -

PREP: 20 min. • **BAKE:** 1¼ hours
MAKES: 20 servings

PINWHEEL
- 3 large eggs
- 1 cup dry bread crumbs
- ½ cup finely chopped onion
- ½ cup finely chopped green pepper
- ¼ cup ketchup
- 2 tsp. minced fresh parsley
- 1 tsp. dried basil
- 1 tsp. dried oregano
- 1 garlic clove, minced
- 2 tsp. salt
- ½ tsp. pepper
- 5 lbs. lean ground beef (90% lean)
- ¾ lb. thinly sliced deli ham
- ¾ lb. thinly sliced Swiss cheese

SAUCE
- ½ cup finely chopped onion
- 2 celery ribs, chopped
- ½ cup chopped green pepper
- 1 garlic clove, minced
- 1 to 2 tsp. olive oil
- 2 cups chopped fresh tomatoes
- 1 cup beef broth
- 1 bay leaf
- 1 tsp. sugar
- ¼ tsp. salt
- ¼ tsp. dried thyme
- 1 Tbsp. cornstarch
- 2 Tbsp. cold water

1. Combine first 11 ingredients. Crumble the beef over mixture and mix lightly but thoroughly. On a piece of heavy-duty foil, pat beef mixture into a 17x15-in. rectangle. Cover with ham and cheese slices to within ½ in. of edges. Roll up tightly jelly-roll style, starting with a short side.
2. Place roll, seam side down, in a roasting pan. Bake, uncovered, at 350° until a thermometer reads 160°, 1¼ - 1½ hours.
3. In a large saucepan, saute onion, celery, green pepper and garlic in oil until tender, 3-5 minutes. Add tomatoes, broth, bay leaf, sugar, salt and thyme. Simmer, uncovered, for 30 minutes. Discard bay leaf.
4. Combine cornstarch and water until smooth; stir into sauce. Bring to a boil; cook and stir until thickened, about 2 minutes. Drain meat loaf. Serve with sauce.
1 piece: 319 cal., 17g fat (7g sat. fat), 124mg chol., 732mg sod., 8g carb. (2g sugars, 1g fiber), 32g pro.

EASY CORNISH PASTIES

These are a bit different from traditional pasties, but the ingredients are probably already in your kitchen. I like to double the recipe and freeze the extras to have on hand for a quick meal when we're on the go.
—*Judy Marsden, Ontario, CA*

- -

PREP: 45 min. • **BAKE:** 20 min.
MAKES: 8 pasties

- ½ lb. ground beef
- 2 Tbsp. all-purpose flour
- ½ to 1 tsp. seasoned salt
- 1 Tbsp. minced fresh parsley
- 1 tsp. beef bouillon granules
- ¼ cup water
- 1 cup diced peeled potatoes
- ½ cup diced carrots
- 2 Tbsp. finely chopped onion
- 2 pkg. (11 oz. each) pie crust mix

1. In a skillet, cook beef over medium heat until no longer pink, 5-7 minutes; crumble the meat; drain. Add flour, seasoned salt and parsley; stir until well coated. Dissolve bouillon in water; stir into meat mixture. Add potatoes, carrots and onion. Cover and cook over medium heat until vegetables are crisp-tender. Cool.
2. Meanwhile, prepare pie crusts according to package directions. On a floured surface, roll each pie crust into a 12-in. square. Cut each square into four 6-in. squares. Place about ⅓ cup meat mixture in center of each square.
3. Moisten edges of crusts with water and fold over meat mixture to form a triangle. Press the edges with a fork to seal. Make a 1-in. slit in the top of each triangle. Place on 2 parchment-lined baking sheets. Bake at 400° until golden brown, 20-25 minutes.
1 pasty: 289 cal., 18g fat (5g sat. fat), 14mg chol., 521mg sod., 24g carb. (1g sugars, 1g fiber), 8g pro.

MEAT LOAF & MASHED RED POTATOES

Satisfy the meat-and-potatoes eaters in your house with a satisfying dish that all cooks up in one pot. Talk about classic comfort food!
—*Faith Cromwell, San Francisco, CA*

- -

PREP: 30 min. • **COOK:** 4 hours + standing
MAKES: 8 servings

- 3 lbs. small red potatoes, quartered
- 1½ cups beef stock, divided
- 3 slices white bread, torn into small pieces
- 2 large portobello mushrooms (about 6 oz.), cut into chunks
- 1 medium onion, cut into wedges
- 1 medium carrot, cut into chunks
- 1 celery rib, cut into chunks
- 3 garlic cloves, halved
- 2 large eggs, lightly beaten
- 1¼ lbs. ground beef
- ¾ lb. ground pork
- 2 Tbsp. Worcestershire sauce
- 2 tsp. salt, divided
- 1 tsp. pepper, divided
- ½ cup ketchup
- 2 Tbsp. tomato paste
- 2 Tbsp. brown sugar
- 3 Tbsp. butter

1. In a large microwave-safe bowl, combine the potatoes and 1 cup stock. Microwave on high, covered, until just softened, 12-15 minutes. Transfer to a 6-qt. slow cooker. Combine bread and remaining ½ cup stock in a large bowl; let stand until liquid is absorbed.

2. Pulse mushrooms, onion, carrot, celery and garlic in a food processor until finely chopped. Add the vegetable mixture, eggs, beef, pork, Worcestershire sauce, 1¼ tsp. salt and ¾ tsp. pepper to bread mixture; mix lightly but thoroughly.

3. Place on an 18x12-in. piece of heavy-duty foil; shape into a 10x6-in. oval loaf. Lifting with foil, place in slow cooker on top of potatoes; press foil up sides and over edges of slow cooker, creating a bowl to contain the juices. Combine last 4 ingredients; spread over loaf.

4. Cook, covered, on low until a thermometer reads 160°, 4-5 hours. Using a turkey baster, remove and discard liquid contained in foil; lifting with foil, remove meat loaf to a platter (or carefully remove meat loaf using foil, draining liquid into a small bowl). Let meat loaf stand 10 minutes before cutting.

5. Drain potatoes, reserving cooking liquid; transfer potatoes to a large bowl. Mash, gradually adding butter, ¾ tsp. salt, ¼ tsp. pepper and enough reserved liquid to reach desired consistency. Serve with meat loaf.

1 piece with ⅔ cup mashed potatoes: 485 cal., 21g fat (9g sat. fat), 130mg chol., 1107mg sod., 46g carb. (12g sugars, 4g fiber), 28g pro.

❄ SOUTHWESTERN SHEPHERD'S PIE

Guests will eat this hearty meal right up! You can freeze one of the pies for another day.
—*Suzette Jury, Keene, CA*

- -

PREP: 35 min. • **BAKE:** 25 min.
MAKES: 2 casseroles (6 servings each)

- 3 lbs. ground beef
- 1 cup chopped onion
- 2 cans (10 oz. each) enchilada sauce
- 2 Tbsp. all-purpose flour
- 2 tsp. chopped chipotle peppers in adobo sauce
- 1 tsp. ground cumin
- 1 tsp. dried oregano
- 2½ cups water
- 2 cups 2% milk
- ⅓ cup butter, cubed
- 1 tsp. salt
- 4 cups mashed potato flakes
- 2 cans (4 oz. each) chopped green chiles, undrained
- 2 cups shredded Mexican cheese blend, divided
- 2 cans (11 oz. each) Mexicorn, drained
- ⅔ cup chopped green onions
  Paprika

1. In a Dutch oven, cook beef and onion over medium heat until the meat is no longer pink; crumble meat; drain. Add the enchilada sauce, flour, chipotle peppers, cumin and oregano; bring to a boil. Reduce heat; simmer mixture uncovered, 5 minutes.

2. Meanwhile, in a large saucepan, combine the water, milk, butter and salt; bring to a boil. Remove from the heat. Stir in potato flakes until combined. Add chiles and ½ cup cheese.

3. Transfer meat mixture to 2 greased 11x7-in. baking dishes. Layer corn, potato mixture and remaining cheese. Sprinkle with green onions.

4. Cover and bake at 375° for 20 minutes. Uncover and bake 5-10 minutes longer or until bubbly. Sprinkle with paprika.

Freeze option: Cover and freeze unbaked casserole for up to 3 months. Thaw in the refrigerator overnight. Remove from the refrigerator 30 minutes before baking. Cover and bake at 375° for 20 minutes. Uncover and bake until bubbly, or until a thermometer inserted in center reads 165°, 15-20 minutes longer. Sprinkle with paprika.

1 serving: 500 cal., 26g fat (12g sat. fat), 104mg chol., 917mg sod., 35g carb. (7g sugars, 3g fiber), 30g pro.

BACON-TOPPED MEAT LOAF

My family loves meat loaf—this one in particular. I created the recipe after trying and adjusting many others over the years. Cheddar cheese tucked inside—plus a flavorful bacon topping—dress it up for Sunday dinner!
—*Sue Call, Beech Grove, IN*

PREP: 10 min. • **BAKE:** 70 min. + standing
MAKES: 8 servings

- ½ cup chili sauce
- 2 large eggs, lightly beaten
- 1 Tbsp. Worcestershire sauce
- 1 medium onion, chopped
- 1 cup shredded cheddar cheese
- ⅔ cup dry bread crumbs
- ½ tsp. salt
- ¼ tsp. pepper
- 2 lbs. lean ground beef (90% lean)
- 2 bacon strips, halved

Preheat oven to 350°. In a large bowl, combine the first 8 ingredients. Crumble beef over the mixture and mix lightly but thoroughly. Shape into a loaf in an ungreased 13x9-in. baking dish. Top with bacon. Bake the loaf, uncovered, 70-80 minutes or until meat is no longer pink and a thermometer reads 160°. Drain; let stand for 10 minutes before cutting.
1 piece: 329 cal., 17g fat (8g sat. fat), 127mg chol., 692mg sod., 13g carb. (5g sugars, 1g fiber), 28g pro.

❄
MUFFIN-CUP CHEDDAR BEEF PIES

My kids love these beef rolls so much that I always make extra since they heat up so quickly. I give the kids their choice of dipping sauces—spaghetti sauce or ranch dressing are the top picks.
—*Kimberly Farmer, Wichita, KS*

PREP: 25 min. + standing • **BAKE:** 20 min.
MAKES: 20 meat pies

- 2 loaves (1 lb. each) frozen bread dough
- 2 lbs. ground beef
- 1 can (8 oz.) mushroom stems and pieces, drained
- 1¼ cups shredded cheddar cheese
- 1½ tsp. Italian seasoning
- 1 tsp. garlic powder
- ½ tsp. salt
- ¼ tsp. pepper
  Spaghetti sauce, warmed

1. Let dough stand at room temperature until softened, about 30 minutes. Preheat oven to 350°. Meanwhile, in a Dutch oven, cook the beef over medium heat until no longer pink, 12-15 minutes; crumble meat; drain. Stir in mushrooms, cheese and seasonings.
2. Divide each loaf of dough into 10 portions; roll each portion into a 4-in. circle. Top each circle with ¼ cup filling; bring edges of dough up over filling and pinch to seal.
3. Place meat pies in greased muffin cups, seam-side down. Bake until golden brown, 20-25 minutes. Serve with spaghetti sauce.
Freeze option: Freeze cooled pies in a freezer container. To use, reheat beef pies on greased baking sheets in a preheated 350° oven until heated through.
2 beef pies: 482 cal., 19g fat (7g sat. fat), 71mg chol., 850mg sod., 45g carb. (4g sugars, 4g fiber), 29g pro.

SUN-DRIED TOMATO MEAT LOAF

Meat loaf gets an Italian flair thanks to classic herbs and tangy sun-dried tomatoes. This recipe yields a large loaf, so the extra slices can be used to fix tasty sandwiches.
—Taste of Home *Test Kitchen*

- -

PREP: 25 min. • **BAKE:** 55 min. + standing
MAKES: 10 servings

- 1¼ cups sun-dried tomatoes (not packed in oil)
- 3 cups boiling water
- ½ cup chopped onion
- ½ cup chopped green pepper
- 2 tsp. canola oil
- 1 large egg, lightly beaten
- ½ cup 2% milk
- 1 cup soft bread crumbs
- 2 tsp. dried basil
- 1 tsp. dried oregano
- 1 tsp. salt
- 1 tsp. pepper
- ½ tsp. dried thyme
- 1½ lbs. ground beef
- ¼ cup ketchup

1. Preheat oven to 350°. In a large bowl, combine tomatoes and water; let stand for 15 minutes or until tomatoes are softened. Meanwhile, in a small skillet, saute onion and green pepper in oil until tender. In a large bowl, combine the egg, milk and bread crumbs.
2. Drain and chop the tomatoes; set aside ¼ cup for topping. Add the onion mixture, basil, oregano, salt, pepper, thyme and the remaining chopped tomatoes to the egg mixture. Crumble beef over mixture and mix lightly but thoroughly. Shape into a loaf in an ungreased 13x9-in. baking dish.
3. Combine ketchup and the ¼ cup reserved tomatoes; spread over loaf. Bake, uncovered, until no pink remains and a thermometer reads 160°, 55-60 minutes. Drain; let meat stand for 10 minutes before slicing.
1 piece: 169 cal., 8g fat (3g sat. fat), 65mg chol., 515mg sod., 10g carb. (4g sugars, 2g fiber), 16g pro.

TEST KITCHEN TIP
If using sun-dried tomatoes in oil, drain, skip the softening step, and use a little less than ¼ cup.

BEEF TACO PIE

I combine taco fixings with biscuit mix to create this zippy main-dish pie. You can make this as mild or as spicy as you'd like. I serve it with a tossed salad.
—Shelly Winkleblack, Interlaken, NY

- -

PREP: 20 min. • **BAKE:** 25 min.
MAKES: 6 servings

- 1 lb. ground beef
- 1 large onion, chopped
- ½ cup salsa
- 2 Tbsp. taco seasoning
- ¼ tsp. pepper
- 1 cup shredded cheddar cheese
- 2 large eggs
- 1 cup 2% milk
- ½ cup biscuit/baking mix

1. Preheat oven to 400°. In a large skillet, cook beef and onion over medium heat until meat is no longer pink; crumble beef; drain. Stir in the salsa, taco seasoning and pepper. Transfer to a greased 9-in. pie plate; sprinkle with cheese.
2. In a large bowl, combine the eggs, milk and biscuit mix just until combined; pour over the cheese. Bake until a knife inserted in the center comes out clean, 25-30 minutes.
1 serving: 332 cal., 19g fat (9g sat. fat), 147mg chol., 685mg sod., 14g carb. (4g sugars, 1g fiber), 23g pro.

Ground Beef

CASSEROLES & OTHER OVEN ENTREES

Tasty and satisfying, these savory oven creations are the definition of comfort and convenience—whether you're eating at home or making a dish to wow the potluck crowd!

EIGHT-LAYER CASSEROLE

My sister shared this original recipe with me, but I adapted it for my family's taste. I like that it's a nutritious meal in one dish. When my boys were young, it was a tasty way to sneak veggies into their diet. This is also a perfect potluck dish.

—*Jo Prusha, Omaha, NE*

- -

PREP: 35 min. • **BAKE:** 40 min. + standing
MAKES: 12 servings

- 1 lb. frozen home-style egg noodles
- 2 lbs. ground beef
- 2 cans (15 oz. each) tomato sauce
- 1 Tbsp. dried minced onion
- 2 tsp. sugar
- 2 tsp. each Italian seasoning, dried basil and dried parsley flakes
- 1½ tsp. garlic powder
- 1 tsp. salt
- ½ tsp. pepper
- 1 pkg. (8 oz.) cream cheese, softened
- 1 cup sour cream
- ½ cup 2% milk
- 2 pkg. (10 oz. each) frozen chopped spinach, thawed and squeezed dry
- 1 cup shredded Colby-Monterey Jack cheese
- 1 cup shredded cheddar cheese
  Minced fresh parsley, optional

1. Preheat oven to 350°. Cook the noodles according to package directions.
2. Meanwhile, in a large skillet, cook beef over medium heat until no longer pink; crumble meat; drain. Add the tomato sauce, onion, sugar and seasonings. Bring to a boil. Reduce heat; cover and simmer for 10 minutes.
3. In a small bowl, combine cream cheese, sour cream and milk.
4. Place half of the noodles in a greased 13x9-in. baking dish; top with 3 cups of meat mixture. Layer with the cream cheese mixture, spinach, the remaining meat mixture and noodles. Sprinkle with cheeses. (Dish will be full.)
5. Bake, uncovered, for 40-45 minutes or until bubbly. Let the casserole stand for 10 minutes before serving. If desired, top with minced fresh parsley.

1 cup: 465 cal., 28g fat (14g sat. fat), 133mg chol., 794mg sod., 30g carb. (5g sugars, 3g fiber), 26g pro.

BAKED BEEF TACOS

We give tacos a fresh approach by baking the shells upright in refried beans and tomatoes. The bottoms gets soft, and the tops stay crisp and crunchy.

—*Patricia Stagich, Elizabeth, NJ*

PREP: 15 min. • **BAKE:** 20 min.
MAKES: 12 servings

- 1½ lbs. ground beef
- 1 envelope taco seasoning
- 2 cans (10 oz. each) diced tomatoes and green chiles, divided
- 1 can (16 oz.) refried beans
- 2 cups shredded Mexican cheese blend, divided
- ¼ cup chopped fresh cilantro
- 1 tsp. hot pepper sauce, optional
- 12 taco shells
  Chopped green onions

1. Preheat oven to 425°. In a large skillet, cook beef over medium heat, 6-8 minutes or until no longer pink; crumble beef; drain. Stir in taco seasoning and 1 can of undrained tomatoes; heat through.
2. Mix the beans, ½ cup cheese, cilantro, remaining can of undrained tomatoes and, if desired, pepper sauce. Spread onto the bottom of a greased 13x9-in. baking dish.
3. Stand taco shells upright on bean mixture. Fill each with 1 Tbsp. cheese and about ⅓ cup beef mixture. Bake, covered, 15 minutes.
4. Uncover; sprinkle with remaining cheese. Bake, uncovered, 5-7 minutes or until cheese is melted and shells are lightly browned. Sprinkle with green onions.
1 taco with ¼ cup bean mixture: 277 cal., 15g fat (7g sat. fat), 52mg chol., 836mg sod., 17g carb. (0 sugars, 3g fiber), 17g pro.

BAKED SHEPHERD'S CASSEROLE

All my kids are grown and most are married, but they often still come home for Sunday dinner, and their most requested meal is this casserole. When you get several people in the kitchen chopping and slicing, it comes together super fast and, at the same time, you get to catch up on all the family happenings.
—*Beverly Matthews, Richland, WA*

PREP: 30 min. • **BAKE:** 1 hour + standing
MAKES: 8 servings

- 1 lb. ground beef
- 2 cups sliced fresh mushrooms
- 1 small onion, chopped
- ½ tsp. salt
- ½ tsp. garlic powder
- ½ tsp. pepper
- 1 can (14½ oz.) petite diced tomatoes, drained
- 1 pkg. (10 oz.) frozen corn
- 2 cups frozen cut green beans
- 1 can (10¾ oz.) condensed cream of mushroom soup, undiluted
- ¾ cup water
- 1 lb. Yukon Gold potatoes, thinly sliced (about 3 cups)
- 1 cup shredded cheddar cheese
  Optional: ¾ cup french-fried onions, ½ cup bacon bits

1. Preheat oven to 375°. In large skillet, cook beef, mushrooms and onion over medium-high heat for 6-8 minutes or until the beef is no longer pink, crumble beef; drain.
2. Stir in salt, garlic powder and pepper. Add the tomatoes, corn and green beans. Heat through, stirring occasionally.
3. In a small bowl, mix soup and water.
4. In a greased 13x9-in. baking dish, layer half each of the beef mixture, potatoes and soup mixture. Repeat the layers. Sprinkle with the cheese and, if desired, french-fried onions and bacon bits.
5. Bake, covered, 1 to 1¼ hours or until bubbly and potatoes are tender. Let stand 10 minutes before serving.
1¼ cups: 298 cal., 14g fat (6g sat. fat), 51mg chol., 638mg sod., 27g carb. (5g sugars, 4g fiber), 17g pro.

BEVERLY MATTHEWS
Richland, WA

BROCCOLI BEEF SUPPER

Broccoli is one of my favorite vegetables, so I'm constantly on the lookout for new ways of preparing it. This casserole is a hearty entree.
—*Connie Bolton, San Antonio, TX*

PREP: 15 min. • **BAKE:** 35 min.
MAKES: 8 servings

- 4 cups frozen cottage fries
- 1 lb. ground beef
- 3 cups frozen chopped broccoli, thawed
- 1 can (2.8 oz.) french-fried onions, divided
- 1 medium tomato, chopped
- 1 can (10¾ oz.) condensed cream of celery soup, undiluted
- 1 cup shredded cheddar cheese, divided
- ½ cup 2% milk
- ¼ tsp. garlic powder
- ¼ tsp. pepper

1. Preheat oven to 400°. Line bottom and sides of a greased 13x9-in. baking dish with cottage fries. Bake, uncovered, for 10 minutes.
2. Meanwhile, in a large skillet, cook beef over medium heat until no longer pink; crumble beef; drain. Layer the beef, broccoli, half of the onions and the tomato over fries. In a small bowl, combine the soup, ½ cup cheese, the milk, garlic powder and pepper; pour over top.
3. Cover and bake for 20 minutes. Uncover; sprinkle with the remaining ½ cup cheese and remaining onions. Bake 2 minutes longer or until cheese is melted.
1 cup: 420 cal., 22g fat (9g sat. fat), 46mg chol., 529mg sod., 40g carb. (3g sugars, 3g fiber), 18g pro.

> **TEST KITCHEN TIP**
> If you like, you can use a different potato in this casserole. Waffle fries or crinkle-cut potatoes are a quick and easy substitution!

❄ ARGENTINE LASAGNA

My family is from Argentina, which has a strong Italian heritage and large cattle ranches. This all-in-one lasagna is packed with meat, cheese and veggies.
—*Sylvia Maenenr, Omaha, NE*

PREP: 30 min. • **BAKE:** 55 min. + standing
MAKES: 12 servings

- 1 lb. ground beef
- 1 large sweet onion, chopped
- ½ lb. sliced fresh mushrooms
- 1 garlic clove, minced
- 1 can (15 oz.) tomato sauce
- 1 can (6 oz.) tomato paste
- ¼ tsp. pepper
- 4 cups shredded part-skim mozzarella cheese, divided
- 1 jar (15 oz.) Alfredo sauce
- 1 carton (15 oz.) ricotta cheese
- 2½ cups frozen peas, thawed
- 1 pkg. (10 oz.) frozen chopped spinach, thawed and squeezed dry
- 1 pkg. (9 oz.) no-cook lasagna noodles
  Fresh basil leaves
  Grated Parmesan cheese, optional

1. Preheat oven to 350°. In a Dutch oven, cook the beef, onion, mushrooms and garlic over medium heat until meat is no longer pink; crumble beef; drain. Stir in the tomato sauce, tomato paste, pepper and 2 cups mozzarella cheese; set aside.
2. In a large bowl, combine the Alfredo sauce, ricotta cheese, peas and spinach.
3. Spread 1 cup meat sauce into a greased 13x9-in. baking dish. Layer with 4 noodles, 1¼ cups meat sauce and 1¼ cups spinach mixture. Repeat layers 3 times. Sprinkle with the remaining 2 cups mozzarella cheese. (Dish will be full.)
4. Cover and bake for 45 minutes. Uncover; bake 10 minutes longer or until cheese is melted. Let stand for 10 minutes before cutting. Garnish with basil and, if desired, serve with Parmesan cheese.
Freeze option: Cover and freeze unbaked lasagna. To use, partially thaw in refrigerator overnight. Remove from the refrigerator 30 minutes before baking. Bake lasagna as directed, increasing time as necessary to heat through and for a thermometer to read 165°.
1 piece: 406 cal., 18g fat (10g sat. fat), 69mg chol., 598mg sod., 33g carb. (8g sugars, 4g fiber), 28g pro.

BEEF & SPINACH LASAGNA

Using no-cook noodles gives you a jump start on assembling this hearty main dish. After it stands a few minutes, It cuts nicely and reveals flavorful layers.

—Carolyn Schmeling, Brookfield, WI

- -

PREP: 40 min. • **BAKE:** 40 min. + standing
MAKES: 12 servings

- 1 lb. lean ground beef (90% lean)
- 1 medium onion, chopped
- 2 jars (24 oz. each) spaghetti sauce
- 4 garlic cloves, minced
- 1 tsp. dried basil
- 1 tsp. dried oregano
- 1 pkg. (10 oz.) frozen chopped spinach, thawed and squeezed dry
- 2 cups ricotta cheese
- 2 cups shredded part-skim mozzarella cheese, divided
- 9 no-cook lasagna noodles
  Minced fresh basil, optional

1. Preheat oven to 375°. In a large skillet, cook beef and onion over medium heat until meat is no longer pink; crumble beef; drain. Stir in the spaghetti sauce, garlic, basil and oregano. Bring to a boil. Reduce heat; cover and simmer for 10 minutes. In a large bowl, mix together the spinach, ricotta cheese and 1 cup of the mozzarella cheese.

2. Spread 1½ cups meat sauce into a greased 13x9-in. baking dish. Top with 3 noodles. Spread 1½ cups sauce to edges of noodles. Top with half the spinach mixture. Repeat layers. Top with the remaining noodles, sauce and 1 cup mozzarella cheese.

3. Cover and bake for 30 minutes. Uncover; bake until bubbly, 10-15 minutes longer. Let stand for 10 minutes before cutting. If desired, top with minced fresh basil.

1 piece: 281 cal., 11g fat (6g sat. fat), 50mg chol., 702mg sod., 26g carb. (11g sugars, 3g fiber), 20g pro.

READER REVIEW

"Straight up simple and delicious. I upped the spices because that's how I roll. Thank you!"

JULIA, TASTEOFHOME.COM

BEEFY NOODLE CASSEROLE

When life calls for a dish for a potluck or family event, we stir up a batch of beef and noodles. That's our cheesy, bubbly comfort food.
—*Susan Lavery, Mckinney, TX*

PREP: 20 min. • **BAKE:** 15 min. + standing
MAKES: 6 servings

- 2 cups uncooked elbow macaroni
- 1 lb. ground beef
- 1 can (14½ oz.) diced tomatoes, drained
- 1 can (8 oz.) tomato sauce
- 1 Tbsp. sugar
- ½ tsp. salt
- ¼ tsp. garlic salt
- ¼ tsp. pepper
- 1 cup sour cream
- 3 oz. cream cheese, softened
- 3 green onions, chopped
- 1 cup shredded cheddar cheese

1. Preheat oven to 350°. In a 6-qt. stockpot, cook macaroni according to the package directions for al dente; drain and return to pot.
2. Meanwhile, in a large skillet, cook beef over medium heat until no longer pink, 6-8 minutes; crumble beef; drain. Stir in tomatoes, tomato sauce, sugar, salt, garlic salt and pepper. Transfer the mixture to a greased 11x7-in. baking dish.
3. Stir the sour cream, cream cheese and green onions into macaroni. Spoon over the beef mixture, spreading evenly. Sprinkle with shredded cheese.
4. Bake, covered, until bubbly, 15-20 minutes. Let stand 10 minutes before serving.
1 cup: 506 cal., 27g fat (15g sat. fat), 107mg chol., 745mg sod., 37g carb. (8g sugars, 3g fiber), 27g pro.

CRESCENT BEEF CASSEROLE

This flavorful meal-in-one dish is all you need to serve a satisfying and quick weeknight dinner. It's on the table in just 30 minutes. Use leftover puree for sauce for the rest of the week.
—*Taste of Home Test Kitchen*

TAKES: 30 min. • **MAKES:** 6 servings

- 1 lb. lean ground beef (90% lean)
- 2 tsp. olive oil
- 1 cup diced zucchini
- ¼ cup chopped onion
- ¼ cup chopped green pepper
- 1 cup tomato puree
- 1 tsp. dried oregano
- ¼ tsp. salt
- ⅛ tsp. pepper
- 1½ cups mashed potatoes
- 1 cup (4 oz.) crumbled feta cheese
- 1 tube (8 oz.) refrigerated crescent rolls
- 1 large egg, beaten, optional

1. Preheat oven to 375°. In a large skillet, cook beef over medium heat until no longer pink; crumble meat; drain and set aside.
2. In the same skillet, heat oil over medium-high heat. Add zucchini, onion and green pepper; cook and stir until crisp-tender, 4-5 minutes. Stir in beef, tomato puree, oregano, salt and pepper; heat through.
3. Spread mashed potatoes in an 11x7-in. baking dish coated with cooking spray. Top with beef mixture; sprinkle with feta cheese.
4. Unroll crescent dough. Separate into 4 rectangles; arrange 3 rectangles over the casserole. If desired, brush with egg wash. Bake until top is browned, 12-15 minutes. Roll the remaining dough into 2 crescent rolls; bake for another use.
1 serving: 443 cal., 22g fat (7g sat. fat), 67mg chol., 981mg sod., 31g carb. (6g sugars, 3g fiber), 26g pro.

BAKED MACARONI & CHEESE PIZZA

Here's a fun and flavorful way to combine pizza and macaroni and cheese. Experiment with other pizza toppings, such as sausage or diced green peppers.
—*Andrew McDowell, Lake Villa, IL*

PREP: 25 min. • **BAKE:** 10 min. + standing
MAKES: 8 servings

- 1   pkg. (7¼ oz.) macaroni and cheese dinner mix
- 2   large eggs, beaten
- ½   lb. ground beef
- ¾   cup chopped onion
- 1¼ cups pizza sauce
- 1   can (4 oz.) mushroom stems and pieces, drained
- 28 pepperoni slices
- 1   cup shredded Mexican cheese blend

1. Preheat oven to 375°. Prepare macaroni and cheese according to package directions; gradually stir in eggs. Spread onto a greased 12-in. pizza pan. Bake for 10 minutes.
2. Meanwhile, in a large skillet, cook beef and onion over medium heat until the meat is no longer pink; crumble beef; drain. Stir in the pizza sauce.
3. Spread meat mixture over macaroni crust. Sprinkle with mushrooms, pepperoni and cheese blend. Bake for 10-15 minutes or until a thermometer inserted in crust reads 160° and the cheese is melted.
1 piece: 332 cal., 20g fat (10g sat. fat), 108mg chol., 723mg sod., 22g carb. (5g sugars, 1g fiber), 17g pro.

> **TEST KITCHEN TIP**
> This pizza dresses up just like one with a bread crust, so feel free to experiment. Use fresh mushrooms instead, or top with mozzarella cheese—try any combo you like!

BEEF CABBAGE ROLL-UPS

Cooking up original recipes is a hobby of mine. My version of classic cabbage rolls is delicious served over rice or noodles.
—*Irma Finely, Lockwood, MO*

PREP: 30 min. • **BAKE:** 30 min.
MAKES: 6 servings

- 1   head cabbage
- 1   large potato, peeled and shredded
- 1   large carrot, shredded
- ½   cup finely chopped celery
- ½   cup finely chopped green pepper
- ½   cup finely chopped onion
- 2   large eggs, lightly beaten
- 2   garlic cloves, minced
- ¾   tsp. salt
- ½   tsp. pepper
- 1   lb. lean ground beef (90% lean)
- 2   cans (8 oz. each) tomato sauce
- ½   tsp. dried basil
- ½   tsp. dried parsley flakes

1. Preheat oven to 350°. Cook cabbage in boiling water just until the leaves fall off head. When cool enough to handle, use V-shaped cuts to remove the thick veins from bottoms of 12 large leaves; set aside. (Refrigerate the remaining cabbage for another use.)
2. In a large bowl, combine the potato, carrot, celery, green pepper, onion, eggs, garlic, salt and pepper. Crumble beef over mixture; mix lightly but thoroughly.
3. Shape into 12 logs. Place 1 log on each cabbage leaf; overlap the cut ends of the leaf. Fold in sides, beginning from the cut end. Roll up completely to enclose filling. Secure with a toothpick.
4. Place roll-ups in a greased 13x9-in. baking dish. Pour tomato sauce over roll-ups and sprinkle with basil and parsley. Cover and bake until a thermometer reads 160° and the cabbage is tender, 30-35 minutes.
2 roll-ups: 251 cal., 8g fat (3g sat. fat), 108mg chol., 584mg sod., 25g carb. (8g sugars, 6g fiber), 21g pro. **Diabetic exchanges:** 3 lean meat, 1 starch, 1 vegetable.

BACON CHEESEBURGER TATER TOT BAKE

Roll your burgers, cheese and taters all into one. It's the perfect dish to use to bribe your kids. Homework, chores, piano practice—consider them done when this is the reward!
—*Deanna Zewen, Union Grove, WI*

- -

PREP: 15 min. • **BAKE:** 35 min.
MAKES: 12 servings

- 2 lbs. ground beef
- 1 large onion, chopped and divided
- 1 can (15 oz.) tomato sauce
- 1 pkg. (8 oz.) Velveeta
- 1 Tbsp. ground mustard
- 1 Tbsp. Worcestershire sauce
- 2 cups shredded cheddar cheese
- 12 bacon strips, cooked and crumbled
- 1 pkg. (32 oz.) frozen Tater Tots
- 1 cup grape tomatoes, chopped
- ⅓ cup sliced dill pickles

1. Preheat oven to 400°. In a large skillet over medium heat, cook beef and 1 cup onion until beef is no longer pink and onion is tender, 6-8 minutes; crumble meat; drain. Stir in tomato sauce, Velveeta, mustard and Worcestershire sauce until cheese is melted, 4-6 minutes.
2. Transfer to a greased 13x9-in. or 3½-qt. baking dish. Sprinkle with cheddar cheese and bacon. Top with Tater Tots. Bake, uncovered, 35-40 minutes or until bubbly. Top with the tomatoes, pickles and remaining onion.
1 cup: 479 cal., 31g fat (12g sat. fat), 92mg chol., 1144mg sod., 24g carb. (4g sugars, 3g fiber), 27g pro.

JENNIFER BECKMAN
Falls Church, VA

FRENCH ONION SHEPHERD'S PIE

This hearty casserole has all the rich flavor of the French onion soup my family loves. The combination of the cheese-topped mashed potatoes and savory beef and onions is ideal for an autumn dinner. It doubles and freezes easily, so make one to eat tonight and one to freeze for later.
—*Jennifer Beckman, Falls Church, VA*

- -

PREP: 45 min. • **BAKE:** 30 min.
MAKES: 4 servings

- 2 large onions, halved and thinly sliced
- 1 Tbsp. canola oil
- 1 lb. ground beef
- 2 Tbsp. all-purpose flour
- ½ tsp. saltcbeef broth
- 2 Tbsp. brandy or additional reduced-sodium beef broth
- 1 Tbsp. Worcestershire sauce
- 1 Tbsp. stone-ground mustard
- 3 cups mashed potatoes
- 1 cup shredded Swiss cheese

1. Preheat oven to 375°. In a large skillet, saute onions in oil until softened. Reduce the heat to medium-low; cook for 35-40 minutes or until the onions are a deep golden brown: stir occasionally.
2. Meanwhile, in a large saucepan, cook the beef over medium heat until no longer pink; crumble beef; drain. Stir in flour and salt until well blended; cook 1 minute longer. Combine the broth, brandy, Worcestershire sauce and mustard. Gradually stir into pan. Bring to a boil; cook and stir for 2 minutes or until thickened. Stir in onions; heat through.
3. Transfer beef mixture to a greased 8-in. square baking dish. Spread with potatoes; sprinkle with cheese. Bake, uncovered, for 30-35 minutes or until bubbly and cheese is melted. If desired, increase heat to 475° and bake an additional 8-10 minutes until top is golden brown.
1½ cups: 563 cal., 27g fat (11g sat. fat), 101mg chol., 1150mg sod., 42g carb. (5g sugars, 2g fiber), 34g pro.

❄️ CHIPOTLE MAC & CHEESE

Beefy and bubbly, this Southwestern pasta bake heats up dinner with a chipotle-pepper kick. Add more cayenne if you like it hot!
—Cyndy Gerken, Naples, FL

- -

PREP: 35 min. • **BAKE:** 30 min.
MAKES: 2 casseroles (4 servings each)

1   pkg. (16 oz.) cavatappi or spiral pasta
2   lbs. ground beef
2   large onions, chopped
2   large green peppers, chopped
3   garlic cloves, minced
1   can (28 oz.) crushed tomatoes
1   can (10¾ oz.) condensed cheddar cheese soup, undiluted
½   cup 2% milk
1   chipotle pepper in adobo sauce, chopped
2   Tbsp. chili powder
1   Tbsp. ground cumin
1   tsp. cayenne pepper
1   tsp. dried oregano
½   tsp. salt
¼   tsp. pepper
2   cups shredded Monterey Jack cheese
2   Tbsp. minced fresh cilantro, optional

1. Preheat oven to 350°. Cook pasta according to package directions to al dente. Meanwhile, in a Dutch oven, cook the beef, onions, green peppers and garlic over medium heat until meat is no longer pink; crumble beef; drain.
2. Stir in the tomatoes, soup, milk, chipotle pepper and seasonings. Bring to a boil. Reduce heat; cover and simmer until thickened, about 15 minutes.
3. Drain pasta; stir into meat mixture. Divide between 2 greased 8-in. square baking dishes; sprinkle with cheese.
4. Cover and bake casseroles for 20 minutes. Uncover; bake until bubbly and cheese is melted, 8-10 minutes longer. If desired, sprinkle with cilantro.
Freeze option: Cover and freeze unbaked casseroles for up to 3 months. To use, partially thaw in refrigerator overnight. Remove from refrigerator 30 minutes before baking. Cover and bake at 350° for 60 minutes. Uncover; bake until bubbly and cheese is melted, 8-10 minutes longer.
1½ cups: 628 cal., 25g fat (12g sat. fat), 98mg chol., 913mg sod., 62g carb. (11g sugars, 7g fiber), 38g pro.

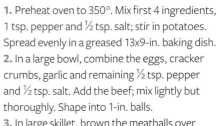

MEATBALL HASH BROWN BAKE

For a seniors potluck at church, I wanted to create a recipe that would incorporate a meat dish and side dish in one. This casserole proved to be a crowd-pleaser, and many people asked for my recipe.
—Joann Fritzler, Belen, NM

- -

PREP: 25 min. • **BAKE:** 1 hour
MAKES: 8 servings

1   can (10¾ oz.) condensed cream of chicken soup, undiluted
1   large onion, chopped
1   cup shredded cheddar cheese
1   cup sour cream
1½ tsp. pepper, divided
1   tsp. salt, divided
1   pkg. (30 oz.) frozen shredded hash brown potatoes, thawed and patted dry
2   large eggs, lightly beaten
¾   cup crushed saltines (20-25 crackers)
6   to 8 garlic cloves, minced
1   lb. lean ground beef (90% lean)

1. Preheat oven to 350°. Mix first 4 ingredients, 1 tsp. pepper and ½ tsp. salt; stir in potatoes. Spread evenly in a greased 13x9-in. baking dish.
2. In a large bowl, combine the eggs, cracker crumbs, garlic and remaining ½ tsp. pepper and ½ tsp. salt. Add the beef; mix lightly but thoroughly. Shape into 1-in. balls.
3. In large skillet, brown the meatballs over medium-high heat. Place over potato mixture, pressing in lightly.
4. Bake, covered, 45 minutes. Uncover; bake until meatballs are cooked through and the potatoes are tender, 10-15 minutes longer.
1 serving: 387 cal., 20g fat (9g sat. fat), 106mg chol., 808mg sod., 32g carb. (4g sugars, 3g fiber), 21g pro.

MINI MEDITERRANEAN PIZZA

I was on a mini-pizza kick and had already served up Mexican and Italian variations, so I opted to create a Mediterranean version!
—*Jenny Dubinsky, Inwood, WV*

PREP: 30 min. • **BAKE:** 5 min.
MAKES: 4 servings

- 1 Tbsp. olive oil
- 8 oz. lean ground beef (90% lean)
- ¼ cup finely chopped onion
- 2 garlic cloves, minced
- 1 can (8 oz.) tomato sauce
- 1 tsp. minced fresh rosemary or ¼ tsp. dried rosemary, crushed
- 2 whole wheat pita breads (6 in.), cut in half horizontally
- 1 medium tomato, seeded and chopped
- ½ cup fresh baby spinach, thinly sliced
- 12 Greek pitted olives, thinly sliced
- ½ cup shredded part-skim mozzarella cheese
- ¼ cup crumbled feta cheese

1. Preheat oven to 400°. Heat oil in a large nonstick skillet; cook the beef, onion and garlic over medium heat until meat is no longer pink, 5-6 minutes; crumble meat; drain. Stir in the tomato sauce and rosemary; bring to a boil. Reduce the heat; simmer, uncovered, until thickened, or 6-9 minutes.
2. Place pita halves, cut side up, on a baking sheet. Top with meat mixture, tomato, spinach and olives. Sprinkle with cheeses. Bake until cheeses are melted, or 4-6 minutes.
1 pizza: 287 cal., 12g fat (5g sat. fat), 47mg chol., 783mg sod., 25g carb. (3g sugars, 4g fiber), 21g pro. **Diabetic exchanges:** 2 lean meat, 1½ starch, 1 fat.

❄ LOADED SPAGHETTI BAKE

We used to go south in our RV for months at a time. One year when we arrived home after being gone for a while, my neighbor Jill came over with a pie plate filled with this wonderful spaghetti bake. Now I make it often for my family. I sometimes use leftover chicken instead of beef.
—*Marian Pappas, Lake Stevens, WA*

PREP: 25 min. • **BAKE:** 30 min.
MAKES: 8 servings

- 12 oz. uncooked spaghetti
- 1 lb. lean ground beef (90% lean)
- 1 cup chopped onion
- 1 cup chopped green pepper
- 1 jar (26 oz.) spaghetti sauce
- 1 can (4 oz.) mushroom stems and pieces, drained
- 1 can (2¼ oz.) sliced ripe olives, drained
- 2 cups shredded cheddar cheese, divided
- 1 can (10¾ oz.) condensed cream of chicken soup, undiluted
- 1 carton (10 oz.) refrigerated Alfredo sauce
- ¼ cup grated Parmesan cheese
- ½ cup cornflake crumbs

1. Preheat oven to 350°. Cook spaghetti according to package directions. Meanwhile, in a large skillet, cook the beef, onion and pepper over medium heat until meat is no longer pink; crumble beef; drain. Add the spaghetti sauce, mushrooms and olives. Drain spaghetti; add to skillet.
2. Transfer to a greased 13x9-in. baking dish. Sprinkle with 1 cup cheddar cheese. In a small bowl, combine the soup, Alfredo sauce and Parmesan cheese; spread over cheddar cheese. In another bowl, combine cornflake crumbs and remaining 1 cup cheddar cheese; sprinkle over the top.
3. Bake, uncovered, until casserole is bubbly and cheese is melted, 30 minutes. Let stand 5 minutes before serving.
Freeze option: Cover and freeze casserole for up to 3 months. To use, remove from the freezer 30 minutes before baking (do not thaw). Cover and bake for 1 hour. Uncover casserole and bake until heated through and a thermometer reads 165°, 15-20 minutes longer.
1½ cups: 612 cal., 30g fat (14g sat. fat), 80mg chol., 1486mg sod., 55g carb. (10g sugars, 4g fiber), 29g pro.

BEEF & BISCUIT BAKE

This satisfying dish is perfect. It has the best flavor and is quick and easy. With its beef and corn combo, I think it's a fine example of Midwest cuisine.

—*Erin Schneider, St. Peters, MO*

TAKES: 30 min. • **MAKES:** 8 servings

- 1 lb. ground beef
- 1 can (16 oz.) kidney beans, rinsed and drained
- 1 can (15¼ oz.) whole kernel corn, drained
- 1 can (10¾ oz.) condensed tomato soup, undiluted
- ¼ cup 2% milk
- 2 Tbsp. finely chopped onion
- ½ tsp. chili powder
- ¼ tsp. salt
- 1 cup cubed Velveeta
- 1 tube (12 oz.) refrigerated biscuits
- 2 to 3 Tbsp. butter, melted
- ⅓ cup yellow cornmeal

1. Preheat oven to 375°. In a saucepan over medium heat, cook beef until no longer pink; crumble meat; drain. Add beans, corn, soup, milk, onion, chili powder and salt; bring to a boil. Remove from heat; stir in cheese until melted. Spoon into a greased 2½-qt. baking dish. Bake, uncovered, 10 minutes.
2. Meanwhile, brush all sides of biscuits with butter; roll in cornmeal. Place on top of bubbling meat mixture. Return to oven for 10-12 minutes or until the biscuits are lightly browned and cooked through.
1 serving: 439 cal., 19g fat (8g sat. fat), 46mg chol., 1180mg sod., 44g carb. (10g sugars, 5g fiber), 21g pro.

READER REVIEW

"Very easy and yummy dish. I did substitute grated cheddar for the Velveeta."

JACQUELINEFRIEDERICHSEN, TASTEOFHOME.COM

BEEF & RICE ENCHILADAS

With a toddler in the house, I look for foods that are a snap to make. Loaded with beef, cheese and a flavorful rice mix, these enchiladas come together without any fuss. But they're so good that guests think I spent hours in the kitchen.
—*Jennifer Smith, Colona, IL*

PREP: 30 min. • **BAKE:** 20 min.
MAKES: 10 enchiladas

- 1 pkg. (6.8 oz.) Spanish rice and pasta mix
- 1 lb. ground beef
- 2 cans (10 oz. each) enchilada sauce, divided
- 10 flour tortillas (8 in.), warmed
- 1⅔ cups shredded cheddar cheese, divided

1. Preheat oven to 350°. Prepare rice mix according to package directions. Meanwhile, in a large skillet, cook beef over medium heat until no longer pink; crumble meat; drain. Stir in Spanish rice and 1¼ cups enchilada sauce.
2. Spoon about ⅔ cup of the beef mixture down the center of each tortilla. Top each with 1 Tbsp. cheese; roll up.
3. Place in an ungreased 13x9-in. baking dish. Top with the remaining enchilada sauce and cheese. Bake, uncovered, until the cheese is melted, 20-25 minutes.

1 enchilada: 415 cal., 17g fat (8g sat. fat), 47mg chol., 1141mg sod., 46g carb. (3g sugars, 3g fiber), 20g pro.

READER REVIEW

"I have been making this for 40 years! Still love the simplicity, taste, and flexibility to add whatever your taste desires!"

BATEMANJ, TASTEOFHOME.COM

SWEET & SOUR SUPPER

My mother shared this recipe with me, and I've been making it for my own family for years. The homemade sweet & sour sauce is the key to this dish's success.
—*Dorothy Reimer, Dewberry, AB*

PREP: 20 min. • **BAKE:** 30 min.
MAKES: 6 servings

- 1 lb. ground beef
- 1½ tsp. chili powder
- 1½ tsp. dried oregano
- 1½ tsp. salt
   Pepper to taste
- 3 cups cooked long grain rice
- 1 can (7 oz.) mushroom stems and pieces, drained
- 1 medium green pepper, sliced

SAUCE
- 1 cup plus 2 Tbsp. sugar
- ⅓ cup cornstarch
- 2½ cups cold water
- ⅓ cup white vinegar
- ⅓ cup ketchup
- 1½ tsp. salt
   Pepper to taste

1. Preheat oven to 350°. In a large skillet, cook beef over medium heat until meat is no longer pink; crumble meat; drain. Stir in the chili powder, oregano, salt and pepper.
2. In a greased 3-qt. baking dish, layer the rice, beef mixture, mushrooms and green pepper; set aside.
3. In a large saucepan, combine sugar and cornstarch; stir in the remaining sauce ingredients until smooth. Bring to a boil; cook and stir for 2 minutes or until thickened.
4. Pour sauce over layered ingredients. Bake, uncovered, for 30 minutes or until heated through.

1 serving: 424 cal., 7g fat (3g sat. fat), 37mg chol., 1518mg sod., 73g carb. (39g sugars, 2g fiber), 17g pro.

BEEF & TATER BAKE

The entire family will enjoy this heartwarming, all-in-one dinner. Plus, it offers easy cleanup!
—*Mike Tchou, Pepper Pike, OH*

- -

PREP: 10 min. • **BAKE:** 35 min.
MAKES: 8 servings

- 4 cups frozen Tater Tots
- 1 lb. ground beef
- ¼ tsp. garlic powder
- ⅛ tsp. pepper
- 1 can (10¾ oz.) condensed cream of broccoli soup, undiluted
- ⅓ cup 2% milk
- 1 pkg. (16 oz.) frozen chopped broccoli, thawed
- 1 can (2.8 oz.) french-fried onions, divided
- 1 cup shredded Colby-Monterey Jack cheese, divided
- 1 medium tomato, chopped

1. Preheat oven to 400°. Spread Tater Tots evenly in an ungreased 13x9-in. baking dish. Bake, uncovered, 10 minutes.
2. Meanwhile, in a large skillet, cook the beef over medium heat until no longer pink, 5-7 minutes; crumble beef; drain. Stir in the seasonings, soup, milk, broccoli, ¾ cup onions, ½ cup cheese and tomato; heat through. Pour over potatoes.
3. Bake, covered, for 20 minutes. Sprinkle with the remaining onions and cheese. Bake, uncovered, until the cheese is melted, 5-10 minutes longer.
1 serving: 400 cal., 24g fat (9g sat. fat), 50mg chol., 805mg sod., 29g carb. (3g sugars, 4g fiber), 17g pro.

❄ PEPPERY PIZZA LOAVES

I often take these French bread pizzas to church picnics or potluck suppers and there are never any left. When I fix them for the two of us, I freeze two halves in foil to enjoy later.
—*Lou Stasny, Poplarville, MS*

- -

PREP: 20 min. • **BAKE:** 20 min.
MAKES: 12 servings

- 1½ lbs. ground beef
- ½ tsp. garlic powder
- ½ tsp. salt
- 2 loaves (8 oz. each) French bread, halved lengthwise
- 1 cup cheese dip
- 1 can (4 oz.) mushroom stems and pieces, drained
- 1 cup chopped green onions
- 1 can (4 oz.) sliced jalapenos, drained
- 1 can (8 oz.) tomato sauce
- ½ cup grated Parmesan cheese
- 4 cups shredded part-skim mozzarella cheese

1. Preheat oven to 350°. In a large skillet, cook beef over medium heat until no longer pink; drain. Stir in garlic powder and salt.
2. Place each bread half on a large piece of heavy-duty foil. Spread with cheese sauce. Top with the beef mixture, mushrooms, onions and jalapenos. Drizzle with tomato sauce. Top with Parmesan and mozzarella cheeses.
3. Bake 10-15 minutes or until golden brown. Serve warm.
1 piece: 323 cal., 19g fat (11g sat. fat), 71mg chol., 907mg sod., 15g carb. (2g sugars, 1g fiber), 23g pro.

TEST KITCHEN TIP
These loaves freeze well for a great last-minute dinner option. Wrap assembled loaves and freeze for up to 3 months. To use, unwrap and thaw on baking sheets in the refrigerator and bake at 350° for 18 minutes.

SPICY NACHO BAKE

I made this hearty, layered Southwestern casserole for a dinner meeting, and now I'm asked to bring it to every potluck. Everybody savors the ground beef and bean filling and crunchy, cheesy topping. The recipe makes two casseroles to feed a crowd, but you can easily halve it for a smaller guest list.
—*Anita Wilson, Mansfield, OH*

- -

PREP: 1 hour • **BAKE:** 20 min.
MAKES: 2 casseroles (15 servings each)

- 2 **lbs. ground beef**
- 2 **large onions, chopped**
- 2 **large green peppers, chopped**
- 2 **cans (28 oz. each) diced tomatoes, undrained**
- 2 **cans (16 oz. each) hot chili beans, undrained**
- 2 **cans (15 oz. each) black beans, rinsed and drained**
- 2 **cans (11 oz. each) whole kernel corn, drained**
- 2 **cans (8 oz. each) tomato sauce**
- 2 **envelopes taco seasoning**
- 2 **pkg. (13 oz. each) spicy nacho-flavored tortilla chips**
- 4 **cups shredded cheddar cheese**

1. In a Dutch oven, cook the beef, onions and green peppers over medium heat until meat is no longer pink, crumble beef; drain. Stir in the tomatoes, beans, corn, tomato sauce and taco seasoning. Bring to a boil. Reduce heat; simmer, uncovered, for 30 minutes (mixture will be thin).
2. In each of 2 greased 13x9-in. baking dishes, layer 5 cups of chips and 4⅔ cups of the meat mixture. Repeat layers. Top each with 4 cups of chips and 2 cups of cheese.
3. Bake, uncovered, at 350° until golden brown, 20-25 minutes.
⅔ cup: 314 cal., 13g fat (6g sat. fat), 31mg chol., 845mg sod., 33g carb. (5g sugars, 5g fiber), 14g pro.

BROWN RICE STUFFED PEPPERS

For extra flavor, I sometimes add beef bouillon to the dish while the peppers bake. It also steams them a little. I also make these with ground chicken or turkey; then, I'd use chicken bouillon instead.
—*Hope Huggins, Santa Cruz, CA*

- -

PREP: 20 min. • **BAKE:** 15 min.
MAKES: 6 servings

- 6 **medium green peppers**
- ¾ **cup uncooked brown rice**
- 1 **lb. lean ground beef (90% lean)**
- 1 **medium onion, chopped**
- 1 **can (8 oz.) tomato sauce**
- ¼ **tsp. dried basil**
- ¼ **tsp. dried oregano**
- ¼ **tsp. dried thyme**
- ½ **tsp. salt**
  Pepper to taste

1. Remove tops and seeds from peppers. In a stockpot, bring 10 cups water to boil; cook peppers for 5 minutes. Remove and drain. Cook rice according to package directions.
2. Preheat oven to 375°. In a large skillet, cook beef and onion over medium heat until meat is no longer pink; crumble meat; drain. Add tomato sauce, herbs, salt and pepper; cook, uncovered, for 5 minutes. Stir in rice. Remove from the heat.
3. Spoon rice mixture into peppers. Place in a shallow ungreased baking dish or casserole. Bake, uncovered, until peppers are tender, 15-20 minutes.
1 serving: 245 cal., 6g fat (2g sat. fat), 37mg chol., 424mg sod., 29g carb. (5g sugars, 3g fiber), 18g pro.

CHEESEBURGER PEPPER CUPS

I like to serve my grandkids something special, and this is one of their favorites. They like red or yellow peppers because they're sweeter.
—*Betty Winscher, Royalton, MN*

- -

PREP: 15 min. • **BAKE:** 35 min.
MAKES: 4 servings

4	medium sweet bell peppers
½	lb. ground beef
¼	cup finely chopped onion
2	cups cooked brown rice
1	can (6 oz.) tomato paste
2	Tbsp. ketchup
1	Tbsp. Worcestershire sauce
1	Tbsp. spicy brown mustard
½	tsp. garlic salt
¼	tsp. pepper
1	cup vegetable broth
1	cup shredded cheddar cheese

1. Preheat oven to 350°. Cut peppers in half lengthwise and remove seeds; set aside.
2. In a large skillet, cook beef and onion over medium heat until meat is no longer pink; crumble beef; drain. Stir in rice, tomato paste, ketchup, Worcestershire sauce, mustard, garlic salt and pepper. Spoon into peppers.
3. Place in a greased 13x9-in. baking dish; pour broth around the peppers. Cover and bake for 30 minutes. Sprinkle with cheese. Bake, uncovered, 5 minutes longer or until cheese is melted.

2 pepper halves: 413 cal., 16g fat (9g sat. fat), 68mg chol., 893mg sod., 45g carb. (12g sugars, 7g fiber), 23g pro.

DID YOU KNOW?
Red bell peppers are simply vine-ripened green bells that, because they've ripened longer, are very sweet. You can use any sweet bell pepper for this recipe.

CREOLE BEEF CASSEROLE

One night, when my husband and I were each cooking something different, we ended up combining them for this dish. Serendipity!
—*Nicki Austin, Lawrenceville, IL*

- -

PREP: 25 min. • **BAKE:** 40 min.
MAKES: 8 servings

- 2 cans (10¾ oz. each) condensed cream of chicken soup, undiluted
- 2 cups sour cream
- 1 small onion, chopped
- ¼ tsp. pepper
- 1 pkg. (30 oz.) frozen shredded hash brown potatoes, thawed
- 2 cups shredded cheddar cheese
- 1½ lbs. ground beef
- 1 cup ketchup
- ¼ cup packed brown sugar
- 3 tsp. Creole seasoning
- 1 tsp. garlic salt
- 1 tsp. dried oregano
- ¼ tsp. cayenne pepper
- ¾ cup crushed cornflakes
- ¼ cup butter, melted

1. Preheat oven to 350°. In a large bowl, combine soup, sour cream, onion and pepper. Stir in potatoes and cheese; transfer to a greased 3-qt. baking dish.
2. In a large skillet, cook beef over medium heat until no longer pink; crumble beef; drain. Stir in ketchup, brown sugar and seasonings; spread over the potatoes. Combine cornflakes and butter; sprinkle over top. Bake, uncovered, for 40-45 minutes or until bubbly.

Note: If you don't have Creole seasoning in your cupboard, you can make your own using ¼ tsp. each salt, garlic powder and paprika; and a pinch each of dried thyme, ground cumin and cayenne pepper.

1¼ cups: 654 cal., 36g fat (21g sat. fat), 133mg chol., 1763mg sod., 51g carb. (19g sugars, 2g fiber), 28g pro.

DILL PICKLE HAMBURGER PIZZA

My husband's favorite foods are pizza and cheeseburgers, so I combined the two in a pizza with mayo and dill pickle juice topping. People who try it always laugh in surprise because it's so good.
—*Angie Zimmerman, Eureka, IL*

- -

TAKES: 30 min. • **MAKES:** 6 servings

- ½ lb. ground beef
- 1 prebaked 12-in. pizza crust
- ½ cup ketchup
- ¼ cup prepared mustard
- 1½ cups shredded cheddar cheese
- 2 cups shredded lettuce
- ½ cup chopped dill pickle
- ¼ cup chopped onion
- ½ cup mayonnaise
- 2 to 3 Tbsp. dill pickle juice

1. Preheat oven to 425°. In a large skillet, cook beef over medium heat until no longer pink, 3-4 minutes; crumble meat; drain.
2. Meanwhile, place crust on an ungreased baking sheet or pizza pan. Mix ketchup and mustard; spread over crust. Add ground beef; bake 5 minutes. Sprinkle with cheese; bake until cheese is bubbly and crust is lightly browned, 8-10 minutes longer.
3. Top with lettuce, pickle and onion. Whisk mayonnaise and enough pickle juice to reach desired consistency; drizzle over pizza.

1 slice: 521 cal., 32g fat (10g sat. fat), 59mg chol., 1192mg sod., 36g carb. (7g sugars, 2g fiber), 21g pro.

MEXICAN MANICOTTI

Serve this hearty entree with Spanish rice, homemade salsa and tortilla chips. I've also made it without ground beef. Our friends who are vegetarians requested the recipe.
—*Lucy Shifton, Wichita, KS*

PREP: 15 min. + chilling
BAKE: 65 min. + standing
MAKES: 8 servings

- 1 lb. lean ground beef
- 1 can (16 oz.) refried beans
- 2½ tsp. chili powder
- 1½ tsp. dried oregano
- 1 pkg. (8 oz.) uncooked manicotti shells
- 2½ cups water
- 1 jar (16 oz.) picante sauce
- 2 cups sour cream
- 1 cup shredded Monterey Jack or Mexican cheese blend
- ¼ cup sliced green onions
  Sliced ripe olives, optional

1. In a large bowl, combine the uncooked beef, beans, chili powder and oregano. Spoon into uncooked manicotti shells; arrange in a greased 13x9-in. baking dish. Combine water and picante sauce; pour over shells. Cover and refrigerate overnight.
2. Remove from the refrigerator 30 minutes before baking. Cover and bake at 350° for 1 hour.
3. Uncover; spoon sour cream over the top. Sprinkle with cheese, onions and olives if desired. Bake 5-10 minutes longer or until the cheese is melted.
1 serving: 431 cal., 20g fat (12g sat. fat), 90mg chol., 554mg sod., 36g carb. (6g sugars, 4g fiber), 23g pro.

> **DID YOU KNOW?**
> The Spanish word *picante* translates to "piquant"—implying it's spicy. However, picante sauce can come in various heat levels. You can choose the one you like, and spice it up with more chili powder, some hot sauce, or finely diced hot peppers.

TASTY HAMBURGER CASSEROLE

I need only a few ingredients to pack a lot of flavor into this hearty ground beef bake. My daughter received this recipe from a missionary when they were both serving in Zambia. It's delicious!
—*Faith Richards, Tampa, FL*

PREP: 10 min. • **BAKE:** 1¼ hours
MAKES: 6 servings

- 5 medium potatoes, peeled and sliced
- 1 small onion, chopped
- 1 lb. lean ground beef (90% lean)
- 1 can (10¾ oz.) condensed cream of mushroom soup, undiluted
- 1 can (10½ oz.) condensed vegetarian vegetable soup, undiluted
- 1 cup crushed potato chips

1. Preheat oven to 350°. In a greased 13x9-in. baking dish, layer potatoes and onion. Crumble beef over onion. Spread soups over beef.
2. Cover and bake for 55 minutes. Uncover; sprinkle with chips. Bake 20 minutes longer or until the meat is no longer pink and the vegetables are tender.
1 serving: 348 cal., 13g fat (4g sat. fat), 49mg chol., 723mg sod., 39g carb. (4g sugars, 3g fiber), 19g pro.

CHILES RELLENOS CASSEROLE

I love green chiles and cook with them often when I entertain. This easy version of the classic Mexican dish gives you big pepper taste in every meaty bite.
—*Nadine Estes, Alto, NM*

PREP: 15 min. • **BAKE:** 45 min.
MAKES: 6 servings

- 1 can (7 oz.) whole green chiles
- 1½ cups shredded Colby-Monterey Jack cheese
- ¾ lb. ground beef
- ¼ cup chopped onion
- 1 cup 2% milk
- 4 large eggs
- ¼ cup all-purpose flour
- ¼ tsp. salt
- ⅛ tsp. pepper

1. Split chiles and remove seeds; dry on paper towels. Arrange chiles on the bottom of a greased 2-qt. baking dish. Top with cheese.
2. In a skillet, cook beef and onion over medium heat until meat is no longer pink; crumble beef; drain. Spoon over the cheese.
3. Beat milk, eggs, flour, salt and pepper until smooth; pour over beef mixture. Bake, uncovered, at 350° until a knife inserted in the center comes out clean, 45-50 minutes. Let stand 5 minutes before serving.
Note: Wear disposable gloves when cutting hot peppers; the oils can burn skin. Avoid touching your face.
1 serving: 321 cal., 20g fat (11g sat. fat), 212mg chol., 406mg sod., 9g carb. (3g sugars, 0 fiber), 24g pro.

❄ SPICY ENCHILADA CASSEROLE

Chili powder, tortillas, cheese and ground beef combine for a winning Tex-Mex casserole. Choose a salsa that suits your family's tastes— mild, medium or hot.
—*Julie Huffman, New Lebanon, OH*

PREP: 20 min. • **BAKE:** 40 min.
MAKES: 2 casseroles (4 servings each)

- 1½ lbs. ground beef
- 1 large onion, chopped
- 1 cup water
- 2 to 3 Tbsp. chili powder
- 1½ tsp. salt
- ½ tsp. pepper
- ¼ tsp. garlic powder
- 2 cups salsa, divided
- 10 flour tortillas (8 in.), cut into ¾-in. strips, divided
- 1 cup sour cream
- 2 cans (15¼ oz. each) whole kernel corn, drained
- 4 cups shredded part-skim mozzarella cheese

1. In a large skillet, cook beef and onion over medium heat until meat is no longer pink; crumble beef; drain. Stir in the water, chili powder, salt, pepper and garlic powder. Bring to a boil. Reduce heat; simmer, uncovered, for 10 minutes.
2. Place ¼ cup salsa in each of two greased 8-in. square baking dishes. Top each with a fourth of the tortilla strips and ¼ cup salsa.
3. Divide the meat mixture, sour cream and corn between the two casseroles. Top with the remaining tortilla strips, salsa and cheese.
4. Cover one casserole and bake at 350° for 35 minutes. Uncover; bake 5-10 minutes longer or until heated through.
Freeze option: Cover the unbaked casserole and freeze for up to 1 month. To use, thaw in the refrigerator for 24 hours. Remove from the refrigerator 30 minutes before baking. Bake as directed above.
1 cup: 592 cal., 26g fat (13g sat. fat), 94mg chol., 1535mg sod., 45g carb. (8g sugars, 4g fiber), 37g pro.

SASSY SOUTHWEST STUFFED SHELLS

When I was a child, my mom made this dish quite often. When I came across her recipe on an index card, I quickly copied it. Over the years, I have made very few changes because I wanted to retain that taste-of-home memory.
—*Kellie Braddell, West Point, CA*

PREP: 45 min. • **BAKE:** 35 min.
MAKES: 8 servings

- 24 uncooked jumbo pasta shells
- ½ lb. lean ground beef (90% lean)
- ½ lb. lean ground pork
- 1 large carrot, shredded
- 3 green onions, chopped
- 3 garlic cloves, minced
- 2 cans (4 oz. each) chopped green chiles
- 2 cups shredded Mexican cheese blend, divided
- 1 can (6 oz.) french-fried onions, divided
- ¼ cup minced fresh cilantro
- 1 jar (16 oz.) picante sauce
- 2 cans (8 oz. each) tomato sauce
- 1 cup water

1. Preheat oven to 350°. Cook pasta according to package directions for al dente. Drain and rinse in cold water.
2. Meanwhile, in a large skillet, cook beef and pork over medium heat until no longer pink, breaking into crumbles, 8-10 minutes; drain.
3. Add carrot, green onions and garlic; cook 1 minute longer. Stir in chiles, 1 cup cheese, half of the fried onions and the cilantro. In a large bowl combine picante sauce, tomato sauce and water; stir 1 cup picante mixture into pan.
4. Spread 1 cup of the remaining picante mixture into a greased 13x9-in. baking dish. Fill pasta shells with meat mixture; place in baking dish, overlapping ends slightly. Top with remaining sauce. Cover and bake 30 minutes.
5. Uncover; top with the remaining 1 cup cheese and the remaining fried onions. Bake until cheese is melted, 5-10 minutes longer.
3 stuffed shells: 487 cal., 26g fat (10g sat. fat), 59mg chol., 1181mg sod., 41g carb. (5g sugars, 3g fiber), 22g pro.

INSIDE-OUT STUFFED PEPPERS

My daughters don't care for the usual green peppers stuffed with a meat-and-rice mixture, so one of the girls dreamed up this alternative. The peppers are simply chopped and combined with the other ingredients in a casserole.
—*Darlene Brenden, Salem, OR*

PREP: 15 min. • **BAKE:** 65 min.
MAKES: 6 servings

- 1 lb. ground beef
- ½ cup chopped onion
- 1 can (14½ oz.) stewed tomatoes, cut up
- 1 large green pepper, chopped
- ½ cup uncooked long grain rice
- ½ cup water
- 2 tsp. Worcestershire sauce
- ½ tsp. salt
- ¼ tsp. pepper
- 1 cup shredded cheddar cheese

1. Preheat oven to 350°. In a large skillet, cook beef over medium heat until no longer pink; drain. Transfer to a greased 2-qt. casserole. Add the next 8 ingredients.
2. Bake, covered, until the rice is tender, about 1 hour.
3. Uncover and sprinkle with cheese; cook until cheese is melted, about 5 minutes longer.
1 serving: 276 cal., 12g fat (7g sat. fat), 57mg chol., 516mg sod., 22g carb. (5g sugars, 2g fiber), 19g pro.

WESTERN BEEF & CORNMEAL PIE

With this hearty main-dish recipe, the bread is baked right in the casserole. The meal covers all four food groups, and it's a guaranteed family pleaser.
—*Darlene Alexander, Nekoosa, WI*

- -

PREP: 25 min. • **BAKE:** 25 min.
MAKES: 8 servings

- 1   lb. ground beef
- 1   can (11 oz.) Mexican-style corn, drained
- 1   can (6 oz.) tomato paste
- 1   cup shredded cheddar cheese
- ¾   cup barbecue sauce
- ½   tsp. salt
- ½   tsp. chili powder

CRUST

- 1   cup all-purpose flour
- ½   cup cornmeal
- ½   cup 2% milk
- ¼   cup butter, softened
- 1   large egg, room temperature
- 2   Tbsp. sugar
- 1   tsp. baking powder
- 1   tsp. salt
- 1   cup shredded cheddar cheese, divided

1. Preheat oven to 400°. In a skillet, brown ground beef; crumble meat; drain. Stir in next 6 ingredients; set aside.
2. In a large bowl, combine flour, cornmeal, milk, butter, egg, sugar, baking powder, salt and ½ cup cheddar cheese; mix well. Spread on the bottom and up the sides of a greased 2½-qt. baking dish or 10-in. ovenproof skillet.
3. Pour filling into prepared crust. Sprinkle with the remaining ½ cup cheese. Bake, uncovered, 25-30 minutes.
1 cup: 452 cal., 23g fat (13g sat. fat), 113mg chol., 1195mg sod., 38g carb. (12g sugars, 4g fiber), 23g pro.

LASAGNA TOSS

This easy skillet dish tastes just like lasagna without all the layering prep work. It's perfect for busy weeknights!
—*Sharon Martin, Denver, PA*

- -

PREP: 15 min. • **BAKE:** 20 min.
MAKES: 6 servings

- 1   lb. ground beef
- ½   cup chopped onion
- 1   garlic clove, minced
- ½   tsp. salt
- 1¾ cups spaghetti sauce
- 6   oz. spiral noodles, cooked and drained
- 1   cup small curd 4% cottage cheese
- 2   cups shredded part-skim mozzarella cheese, divided
-     Grated Parmesan cheese
-     Minced fresh basil

1. Preheat oven to 350°. In a large skillet, brown beef with onion, garlic and salt. Stir in spaghetti sauce; simmer until heated. Remove 1 cup meat sauce; set aside. Stir noodles into the remaining sauce.
2. Place half of the noodle mixture in a greased 2-qt. baking dish. Cover with cottage cheese and 1 cup mozzarella cheese.
3. Add remaining noodle mixture; top with reserved meat sauce and remaining 1 cup mozzarella cheese. Sprinkle with Parmesan cheese. Cover; bake for 20-25 minutes.
4. Let stand 5 minutes before serving. If desired, sprinkle with basil.
1½ cups: 436 cal., 19g fat (9g sat. fat), 74mg chol., 885mg sod., 34g carb. (10g sugars, 3g fiber), 31g pro.

REFRIED BEAN-TACO PIZZA

I like to make pizzas, and this one's my favorite. I use a ready-to-use pizza crust when time is tight. If you like taco salad, you'll love this pizza.
—*Mary Detweiler, Middlefield, OH*

PREP: 30 min. • **BAKE:** 20 min.
MAKES: 8 servings

- 1¼ lbs. ground beef
- 1 small onion, chopped
- ½ cup water
- 1 envelope taco seasoning
- 1 prebaked 12-in. pizza crust
- 1 can (16 oz.) refried beans
- 2 taco shells, coarsely crushed
- 1 cup shredded cheddar cheese
- 1 cup shredded part-skim mozzarella cheese
- 2 cups torn iceberg lettuce
- 2 medium tomatoes, chopped
- 1 Tbsp. sliced ripe olives

1. Preheat oven to 450°. In a large skillet, cook beef and onion over medium heat until meat is no longer pink; crumble meat; drain. Stir in water and taco seasoning. Bring to a boil. Reduce the heat; simmer, uncovered, for 5 minutes.

2. Place crust on an ungreased baking sheet. Spread with refried beans. Top with the beef mixture, taco shells and cheeses. Bake for 10-15 minutes or until the cheese is melted. Top with lettuce, tomatoes and olives.

1 piece: 420 cal., 17g fat (8g sat. fat), 62mg chol., 1051mg sod., 39g carb. (3g sugars, 5g fiber), 28g pro.

READER REVIEW

"I made two separate pizzas. One with ground beef for me and my husband and the other with vegetarian 'crumbles' for my vegetarian daughters—we all were very pleased!"

RUSTEDGOLD1, TASTEOFHOME.COM

Ground Beef

STOVETOP DINNERS

For convenience, nothing beats a stovetop supper! Simmered in a Dutch oven or whipped up in a skillet, these dishes are perfect for a busy weeknight and guaranteed to satisfy every time.

CHILI-GHETTI

I came up with this recipe when unexpected guests stopped by and I didn't have enough chili to go around. This spur-of-the-moment main dish is now a family favorite.
—*Cindy Cuykendall, Skaneateles, NY*

TAKES: 30 min. • **MAKES:** 6 servings

1 pkg. (7 oz.) spaghetti
1 lb. ground beef
1 small onion, chopped
1 can (16 oz.) kidney beans, rinsed and drained
1 can (14½ oz.) no-salt-added diced tomatoes, undrained
1 can (4 oz.) mushroom stems and pieces, drained
⅓ cup water
1 envelope chili seasoning
2 Tbsp. grated Parmesan cheese
¼ cup shredded part-skim mozzarella cheese

1. Cook spaghetti according to the package directions. Meanwhile, in a large skillet, cook beef and onion over medium heat until meat is no longer pink; crumble beef; drain.
2. Drain spaghetti; add to beef mixture. Stir in the beans, tomatoes, mushrooms, water, chili seasoning and Parmesan cheese. Cover and simmer for 10 minutes. Sprinkle with mozzarella cheese.

1¼ cups: 374 cal., 11g fat (4g sat. fat), 51mg chol., 706mg sod., 43g carb. (5g sugars, 6g fiber), 25g pro.

READER REVIEW
"Great flavor and super easy to put together on a busy weeknight."
ANGEL182009, TASTEOFHOME.COM

HEARTY SKILLET SUPPER

When the weather starts turning cooler, I start to hear requests for this dish. The light soy, onion and garlic flavors blend nicely with fresh carrots and potatoes in this budget-minded recipe.

—*Pat Jensen, Cottonwood, MN*

PREP: 5 min. • **COOK:** 45 min.
MAKES: 4 servings

- 1 **lb. ground beef**
- 1 **large onion, chopped**
- 1 **garlic clove, minced**
- 1 **cup chopped carrots**
- 1 **cup cubed peeled potatoes**
- 1 **cup water**
- ½ **cup uncooked long grain rice**
- 2 **Tbsp. soy sauce**
- 1 **tsp. salt**
- ⅛ **tsp. pepper**

1. In a large skillet, cook the beef, onion and garlic over medium heat until the meat is no longer pink; crumble beef; drain. Stir in the carrots, potatoes, water and rice.

2. Cover and simmer for 30 minutes or until the rice and vegetables are tender. Just before serving, stir in the soy sauce, salt and pepper.

1 serving: 329 cal., 11g fat (5g sat. fat), 56mg chol., 1140mg sod., 33g carb. (5g sugars, 3g fiber), 24g pro.

STOVETOP CHEESEBURGER PASTA

Cheeseburgers are delicious in any form, but I'm partial to this creamy pasta dish that seriously tastes just like the real thing. It's weeknight comfort in a bowl.

—*Tracy Avis, Peterborough, ON*

TAKES: 30 min. • **MAKES:** 8 servings

- 1 **pkg. (16 oz.) penne pasta**
- 1 **lb. ground beef**
- ¼ **cup butter, cubed**
- ½ **cup all-purpose flour**
- 2 **cups 2% milk**
- 1¼ **cups beef broth**
- 1 **Tbsp. Worcestershire sauce**
- 3 **tsp. ground mustard**
- 2 **cans (14½ oz. each) diced tomatoes, drained**
- 4 **green onions, chopped**
- 3 **cups shredded Colby-Monterey Jack cheese, divided**
- ⅔ **cup grated Parmesan cheese, divided**

1. Cook pasta according to the package directions; drain.

2. Meanwhile, in a Dutch oven, cook beef over medium heat until no longer pink, 5-7 minutes; crumble beef. Remove from pan with a slotted spoon; pour off drippings.

3. In the same pan, melt butter over low heat; stir in flour until smooth. Cook and stir until lightly browned, 2-3 minutes (do not burn). Gradually whisk in milk, broth, Worcestershire sauce and mustard. Bring to a boil, stirring constantly; cook and stir until thickened, 1-2 minutes. Stir in tomatoes; return to a boil. Reduce heat; simmer, covered, 5 minutes.

4. Stir in the green onions, pasta and beef; heat through. Stir in half of each cheese until melted. Sprinkle with the remaining cheeses; remove from heat. Let stand, covered, until cheese is melted.

1½ cups: 616 cal., 29g fat (17g sat. fat), 98mg chol., 727mg sod., 56g carb. (7g sugars, 3g fiber), 33g pro.

❄ BEEF & PEPPER SKILLET

I love Mexican-inspired food. I also enjoy experimenting with recipes like this one and making them healthier—and downright good!
—*Jenny Dubinsky, Inwood, WV*

- -

TAKES: 30 min. • **MAKES:** 6 servings

- 1 lb. lean ground beef (90% lean)
- 1 can (14½ oz.) diced tomatoes with mild green chiles, undrained
- 1 can (14½ oz.) beef broth
- 1 Tbsp. chili powder
- ¼ tsp. salt
- ⅛ tsp. garlic powder
- 2 cups instant brown rice
- 1 medium sweet red pepper, sliced
- 1 medium green pepper, sliced
- 1 cup shredded Colby-Monterey Jack cheese

1. In a large cast-iron or other heavy skillet, cook beef over medium heat until the meat is no longer pink, 6-8 minutes; crumble the beef; drain.

2. Add tomatoes, broth, chili powder, salt and garlic powder; bring to a boil. Stir in rice and peppers. Reduce heat; simmer, covered, until liquid is absorbed, 8-10 minutes. Remove from heat; sprinkle with cheese. Let stand, covered, until cheese is melted.

Freeze option: Before adding cheese, cool the beef mixture. Freeze beef mixture in a freezer container. To use, partially thaw in refrigerator overnight. Heat through in a saucepan, stirring occasionally; add broth if necessary. Sprinkle with cheese.

1⅓ cups: 340 cal., 13g fat (7g sat. fat), 64mg chol., 807mg sod., 31g carb. (5g sugars, 4g fiber), 23g pro.

ZUCCHINI BEEF SKILLET

This is a speedy summer recipe that uses up those abundant garden goodies: zucchini, tomatoes and green peppers.
—*Becky Calder, Kingston, MO*

- -

TAKES: 30 min. • **MAKES:** 4 servings

- 1 lb. ground beef
- 1 medium onion, chopped
- 1 small green pepper, chopped
- 2 tsp. chili powder
- ¾ tsp. salt
- ¼ tsp. pepper
- 3 medium zucchini, cut into ¾-in. cubes
- 2 large tomatoes, chopped
- ¼ cup water
- 1 cup uncooked instant rice
- 1 cup shredded cheddar cheese

1. In a large skillet, cook beef with onion and pepper over medium-high heat until beef is no longer pink, 5-7 minutes; crumble beef; drain.

2. Stir in vegetables, seasonings, water and rice; bring to a boil. Reduce heat; simmer, covered, until rice is tender, 10-15 minutes.

3. Sprinkle with cheese. Remove from heat; let stand until cheese is melted.

2 cups: 470 cal., 24g fat (11g sat. fat), 98mg chol., 749mg sod., 33g carb. (8g sugars, 4g fiber), 32g pro.

BEEF CHIMICHANGAS

My husband loves this beef chimichanga recipe! I often double the recipe and freeze the chimichangas individually to take out as needed. I serve them with shredded lettuce and sour cream.

—*Schelby Thompson, Camden Wyoming, DE*

- -

PREP: 25 min. • **COOK:** 15 min.
MAKES: 1 dozen

1	lb. ground beef
1	can (16 oz.) refried beans
½	cup finely chopped onion
3	cans (8 oz. each) tomato sauce, divided
2	tsp. chili powder
1	tsp. minced garlic
½	tsp. ground cumin
12	flour tortillas (10 in.), warmed
1	can (4 oz.) chopped green chiles
1	can (4 oz.) chopped jalapeno peppers
	Oil for deep-fat frying
1½	cups shredded cheddar cheese

1. In a large skillet, cook beef over medium heat until no longer pink; crumble meat; drain. Stir in the beans, onion, ½ cup tomato sauce, chili powder, garlic and cumin.

2. Spoon about ⅓ cup of the beef mixture off-center on each tortilla. Fold edge nearest filling up and over to cover. Fold in both sides and roll up. Fasten with toothpicks. In a large saucepan, combine the chiles, peppers and remaining tomato sauce; heat through.

3. In an electric skillet or deep-fat fryer, heat 1 in. of oil to 375°. Fry the chimichangas for 1½ -2 minutes on each side or until browned. Drain on paper towels. Sprinkle with cheese. Serve with sauce.

1 chimichanga: 626 cal., 41g fat (9g sat. fat), 37mg chol., 1094mg sod., 46g carb. (5g sugars, 6g fiber), 19g pro.

SKILLET BEEF & MACARONI

I found this simple skillet recipe many years ago on a can label. I made some tweaks, and my family loved it. Because it's so easy to put together, it's a real timesaver for people with super busy schedules.

—*Maxine Neuhauser, Arcadia, CA*

- -

TAKES: 30 min. • **MAKES:** 6 servings

1½	lb. ground beef
½	cup chopped onion
2	cans (8 oz. each) tomato sauce
1	cup water
1	pkg. (7 oz.) macaroni
½	cup chopped green pepper
2	Tbsp. Worcestershire sauce
1	tsp. salt
¼	tsp. pepper

In a large skillet over medium-high heat, cook beef and onion until the meat is no longer pink; crumble meat; drain. Stir in rest of ingredients; bring to a boil. Reduce heat; simmer, covered, until the macaroni is tender, 20-25 minutes; stirring occasionally. Add water if needed.

1 cup: 317 cal., 11g fat (5g sat. fat), 56mg chol., 700mg sod., 29g carb. (3g sugars, 2g fiber), 25g pro.

TEST KITCHEN TIP
To make things more convenient, keep a stash of frozen chopped peppers and onions on hand. Place the veggies in a single layer on a parchment-lined baking sheet; freeze for 2-3 hours, then transfer to airtight containers and keep in the freezer for up to 6 months.

❄ 🍎
SKILLET BEEF TAMALES

This southwestern skillet dinner is so cheesy and delicious that no one will guess it's light. It's sure to become a much-requested recipe.
—*Deborah Williams, Peoria, AZ*

- -

TAKES: 30 min. • **MAKES:** 5 servings

- 1 lb. lean ground beef (90% lean)
- ⅓ cup chopped sweet red pepper
- ⅓ cup chopped green pepper
- 2 cups salsa
- ¾ cup frozen corn
- 2 Tbsp. water
- 6 corn tortillas (6 in.), halved and cut into ½-in. strips
- ¾ cup shredded reduced-fat cheddar cheese
- 5 Tbsp. fat-free sour cream

1. In a large skillet coated with cooking spray, cook the beef and peppers over medium heat 6-8 minutes or until beef is no longer pink and vegetables are tender; crumble beef; drain. Stir in salsa, corn and water; bring to a boil.
2. Stir in tortilla strips. Reduce heat; simmer, covered, 10-15 minutes or until tortillas are softened. Sprinkle with cheese; cook, covered, 2-3 minutes longer or until cheese is melted. Serve with sour cream.
Freeze option: Freeze cooled meat mixture in freezer containers. To use, partially thaw in refrigerator overnight. Heat through in a saucepan, stirring occasionally; add water if necessary. Serve with sour cream.
1 cup meat mixture with 1 Tbsp. sour cream: 329 cal., 11g fat (5g sat. fat), 59mg chol., 679mg sod., 28g carb. (6g sugars, 6g fiber), 25g pro. **Diabetic exchanges:** 3 lean meat, 1½ starch, 1 vegetable, ½ fat.

ONE-POT DINNER

Everyone comes back for seconds when I serve this well-seasoned skillet supper. I like the fact that it's on the table in just 30 minutes.
—*Bonnie Morrow, Spencerport, NY*

- -

TAKES: 30 min. • **MAKES:** 5 servings

- ½ lb. ground beef
- 1 medium onion, chopped
- 1 cup chopped celery
- ¾ cup chopped green pepper
- 2 tsp. Worcestershire sauce
- 1 tsp. salt, optional
- ½ tsp. dried basil
- ¼ tsp. pepper
- 2 cups uncooked medium egg noodles
- 1 can (16 oz.) kidney beans, rinsed and drained
- 1 can (14½ oz.) stewed tomatoes
- ¾ cup water
- 1 beef bouillon cube

1. In a large saucepan or skillet, cook the beef, onion, celery and green pepper over medium heat until the vegetables are crisp-tender and meat is no longer pink; crumble meat; drain.
2. Add Worcestershire sauce, salt if desired, basil and pepper. Stir in the noodles, beans, tomatoes, water and bouillon. Bring to a boil.
3. Reduce the heat; cover and simmer for 20 minutes or until the noodles are tender, stirring occasionally.
1 cup: 263 cal., 6g fat (2g sat. fat), 41mg chol., 535mg sod., 36g carb. (8g sugars, 7g fiber), 17g pro.

PIZZA POTATO TOPPERS

Not only is this recipe quick and easy to make, but it's an economical dinner as well. I don't know of a more satisfying way to stretch a half-pound of meat!
—*Sheila Friedrich, Antelope, MT*

TAKES: 25 min. • **MAKES:** 4 servings

- 4 medium baking potatoes
- ½ lb. ground beef
- ½ cup chopped green pepper
- 1 small onion, chopped
- 1 tomato, chopped
- ½ to ¾ cup pizza sauce
- 1 cup shredded part-skim mozzarella cheese
  Optional: Fresh oregano, basil or parsley

1. Prick potatoes with a fork; cook in a microwave until tender. In a large skillet, cook beef and green pepper with onion until meat is no longer pink; crumble meat; drain. Stir in tomato and pizza sauce; heat through.
2. Split potatoes lengthwise; flake potato centers with a fork. Spoon meat mixture into each; top with mozzarella cheese. Sprinkle with herbs if desired.
1 serving: 486 cal., 11g fat (5g sat. fat), 44mg chol., 325mg sod., 74g carb. (10g sugars, 7g fiber), 26g pro.

READER REVIEW
"I made one with sweet potato as well because my husband prefers sweet potatoes. The whole family enjoyed this, even the teenager!"

SKIMBA, TASTEOFHOME.COM

ITALIAN BEEF & SHELLS

I fix this supper when I'm pressed for time. It's as tasty as it is fast. Team it with salad, bread and fresh fruit for a healthy meal that really satisfies.

—*Mike Tchou, Pepper Pike, OH*

TAKES: 30 min. • **MAKES:** 4 servings

- 1½ cups uncooked medium pasta shells
- 1 lb. lean ground beef (90% lean)
- 1 small onion, chopped
- 1 garlic clove, minced
- 1 jar (24 oz.) marinara sauce
- 1 small yellow summer squash, quartered and sliced
- 1 small zucchini, quartered and sliced
- ¼ cup dry red wine or reduced-sodium beef broth
- ½ tsp. salt
- ½ tsp. Italian seasoning
- ½ tsp. pepper

1. Cook pasta according to the package directions. Meanwhile, in a Dutch oven, cook beef, onion and garlic over medium heat until meat is no longer pink; crumble meat; drain.

2. Stir in the marinara sauce, squash, zucchini, wine and seasonings. Bring to a boil. Reduce heat; simmer, uncovered, 10-15 minutes or until thickened.

3. Drain pasta; stir into the beef mixture and heat through.

1¾ cups: 396 cal., 10g fat (4g sat. fat), 71mg chol., 644mg sod., 45g carb. (16g sugars, 5g fiber), 29g pro. **Diabetic exchanges:** 3 starch, 3 lean meat.

RAMEN-VEGETABLE BEEF SKILLET

This ramen stir-fry is flavorful and unusual. The whole gang will enjoy this hearty, colorful meal-in-one recipe.

—*Marlene McAllister, Portland, MI*

TAKES: 30 min. • **MAKES:** 4 servings

- 1 lb. ground beef
- 1½ cups sliced fresh carrots
- ¾ cup sliced onion
- 1 cup water
- 1 cup shredded cabbage
- 1 cup sliced fresh mushrooms
- 1 cup chopped green pepper
- 3 Tbsp. soy sauce
- 1 pkg. (3 oz.) beef ramen noodles

1. In a large skillet, cook the beef, carrots and onion over medium heat until beef is no longer pink and carrots are crisp-tender, 7-9 minutes; crumble beef; drain.

2. Add water, cabbage, mushrooms, green pepper, soy sauce and the contents of the seasoning packet from noodles. Break noodles into small pieces; add to pan. Cover and cook until liquid is absorbed and noodles are tender, 8-10 minutes.

1½ cups: 379 cal., 18g fat (8g sat. fat), 86mg chol., 1202mg sod., 24g carb. (5g sugars, 3g fiber), 29g pro.

BEEF BARLEY SKILLET

This versatile dish goes together fast since it's made with quick-cooking barley. You can make it with ground turkey or chicken and any color bell pepper that you have on hand.
—*Irene Tetreault, South Hadley, MA*

TAKES: 30 min. • **MAKES:** 4 servings

1	lb. lean ground beef (90% lean)
1	small onion, chopped
¼	cup chopped celery
¼	cup chopped green pepper
1	can (14½ oz.) diced tomatoes, undrained
1½	cups water
¾	cup quick-cooking barley
½	cup chili sauce
1	tsp. Worcestershire sauce
½	tsp. dried marjoram
⅛	tsp. pepper
	Chopped parsley, optional

1. In a large skillet, cook beef, onion, celery and green pepper over medium-high heat until beef is no longer pink and vegetables are tender, 5-7 minutes; crumble the beef and drain.

2. Stir in the next 7 ingredients. Bring to a boil; reduce heat. Simmer, uncovered, until barley is tender, 5-10 minutes. If desired, top with chopped parsley.

1½ cups: 362 cal., 10g fat (4g sat. fat), 71mg chol., 707mg sod., 41g carb. (11g sugars, 8g fiber), 27g pro. **Diabetic exchanges:** 3 lean meat, 2 starch, 1 vegetable.

CHUCK WAGON TORTILLA STACK

I make this skillet specialty on those nights when I'm craving southwestern fare. It's easy to cut and remove the pieces from the pan.
—*Bernice Janowski, Stevens Point, WI*

PREP: 15 min. • **COOK:** 40 min.
MAKES: 6 servings

1	lb. ground beef
2	to 3 garlic cloves, minced
1	can (16 oz.) baked beans
1	can (14½ oz.) stewed tomatoes, undrained
1	can (11 oz.) whole kernel corn, drained
1	can (4 oz.) chopped green chiles
¼	cup barbecue sauce
4½	tsp. chili powder
1½	tsp. ground cumin
4	flour tortillas (10 in.)
1⅓	cups shredded pepper jack cheese
	Optional: Shredded lettuce, chopped red onion, sour cream and chopped tomatoes

1. In a large skillet, cook beef until meat is no longer pink; crumble the beef; drain. Add the garlic, beans, tomatoes, corn, chiles, barbecue sauce, chili powder and cumin. Bring to a boil. Reduce the heat and simmer uncovered for 10-12 minutes or until liquid is reduced.

2. Coat a large deep skillet with cooking spray. Place 1 tortilla in skillet; spread with 1½ cups meat mixture. Sprinkle with ⅓ cup cheese. Repeat layers 3 times. Cover and cook on low for 15 minutes or until cheese is melted and tortillas are heated through. Cut into wedges. Serve with toppings of your choice.

1 piece: 539 cal., 23g fat (10g sat. fat), 79mg chol., 1383mg sod., 56g carb. (12g sugars, 9g fiber), 30g pro.

SANTA FE SKILLET

As a mother who works full time, I'm always looking for quick, easy meals to prepare. This is a timeless recipe.
—*Lorie VanHorn, Waddell, AZ*

TAKES: 30 min. • **MAKES:** 6 servings

- 1 lb. lean ground beef (90% lean)
- 1 small onion, chopped
- 1 pkg. (6 oz.) four-cheese corkscrew pasta mix
- 2 cups salsa
- 1 cup hot water
- 1 Tbsp. chili powder
- ½ tsp. salt
  Dash cayenne pepper
- 1 can (14½ oz.) diced tomatoes, undrained
- 1 can (2¼ oz.) sliced ripe olives, drained
- 1 cup shredded cheddar cheese
  Sour cream, optional

1. In a large skillet, cook the beef and onion over medium heat until the meat is no longer pink; crumble meat; drain.
2. Stir in pasta, contents of seasoning packet, salsa, water, chili powder, salt and cayenne. Bring to a boil. Reduce heat; cover and simmer until pasta is tender, about 15 minutes, adding more water if necessary.
3. Stir in tomatoes; sprinkle with the olives and cheese. Cover and simmer until heated through, 3-4 minutes. Serve with sour cream if desired.
Note: This recipe was tested with Pasta Roni mix.
1¼ cups: 287 cal., 10g fat (3g sat. fat), 49mg chol., 1061mg sod., 29g carb. (7g sugars, 3g fiber), 19g pro.

ARRABBIATA SAUCE WITH ZUCCHINI NOODLES

This popular Italian dish is flavorful and spicy. We decided to re-create one of our favorite sauces and serve it over zucchini pasta for a lighter, healthier meal that's naturally gluten-free. The results were amazing!
—*Courtney Stultz, Weir, KS*

PREP: 10 min. • **COOK:** 35 min.
MAKES: 4 servings

- 1 lb. lean ground beef (90% lean)
- ½ cup finely chopped onion
- 2 garlic cloves, minced
- 1 can (14½ oz.) petite diced tomatoes, undrained
- ¼ cup dry red wine or beef broth
- 3 Tbsp. tomato paste
- 2 tsp. honey
- 1 tsp. cider vinegar
- ¾ tsp. dried basil
- ½ to 1 tsp. crushed red pepper flakes
- ½ tsp. salt
- ¼ tsp. dried oregano
- ¼ tsp. dried thyme

ZUCCHINI NOODLES
- 2 large zucchini
- 1 Tbsp. olive oil
- ¼ tsp. salt
  Chopped fresh parsley, optional

1. In a large saucepan, cook beef with onion and garlic over medium-high heat until meat is no longer pink, 5-7 minutes; crumble beef. Stir in tomatoes, wine, tomato paste, honey, vinegar and seasonings; bring to a boil. Reduce heat; simmer, uncovered, until the flavors are blended, about 25 minutes; stir occasionally.
2. For noodles, trim ends of zucchini. Using a spiralizer, shave zucchini into thin strands. In a large cast-iron or other heavy skillet, heat oil over medium-high heat. Add zucchini; cook until slightly softened, 1-2 minutes, tossing constantly with tongs (do not overcook). Sprinkle with salt. Serve with sauce. If desired, sprinkle with parsley.
Freeze option: Freeze cooled sauce in freezer containers. To use, partially thaw in refrigerator overnight. Heat through in a saucepan, stirring occasionally.
1 cup sauce with 1 cup zucchini noodles: 287 cal., 13g fat (4g sat. fat), 71mg chol., 708mg sod., 17g carb. (11g sugars, 4g fiber), 26g pro.
Diabetic exchanges: 3 lean meat, 2 vegetable, ½ starch.

CREAMY BEEF & POTATOES

One of my husband's favorite childhood memories was eating his Grandma Barney's Tater Tot casserole. One day I prepared it using potatoes O'Brien instead. Now I always make it this way.
—*Heather Matthews, Keller, TX*

TAKES: 20 min. • **MAKES:** 4 servings

- 4 cups frozen potatoes O'Brien
- 1 Tbsp. water
- 1 lb. ground beef
- ½ tsp. salt
- ¼ tsp. pepper
- 2 cans (10¾ oz. each) condensed cream of mushroom soup, undiluted
- ⅔ cup 2% milk
- 2 cups shredded Colby-Monterey Jack cheese

1. Place potatoes and water in a microwave-safe bowl. Microwave, covered, on high until tender, 8-10 minutes, stirring twice.

2. Meanwhile, in a Dutch oven, cook beef over medium heat until no longer pink, 6-8 minutes; crumble beef; drain. Stir in salt and pepper.

3. In a small bowl, whisk soup and milk until blended; add to beef. Stir in the potatoes. Sprinkle with cheese. Reduce heat to low; cook, covered, until cheese is melted.

1¾ cups: 664 cal., 38g fat (19g sat. fat), 130mg chol., 1851mg sod., 40g carb. (5g sugars, 6g fiber), 37g pro.

SKILLET BBQ BEEF POTPIE

Beef potpie is a classic comfort food, but who's got time to see it through? My crowd-pleaser is not only speedy but an excellent way to use leftover stuffing.
—*Priscilla Yee, Concord, CA*

TAKES: 25 min. • **MAKES:** 4 servings

- 1 lb. lean ground beef (90% lean)
- ⅓ cup thinly sliced green onions, divided
- 2 cups frozen mixed vegetables, thawed
- ½ cup salsa
- ½ cup barbecue sauce
- 3 cups cooked cornbread stuffing
- ½ cup shredded cheddar cheese
- ¼ cup chopped sweet red pepper

1. In a large skillet, cook beef and ¼ cup green onions over medium heat until beef is no longer pink, 6-8 minutes; crumble beef; drain.

2. Stir in mixed vegetables, salsa and barbecue sauce; cook, covered, over medium-low heat 4-5 minutes or until heated through

3. Layer stuffing over beef; sprinkle with cheese, red pepper and remaining green onion. Cook, covered, 3-5 minutes longer or until heated through and cheese is melted.

1½ cups: 634 cal., 27g fat (9g sat. fat), 85mg chol., 1372mg sod., 62g carb. (19g sugars, 9g fiber), 33g pro.

READER REVIEW

"Delicious and very quick to make! Great summer meal that doesn't use the oven!"

DSCHULTZ01, TASTEOFHOME.COM

HEARTY VEGETABLE BEEF RAGOUT

This recipe is healthy yet satisfying, quick yet delicious. I can have a hearty meal on the table in under 30 minutes, and it's something that my children will gobble up! If you are not fond of kale, stir in baby spinach or chopped broccoli instead—it tastes just as delicious!

—*Kim Van Dunk, Caldwell, NJ*

TAKES: 30 min. • **MAKES:** 8 servings

- 4 cups uncooked whole wheat spiral pasta
- 1 lb. lean ground beef (90% lean)
- 1 large onion, chopped
- 3 garlic cloves, minced
- 2 cans (14½ oz. each) Italian diced tomatoes, undrained
- 1 jar (24 oz.) meatless spaghetti sauce
- 2 cups finely chopped fresh kale
- 1 pkg. (9 oz.) frozen peas, thawed
- ¾ tsp. garlic powder
- ¼ tsp. pepper
  Grated Parmesan cheese, optional

1. Cook spiral pasta according to package directions; drain. Meanwhile, in a Dutch oven, cook the beef, onion and garlic over medium heat 6-8 minutes or until beef is no longer pink; crumble beef; drain.
2. Stir in the tomatoes, spaghetti sauce, kale, peas, garlic powder and pepper. Bring to a boil. Reduce heat; simmer, uncovered, until kale is tender, 8-10 minutes.
3. Stir pasta into sauce. If desired, serve with Parmesan cheese.
1½ cups: 302 cal., 5g fat (2g sat. fat), 35mg chol., 837mg sod., 43g carb. (15g sugars, 7g fiber), 20g pro. **Diabetic exchanges:** 2 starch, 2 lean meat, 2 vegetable.

RANCHERO SUPPER

This hearty dish is fast and easy to fix after a busy workday. We like to use hickory and bacon baked beans and serve it with fruit or a green salad for a complete meal.

—*Karen Roberts, Lawrence, KS*

TAKES: 15 min. • **MAKES:** 7 servings

- 1½ lbs. ground beef
- 1 can (28 oz.) baked beans
- 1 can (11 oz.) whole kernel corn, drained
- ¼ cup barbecue sauce
- 2 Tbsp. ketchup
- 1 Tbsp. prepared mustard
- ¾ cup shredded cheddar cheese
  Optional: Sliced green onions and sour cream
- 7 cups tortilla chips

1. In a large skillet, cook beef over medium heat until no longer pink; crumble beef; drain.
2. Stir in the baked beans, corn, barbecue sauce, ketchup and mustard; heat through. Sprinkle with cheese; cook until melted.
3. Garnish with onions and sour cream if desired. Serve with tortilla chips.
1 cup: 511 cal., 23g fat (9g sat. fat), 85mg chol., 947mg sod., 46g carb. (11g sugars, 8g fiber), 30g pro.

KIM VAN DUNK
Caldwell, NJ

SPAGHETTI SQUASH WITH MEAT SAUCE

Neither my mother nor I had tried spaghetti squash before, so when we cooked this recipe together, all we could do was grin and say, "Wow!" It's fun to separate the noodle-like strands from the squash shell, but the eating is the best part!

—*Lina Vainauskas, Shaw Air Force Base, SC*

PREP: 10 min. • **COOK:** 25 min.
MAKES: 6 servings

- 1 medium spaghetti squash (about 8 in.)
- 1 cup water
- 1 lb. lean ground beef (90% lean)
- 1 large onion, chopped
- 1 medium green pepper, chopped
- 1 tsp. garlic powder
- 2 tsp. dried basil
- 1½ tsp. dried oregano
- 1 tsp. salt
- ½ tsp. pepper
- ¼ to ½ tsp. chili powder
- 1 can (28 oz.) tomato puree
- 1 cup grated Parmesan cheese, divided

1. Preheat oven to 375°. Slice squash lengthwise and scoop out seeds. Place squash, cut side down, in a baking dish. Add water and cover tightly with foil. Bake until easily pierced with a fork, 20-30 minutes.
2. Meanwhile, in a large skillet, cook beef over medium heat until no longer pink; crumble meat; drain. Add onion, green pepper, herbs and seasonings; cook and stir until onion is tender, 5-7 minutes. Stir in tomato puree. Cover and cook over low heat, stirring occasionally.
3. Scoop out squash, separating the strands with a fork. Just before serving; stir ½ cup Parmesan cheese into meat sauce. Serve sauce over spaghetti squash with remaining ½ cup Parmesan cheese.
1 serving: 351 cal., 12g fat (5g sat. fat), 59mg chol., 763mg sod., 36g carb. (4g sugars, 8g fiber), 23g pro. **Diabetic exchanges:** 3 lean meat, 2 starch.

HAWAIIAN BEEF DISH

My dad, who still enjoys experimenting in the kitchen, created this elegant dish when I was a little girl. Sometimes I prepare it the day before and warm it up while I'm cooking the rice.
—*Marilyn Taus, Mississauga, ON*

TAKES: 25 min. • **MAKES:** 2 servings

- ½ lb. lean ground beef (90% lean)
- 1 medium onion, halved and sliced
- ⅓ cup sliced celery
- ⅓ cup chopped green pepper
- 1 garlic clove, minced
- 2 tsp. butter
- 1 can (8 oz.) unsweetened pineapple chunks
- ¼ cup packed brown sugar
- 1 Tbsp. all-purpose flour
- 1 Tbsp. white wine vinegar
- ¼ tsp. salt
- 1 cup hot cooked rice

1. In a small skillet, cook beef over medium heat until no longer pink; crumble meat; drain and set aside. In the same skillet, saute onion, celery, green pepper and garlic in butter until crisp-tender, 5 minutes.

2. Drain pineapple chunks, reserving juice; set pineapple aside. Add enough water to the juice to measure ½ cup. In a bowl, combine the brown sugar, flour, vinegar, salt and pineapple juice mixture until smooth. Add to skillet. Bring to a boil. Cook and stir over medium heat for 2 minutes. Stir in beef and pineapple; heat through. Serve with rice.

1½ cups: 515 cal., 12g fat (6g sat. fat), 66mg chol., 440mg sod., 75g carb. (44g sugars, 4g fiber), 26g pro.

INSIDE-OUT STUFFED CABBAGE

Making stuffed cabbage can be time-consuming, but this version is table-ready in just 30 minutes—and it's got all the classic flavors, plus butternut squash.
—*Taste of Home Test Kitchen*

PREP: 10 min. • **COOK:** 25 min.
MAKES: 4 servings

- 1 lb. ground beef
- 2 cups cubed peeled butternut squash (about 12 oz.)
- 1 medium green pepper, chopped
- 1 envelope Lipton beefy onion soup mix
- 1 Tbsp. brown sugar
- 1 can (11½ oz.) Spicy Hot V8 juice
- 1 cup water
- 6 cups chopped cabbage (about 1 small head)
- ½ cup uncooked instant brown rice

1. In a Dutch oven, cook beef with squash and pepper over medium-high heat until no longer pink; crumble beef; drain.

2. Stir in soup mix, brown sugar, V8 juice, water and cabbage; bring to a boil. Reduce heat; simmer, covered, until cabbage is tender, 8-10 minutes, stirring occasionally.

3. Stir in rice; return to a boil. Simmer, covered, 5 minutes. Remove from the heat; let stand, covered, until rice is tender, about 5 minutes.

1½ cups: 382 cal., 15g fat (5g sat. fat), 70mg chol., 841mg sod., 40g carb. (13g sugars, 7g fiber), 25g pro.

BEEF SKILLET SUPPER

Sometimes, I'll make extra of this comforting, noodle-y supper to guarantee leftovers. It's a great take-along dish for work or school. Trim calories from the entree by using ground turkey and low-fat cheese.
—*Tabitha Allen, Cypress, TX*

- -

TAKES: 30 min. • **MAKES:** 8 servings

- 8 oz. uncooked medium egg noodles (about 4 cups)
- 1½ lbs. ground beef
- 1 medium onion, chopped
- ½ tsp. salt
- ¼ tsp. pepper
- 1 can (8 oz.) tomato sauce
- ½ cup water
- 1 can (11 oz.) Mexicorn, drained
- 1 cup shredded cheddar cheese

1. Cook noodles according to the package directions; drain. Meanwhile, in a large skillet, cook beef with onion over medium-high heat until no longer pink, 6-8 minutes; crumble beef. Stir in salt, pepper, tomato sauce and water; bring to a boil. Reduce heat; simmer, covered, 10 minutes.

2. Stir in corn and noodles; heat through. Sprinkle with cheese; let stand, covered, until cheese is melted.

1 serving: 368 cal., 16g fat (7g sat. fat), 90mg chol., 548mg sod., 30 g carb. (4g sugars, 2g fiber), 24g pro.

TEST KITCHEN TIP
Buying ground beef in bulk makes good budget sense; break it into smaller ½- to 1-lb. portions to freeze it. That lets you select the amount you need for a recipe, and also makes it quicker to thaw.

SAUCY BEEF & CABBAGE DINNER

Using cabbage is a great way to bulk up a meal without adding extra fat and calories. The cabbage in this dish is tender but still has a nice crunch.
—*Marcia Doyle, Pompano, FL*

- -

PREP: 15 min. • **COOK:** 25 min.
MAKES: 8 servings

- 1 lb. lean ground beef (90% lean)
- 1 large onion, chopped
- 1 cup sliced fresh mushrooms
- 1 medium head cabbage, chopped
- 1 can (46 oz.) reduced-sodium tomato juice
- 1 cup instant brown rice
- 1 can (6 oz.) tomato paste
- ¼ cup packed brown sugar
- 2 Tbsp. lemon juice
- 1 tsp. dried thyme
- 1 tsp. dried parsley flakes
- ½ tsp. pepper
  Optional: Fresh thyme and fresh parsley, chopped

1. In a Dutch oven, cook the beef, onion and mushrooms over medium heat until meat is no longer pink; crumble beef; drain.

2. Add next 9 ingredients. Bring to a boil. Reduce heat; cover and simmer until the cabbage and rice are tender, 15-20 minutes. If desired, sprinkle with thyme and parsley.

1⅓ cups: 253 cal., 5g fat (2g sat. fat), 35mg chol., 170mg sod., 36g carb. (19g sugars, 5g fiber), 17g pro. **Diabetic exchanges:** 2 vegetable, 2 lean meat, 1½ starch.

HAMBURGER STROGANOFF

This easy ground beef Stroganoff makes a quick weeknight dinner. I like to serve it with a side salad for a complete meal.
—Deb Helmer, Lynden, WA

TAKES: 30 min. • **MAKES:** 6 servings

1½ lbs. ground beef
½ cup chopped onion
    Dash garlic salt
2 Tbsp. all-purpose flour
1 cup water or beef broth
1 can (10¾ oz.) condensed cream of mushroom soup, undiluted
1 can (4½ oz.) mushrooms, drained
1 cup sour cream
    Salt and pepper to taste
    Cooked noodles or rice
    Chopped fresh parsley, optional

1. In a skillet, cook beef over medium heat until no longer pink, 5-7 minutes; crumble meat; drain.
2. Add onion and garlic salt to beef; continue to cook until onion is soft. Stir in flour; cook and stir 2-3 minutes. Add water or broth, soup and mushrooms; bring to a simmer. Reduce heat; cook, stirring occasionally, 8-10 minutes.
3. Gently fold in sour cream; heat only until warm. Add salt and pepper to taste. Serve over noodles or rice and, if desired, top with parsley.
1 serving: 318 cal., 19g fat (10g sat. fat), 84mg chol., 561mg sod., 10g carb. (3g sugars, 1g fiber), 23g pro.

🍎
HEARTY GARDEN SPAGHETTI

My husband and I wanted a pleasing dish that didn't leave a ton of leftovers. My spaghetti with beef and fresh veggies is perfectly filling for four.
—Wanda Quist, Loveland, CO

PREP: 15 min. • **COOK:** 30 min.
MAKES: 4 servings

1 lb. lean ground beef (90% lean)
1 small onion, finely chopped
1 medium sweet red pepper, finely chopped
1 medium zucchini, finely chopped
½ lb. sliced fresh mushrooms
1 can (8 oz.) tomato sauce
2 tsp. Italian seasoning
½ tsp. salt
¼ tsp. pepper
8 oz. uncooked multigrain spaghetti
    Grated Parmesan cheese, optional

1. In a Dutch oven coated with cooking spray, cook beef, onion and red pepper over medium-high heat until beef is no longer pink, 5-7 minutes; crumble beef; drain.
2. Add zucchini and mushrooms; cook 3-5 minutes longer or until tender. Stir in tomato sauce and seasonings; bring to a boil. Reduce heat; simmer, covered, 15 minutes to allow flavors to blend. Meanwhile, cook spaghetti according to package directions.
3. Serve spaghetti with sauce and, if desired, grated cheese.
1¼ cups sauce with 1 cup spaghetti: 432 cal., 11g fat (4g sat. fat), 71mg chol., 649mg sod., 48g carb. (6g sugars, 7g fiber), 36g pro.
Diabetic exchanges: 3 lean meat, 2½ starch, 2 vegetable.

🍎 CAJUN BEEF & RICE

Dirty rice from a restaurant or box can have a lot of sodium and fat. Here's a hearty, healthy way to trim it down.
—*Raquel Haggard, Edmond, OK*

TAKES: 30 min. • **MAKES:** 4 servings

- 1   lb. lean ground beef (90% lean)
- 3   celery ribs, chopped
- 1   small green pepper, chopped
- 1   small sweet red pepper, chopped
- ¼   cup chopped onion
- 2   cups water
- 1   cup instant brown rice
- 1   Tbsp. minced fresh parsley
- 1   Tbsp. Worcestershire sauce
- 2   tsp. reduced-sodium beef bouillon granules
- 1   tsp. Cajun seasoning
- ¼   tsp. crushed red pepper flakes
- ¼   tsp. pepper
- ⅛   tsp. garlic powder

1. In a large skillet, cook the beef, celery, peppers and onion over medium heat until beef is no longer pink, 8-10 minutes; crumble meat; drain.

2. Stir in the remaining ingredients. Bring to a boil. Reduce heat; simmer, covered, until the rice is tender, 12-15 minutes.

1½ cups: 291 cal., 10g fat (4g sat. fat), 71mg chol., 422mg sod., 23g carb. (3g sugars, 2g fiber), 25g pro. **Diabetic exchanges:** 3 lean meat, 1 starch, 1 vegetable.

GREEK TORTELLINI SKILLET

Looking to please picky little palates? One tester loved this simple skillet entree so much, she made it at home for her 2-year-old daughter, who said "Mmmmm!" after every single bite.
—*Taste of Home Test Kitchen*

TAKES: 30 min. • **MAKES:** 6 servings

- 1   pkg. (19 oz.) frozen cheese tortellini
- 1   lb. ground beef
- 1   medium zucchini, sliced
- 1   small red onion, chopped
- 3   cups marinara or spaghetti sauce
- ½   cup water
- ¼   tsp. pepper
- 2   medium tomatoes, chopped
- ½   cup cubed feta cheese
- ½   cup pitted Greek olives, halved
- 2   Tbsp. minced fresh basil, divided

1. Cook tortellini according to package directions. Meanwhile, in a large skillet, cook the beef, zucchini and onion over medium heat until meat is no longer pink; crumble beef; drain.

2. Drain tortellini; add to skillet. Stir in the marinara sauce, water and pepper. Bring to a boil. Reduce heat; simmer, uncovered, for 5 minutes. Add the tomatoes, cheese, olives and 1 Tbsp. basil. Sprinkle with remaining basil.

1½ cups: 543 cal., 20g fat (8g sat. fat), 89mg chol., 917mg sod., 58g carb. (13g sugars, 6g fiber), 32g pro.

CHEESY HAMBURGER SUPPER

I have wonderful memories of eating this comforting meal-in-one while growing up. We loved the flavor and seldom had leftovers.
—*Andrea Brandt, Newton, KS*

TAKES: 30 min. • **MAKES:** 4 servings

- 1 lb. ground beef
- 1½ cups water
- ½ tsp. poultry seasoning
- ¼ tsp. pepper
- 1 envelope brown gravy mix
- 1 medium onion, sliced and separated into rings
- 1 medium carrot, sliced
- 2 medium potatoes, sliced
- 1 cup shredded cheddar cheese

1. In a large skillet, cook beef over medium heat until no longer pink; crumble meat; drain. Stir in the water, poultry seasoning and pepper. Bring to a boil. Stir in gravy mix. Cook and stir until slightly thickened, about 2 minutes.

2. Arrange the onion, carrot and potatoes over beef. Reduce heat; cover and simmer until vegetables are tender, 10-15 minutes. Sprinkle with cheese. Cover and cook until cheese is melted, 3-5 minutes longer.

1 serving: 412 cal., 19g fat (11g sat. fat), 86mg chol., 796mg sod., 30g carb. (6g sugars, 3g fiber), 30g pro.

INDIAN-SPICED BEEFY LETTUCE WRAPS

Since I love Indian flavors, I almost always have coconut milk, a jar of mango chutney and some garam masala seasoning in my pantry. This recipe is one of my go-tos when I am short on time but still want something that will taste spectacular. If you'd like to give this a different style of Asian flair, use hoisin sauce in place of chutney and Chinese five-spice powder in place of garam masala.
—*Noelle Myers, Grand Forks, ND*

TAKES: 30 min. • **MAKES:** 4 servings

- 1 lb. ground beef
- 1 medium onion, finely chopped
- 2 garlic cloves, minced
- ⅓ cup mango chutney
- 2 Tbsp. soy sauce
- 1 tsp. garam masala
- 1 pkg. (12.70 oz.) Asian crunch salad mix
- ¼ cup canned coconut milk
- 12 Bibb or Boston lettuce leaves
- 1 medium mango, peeled and sliced

1. In a large skillet, cook beef, onion and garlic over medium heat until beef is no longer pink and onion is tender, 6-8 minutes; crumble meat; drain.

2. Stir in chutney, soy sauce and garam masala; heat through. Add salad mix (reserve dressing and topping packets); cook and stir until slightly wilted, about 5 minutes.

3. Combine coconut milk and reserved dressing packet until smooth. Spoon beef mixture into lettuce leaves; sprinkle with contents from toppings packet. Drizzle with coconut milk mixture and top with mango.

3 filled lettuce wraps: 493 cal., 22g fat (8g sat. fat), 74mg chol., 957mg sod., 48g carb. (33g sugars, 5g fiber), 24g pro.

NOELLE MYERS
Grand Forks, ND

GROUND BEEF CHOW MEIN

My grandma used to make a fabulous chop suey with pork, but I found this recipe that uses ground beef and has the same flavor. It's quick and tasty, and the leftovers are wonderful.
—*Ann Nolte, Riverview, FL*

- -

TAKES: 30 min. • **MAKES:** 5 servings

- 2 cups uncooked instant rice
- 1 lb. ground beef
- 1 can (14½ oz.) beef broth
- 1½ cups chopped celery
- 1 can (14 oz.) bean sprouts, drained
- 1 can (8 oz.) sliced water chestnuts, drained
- 1 jar (4½ oz.) sliced mushrooms, drained
- 1 jar (2 oz.) pimientos, drained and diced
- 2 Tbsp. soy sauce
- ½ tsp. ground ginger
- 2 Tbsp. cornstarch
- 3 Tbsp. water

1. Cook rice according to package directions. Meanwhile, in a large skillet, cook beef over medium heat until no longer pink; crumble meat; drain.

2. Add broth, celery, bean sprouts, water chestnuts, mushrooms, pimientos, soy sauce and ginger. Bring to a boil. Reduce heat; cover and simmer 10 minutes, stirring occasionally.

3. In a small bowl, combine cornstarch and water until smooth. Gradually stir into skillet. Bring to a boil; cook and stir for 2 minutes or until thickened. Serve with rice.

1 cup chow mein with ¾ cup rice: 380 cal., 11g fat (4g sat. fat), 56mg chol., 949mg sod., 45g carb. (2g sugars, 4g fiber), 23g pro.

READER REVIEW

"This is excellent to put together after work. I used fresh ginger and fresh mushrooms because I had them on hand. I also added bamboo shoots and sprinkled with chow mein noodles."

MARICAM3, TASTEOFHOME.COM

MEXI-MAC SKILLET

My husband loves this recipe, and I love how simple it is to put together! Because you don't need to precook the macaroni, it's a timesaving dish.

—Maurane Ramsey, Fort Wayne, IN

TAKES: 30 min. • **MAKES:** 4 servings

- 1   lb. extra-lean ground beef (95% lean)
- 1   large onion, chopped
- 1¼ tsp. chili powder
- 1   tsp. dried oregano
- ¼   tsp. salt
- 1   can (14½ oz.) diced tomatoes, undrained
- 1   can (8 oz.) tomato sauce
- 1   cup fresh or frozen corn
- ½   cup water
- ⅔   cup uncooked elbow macaroni
- ½   cup shredded reduced-fat cheddar cheese

1. In a large nonstick skillet, cook beef with onion over medium-high heat until no longer pink, 5-7 minutes; crumble meat.
2. Stir in seasonings, tomatoes, tomato sauce, corn and water; bring to a boil. Stir in macaroni. Reduce heat; simmer, covered, until macaroni is tender, 15-20 minutes, stirring occasionally. Sprinkle with cheese.

1¼ cups: 318 cal., 10g fat (4g sat. fat), 75mg chol., 755mg sod., 28g carb. (9g sugars, 5g fiber), 32g pro. **Diabetic exchanges:** 1 starch, 3 lean meat, 1 vegetable.

BLACK BEAN & BEEF TOSTADAS

Just a handful of ingredients add up to one of our family's favorites. It's also easy to double for company!

—Susan Brown, Kansas City, KS

TAKES: 30 min. • **MAKES:** 4 servings

- ½   lb. lean ground beef (90% lean)
- 1   can (10 oz.) diced tomatoes and green chiles, undrained
- 1   can (15 oz.) black beans, rinsed and drained
- 1   can (16 oz.) refried beans, warmed
- 8   tostada shells
     Optional: Shredded reduced-fat Mexican cheese blend, shredded lettuce, salsa and sour cream

1. In a large skillet, cook beef over medium-high heat until the meat is no longer pink, 4-6 minutes; crumble beef.
2. Stir in tomatoes; bring to a boil. Reduce heat; simmer, uncovered, until liquid is almost evaporated, 6-8 minutes. Stir in black beans; heat through.
3. To serve, spread refried beans over the tostada shells. Top with beef mixture; add toppings as desired.

2 tostadas: 392 cal., 14g fat (4g sat. fat), 35mg chol., 1011mg sod., 46g carb. (2g sugars, 10g fiber), 23g pro.

SPANISH NOODLES & GROUND BEEF

Bacon adds smoky flavor to this comforting stovetop supper my mom frequently made when we were growing up. Now I prepare it for my family.
—*Kelli Jones, Peris, CA*

- -

TAKES: 25 min. • **MAKES:** 4 servings

- 1   lb. ground beef
- 1   small green pepper, chopped
- ⅓   cup chopped onion
- 3¼ cups uncooked medium egg noodles (about 6 oz.)
- 1   can (14½ oz.) diced tomatoes, undrained
- 1½ cups water
- ¼   cup chili sauce
- ¼   tsp. salt
- ⅛   tsp. pepper
- 4   bacon strips, cooked and crumbled

1. In a large skillet, cook beef with green pepper and onion over medium heat until no longer pink, 5-7 minutes; crumble meat; drain.
2. Stir in the noodles, tomatoes, water, chili sauce, salt and pepper; bring to a boil. Reduce heat; simmer, covered, until the noodles are tender, 15-20 minutes, stirring frequently. Top with bacon.

1½ cups: 409 cal., 18g fat (6g sat. fat), 104mg chol., 756mg sod., 33g carb. (8g sugars, 3g fiber), 28g pro.

TEST KITCHEN TIP
While supper cooks on the stovetop, use the oven for crispy bacon. Lay the bacon on a metal rack over a foil-lined rimmed baking pan and bake at 350° for 15-20 minutes. Let the bacon rest on paper towels before crumbling it.

🄵🄸 5i

ASIAN BEEF & NOODLES

This yummy, economical dish takes only five ingredients—all of which are easy to keep on hand. Serve with a dash of soy sauce and a side of fresh pineapple slices.
—*Laura Shull Stenberg, Wyoming, MN*

- -

TAKES: 20 min. • **MAKES:** 4 servings

- 1   lb. lean ground beef (90% lean)
- 2   pkg. (3 oz. each) ramen noodles, crumbled
- 2½ cups water
- 2   cups frozen broccoli stir-fry vegetable blend
- ¼   tsp. ground ginger
- 2   Tbsp. thinly sliced green onion

1. In a large skillet, cook beef over medium heat until no longer pink; crumble meat; drain. Add the contents of 1 ramen noodle flavoring packet; stir until dissolved. Remove beef and set aside.
2. In the same skillet, combine the water, vegetables, ginger, noodles and contents of remaining flavoring packet. Bring to a boil. Reduce heat; cover and simmer for 3-4 minutes or until noodles are tender, stirring occasionally.
3. Return beef to the pan and heat through. Stir in onion.

1½ cups: 383 cal., 16g fat (7g sat. fat), 71mg chol., 546mg sod., 29g carb. (2g sugars, 2g fiber), 27g pro.

PIZZA SPAGHETTI

The idea for this recipe came to me when I saw someone dip a slice of pizza into a pasta dish. My wife and kids love it and so do my friends!
—*Robert Smith, Las Vegas, NV*

PREP: 20 min. • **COOK:** 30 min.
MAKES: 6 servings

- ½ lb. lean ground beef (90% lean)
- ½ lb. Italian turkey sausage links, casings removed
- ½ cup chopped sweet onion
- 4 cans (8 oz. each) no-salt-added tomato sauce
- 3 oz. sliced turkey pepperoni
- 1 Tbsp. sugar
- 2 tsp. minced fresh parsley or ½ tsp. dried parsley flakes
- 2 tsp. minced fresh basil or ½ tsp. dried basil
- 9 oz. uncooked whole wheat spaghetti
- 3 Tbsp. grated Parmesan cheese

1. In a large nonstick skillet, cook beef and sausage with onion over medium-high heat until no longer pink, 5-7 minutes; crumble meat. Stir in tomato sauce, pepperoni, sugar and herbs; bring to a boil. Reduce heat; simmer, uncovered, until thickened, 20-25 minutes.
2. Meanwhile, in a 6-qt. stockpot, cook spaghetti according to package directions; drain and return to pot. Toss with sauce. Sprinkle with cheese.
1⅓ cups: 354 cal., 9g fat (3g sat. fat), 57mg chol., 512mg sod., 45g carb. (11g sugars, 7g fiber), 25g pro. **Diabetic exchanges:** 3 starch, 3 lean meat.

❄ HAMBURGER GOULASH

Goulash over mashed potatoes was my birthday meal of choice when I was growing up. Now I make my mother's tangy recipe for my family, and they like it, too.
—*Jennifer Willingham, Kansas City, MO*

PREP: 5 min. • **COOK:** 30 min. • **MAKES:** 6 cups

- 2½ lbs. ground beef
- 1 medium onion, chopped
- 2 cups water
- ¾ cup ketchup
- 2 Tbsp. Worcestershire sauce
- 2 tsp. paprika
- 1 to 2 tsp. sugar
- 1 tsp. salt
- ½ tsp. ground mustard
- ¼ tsp. garlic powder
- 2 Tbsp. all-purpose flour
- ¼ cup cold water
  Hot cooked noodles or mashed potatoes

1. In a Dutch oven, cook beef and onion over medium heat until meat is no longer pink; crumble beef; drain. .
2. Add the water, ketchup, Worcestershire sauce, paprika, sugar, salt, mustard and garlic powder. Bring to a boil. Reduce heat; simmer, uncovered, for 20 minutes
3. In a small bowl, combine flour and cold water until smooth; stir into the meat mixture. Bring to a boil; cook and stir for 2 minutes or until mixture is thickened. Serve over noodles or potatoes.
Freeze option: Freeze cooled meat mixture in freezer containers. To use, partially thaw in the refrigerator overnight. Heat through in a saucepan, stirring occasionally; add broth or water if necessary.
1 cups: 431 cal., 24g fat (9g sat. fat), 125mg chol., 896mg sod., 15g carb. (6g sugars, 1g fiber), 39g pro.

ONE-PAN ROTINI WITH TOMATO CREAM SAUCE

I like to make one-pan recipes and this one was proclaimed a winner by my family. Bonus: It's also easy to clean up. Serve with crusty bread to dip into the sauce.
—*Angela Lively, Conroe, TX*

- -

PREP: 15 min. • **COOK:** 30 min.
MAKES: 6 servings

- 1 lb. lean ground beef (90% lean)
- 1 medium onion, chopped
- 2 garlic cloves, minced
- 1 tsp. Italian seasoning
- ½ tsp. pepper
- ¼ tsp. salt
- 2 cups beef stock
- 1 can (14½ oz.) fire-roasted diced tomatoes, undrained
- 2 cups uncooked spiral pasta
- 1 cup frozen peas
- 1 cup heavy whipping cream
- ½ cup grated Parmesan cheese

1. In a large skillet, cook beef and onion over medium heat until the beef is no longer pink and the onion is tender, 5-10 minutes; crumble beef; drain.
2. Add garlic and seasonings; cook 1 minute longer. Add the stock and tomatoes; bring to a boil. Add pasta and peas; reduce heat. Simmer, covered, until pasta is tender, 10-12 minutes.
3. Gradually stir in cream and cheese; heat through (do not allow to boil).

1 cup: 443 cal., 23g fat (13g sat. fat), 98mg chol., 646mg sod., 33g carb. (6g sugars, 3g fiber), 25g pro.

5i

BEEFY TORTELLINI SKILLET

This tortellini dish is a one-skillet-wonder the family craves. From browning beef to cooking the pasta and melting the cheese, everything happens in one pan. You can add basil or chives for a touch of freshness.
—*Juli Meyers, Hinesville, GA*

- -

TAKES: 20 min. • **MAKES:** 4 servings

- 1 lb. ground beef
- ½ tsp. Montreal steak seasoning
- 1 cup water
- 1 tsp. beef bouillon granules
- 1 pkg. (19 oz.) frozen cheese tortellini
- 1 cup shredded Italian cheese blend

1. In a large skillet, cook beef over medium heat until no longer pink, 5-6 minutes; crumble meat; drain. Stir in steak seasoning. Add water and bouillon; bring to a boil. Stir in tortellini; return to a boil. Reduce heat; simmer, covered, 3-4 minutes or until tortellini are tender.
2. Remove from heat; sprinkle with cheese. Let stand, covered, until cheese is melted.

1½ cups: 566 cal., 28g fat (13g sat. fat), 111mg chol., 899mg sod., 37g carb. (2g sugars, 2g fiber), 39g pro.

BARLEY BEEF SKILLET

Even my 3-year-old loves this family favorite. It's filling, inexpensive and full of veggies. If you like things spicy, heat it up with chili powder, cayenne or a dash of hot pepper sauce.
—*Kit Tunstall, Boise, ID*

- -

PREP: 20 min. • **COOK:** 20 min.
MAKES: 4 servings

- 1   lb. lean ground beef (90% lean)
- ¼   cup chopped onion
- 1   garlic clove, minced
- 1   can (14½ oz.) reduced-sodium beef broth
- 1   can (8 oz.) tomato sauce
- 1   cup water
- 2   small carrots, chopped
- 1   small tomato, seeded and chopped
- 1   small zucchini, chopped
- 1   cup medium pearl barley
- 2   tsp. Italian seasoning
- ¼   tsp. salt
- ⅛   tsp. pepper

In a large skillet, cook beef and onion over medium heat until meat is no longer pink. Add garlic; cook 1 minute longer. Crumble beef; drain. Add the broth, tomato sauce and water; bring to a boil. Stir in remaining ingredients. Reduce heat; cover and simmer until barley is tender, 20-25 minutes.

1½ cups: 400 cal., 10g fat (4g sat. fat), 73mg chol., 682mg sod., 48g carb. (4g sugars, 10g fiber), 30g pro.

SAUCY SKILLET LASAGNA

Thanks to no-cook noodles, this skillet lasagna makes a fast and filling Italian entree.
—*Meghan Crihfield, Ripley, WV*

- -

TAKES: 30 min. • **MAKES:** 8 servings

- 1   lb. ground beef
- 1   can (14½ oz.) diced tomatoes, undrained
- 2   large eggs, lightly beaten
- 1½   cups ricotta cheese
- 4   cups marinara sauce
- 1   pkg. (9 oz.) no-cook lasagna noodles
- 1   cup shredded part-skim mozzarella cheese, optional

1. In a large skillet, cook beef over medium heat until no longer pink, 6-8 minutes; crumble beef; drain. Transfer to a large bowl; stir in tomatoes. In a small bowl, combine eggs and ricotta cheese.

2. Return 1 cup meat mixture to the skillet; spread evenly. Layer with 1 cup ricotta mixture, 1½ cups marinara sauce and half of the noodles, breaking noodles to fit as necessary. Repeat layers. Top with remaining marinara sauce.

3. Bring to a boil. Reduce heat; simmer, covered, 15-17 minutes or until noodles are tender. Remove from heat. If desired, sprinkle with mozzarella cheese. Let stand 2 minutes or until cheese is melted.

1 serving: 426 cal., 18g fat (8g sat. fat), 112mg chol., 858mg sod., 39g carb. (12g sugars, 4g fiber), 26g pro.

SOUTHWESTERN BEEF & RICE SKILLET

I like to serve this kicked-up skillet dish with warm flour tortillas and a side of guacamole. Feel free to add more jalapeno and enjoy the heat!
—*Pat Hockett, Ocala, FL*

- -

TAKES: 30 min. • **MAKES:** 4 servings

- 1 lb. lean ground beef (90% lean)
- 1 medium onion, chopped
- 1 medium green pepper, chopped
- 1 jalapeno pepper, seeded and finely chopped
- 1½ cups uncooked instant rice
- 1 can (14½ oz.) diced tomatoes with mild green chiles
- 1½ cups beef broth
- 1 tsp. ground cumin
- ¼ tsp. salt
- ¼ tsp. pepper
- 1 cup shredded Mexican cheese blend

1. In a large skillet, cook beef, onion, green pepper and jalapeno over medium heat until meat is no longer pink and vegetables are tender, 8-10 minutes; crumble beef; drain.

2. Add rice, tomatoes, broth and seasonings. Bring to a boil, then reduce heat. Simmer, covered, until liquid is absorbed, about 5 minutes. Fluff with a fork.

3. Remove from heat; sprinkle with cheese. Let stand, covered, until cheese is melted.

1½ cups: 482 cal., 19g fat (8g sat. fat), 96mg chol., 962mg sod., 41g carb. (5g sugars, 4g fiber), 33g pro.

> **TEST KITCHEN TIP**
> To make this dish healthier, use instant brown rice instead of white, switch to reduced-sodium broth, skip the added salt and sprinkle with just ¼ cup of sharp cheddar instead of 1 cup of the mild blend. The result: only 400 calories, 13 grams fat and 540 milligrams sodium per serving.

SKILLET BOW TIE LASAGNA

This quick recipe tastes just like lasagna, but you make it on the stovetop. It's delicious and always a hit with my family.
—*Arleta Schurle, Clay Center, KS*

PREP: 5 min. • **COOK:** 35 min.
MAKES: 4 servings

- 1   lb. ground beef
- 1   small onion, chopped
- 1   garlic clove, minced
- 1   can (14½ oz.) diced tomatoes, undrained
- 1½ cups water
- 1   can (6 oz.) tomato paste
- 1   Tbsp. dried parsley flakes
- 2   tsp. dried oregano
- 1   tsp. salt
- 2½ cups uncooked bow tie pasta
- ¾   cup 4% cottage cheese
- ¼   cup grated Parmesan cheese

1. In a large cast-iron or other heavy skillet, cook beef, onion and garlic until meat is no longer pink; crumble beef; drain.
2. Add the tomatoes, water, tomato paste, parsley, oregano and salt. Stir in pasta; bring to a boil. Reduce heat; cover and simmer until pasta is tender, 20-25 minutes, stirring once.
3. Combine the cheeses; drop by rounded tablespoonfuls onto pasta mixture. Cover and cook for 5 minutes. If desired, sprinkle with additional dried oregano.

1 cup: 505 cal., 18g fat (7g sat. fat), 77mg chol., 1064mg sod., 52g carb. (11g sugars, 5g fiber), 36g pro.

TEST KITCHEN TIP
Just as with a traditional baked lasagna, you can use ricotta cheese in this dish instead of cottage cheese if you prefer, or mix in a bit of grated mozzarella.

MOM'S SLOPPY TACOS

No matter how hectic the weeknight, there's always time to serve your family a healthy meal with recipes this easy and delicious!
—*Kami Jones, Avondale, AZ*

TAKES: 30 min. • **MAKES:** 6 servings

- 1½ lbs. extra-lean ground beef (95% lean)
- 1   can (15 oz.) tomato sauce
- ¾   tsp. garlic powder
- ½   tsp. salt
- ¼   tsp. pepper
- ¼   tsp. cayenne pepper
- 12 taco shells, warmed
     Optional: Shredded lettuce, shredded cheese and chopped tomatoes, avocado and olives

1. In a large skillet, cook beef over medium heat until no longer pink; crumble beef. Stir in the tomato sauce, garlic powder, salt, pepper and cayenne. Bring to a boil. Reduce heat; simmer, uncovered, for 10 minutes.
2. Fill each taco shell with ¼ cup of the beef mixture and toppings of your choice.

2 tacos: 264 cal., 10g fat (4g sat. fat), 65mg chol., 669mg sod., 17g carb. (1g sugars, 1g fiber), 25g pro. **Diabetic exchanges:** 3 lean meat, 1 starch, 1 fat.

CHILI BEEF NOODLE SKILLET

A friend gave me this recipe. My husband likes the hearty blend of beef, onion and tomatoes. I like it because I can get it to the table so quickly.

—*Deborah Elliott, Ridge Spring, SC*

- -

TAKES: 30 min. • **MAKES:** 8 servings

- 1   pkg. (8 oz.) egg noodles
- 2   lbs. ground beef
- 1   medium onion, chopped
- ¼   cup chopped celery
- 2   garlic cloves, minced
- 1   can (28 oz.) diced tomatoes, undrained
- 1   Tbsp. chili powder
- ¼   to ½ tsp. salt
- ⅛   tsp. pepper
- ½   to 1 cup shredded cheddar cheese

1. Cook noodles according to the package directions. Meanwhile, in a large skillet, cook the beef, onion, celery and garlic over medium heat until the meat is no longer pink and the vegetables are tender; crumble meat; drain.
2. Add the tomatoes, chili powder, salt and pepper to the beef mixture. Cook and stir for 2 minutes or until heated through.
3. Drain noodles; stir into beef mixture and heat through. Remove from the heat. Sprinkle with cheese; cover and let stand for 5 minutes or until cheese is melted.
1 cup: 344 cal., 14g fat (6g sat. fat), 90mg chol., 351mg sod., 28g carb. (5g sugars, 3g fiber), 27g pro.

HEARTY SALISBURY STEAKS

I love serving Salisbury steak with mashed potatoes and vegetables. It's the essence of down-home goodness, and it always disappears fast!

—*Dorothy Bayes, Sardis, OH*

- -

TAKES: 30 min. • **MAKES:** 5 servings

- 1   medium onion, finely chopped
- ½   cup crushed saltines (about 15 crackers)
- ¼   cup egg substitute
- ½   tsp. pepper
- 1   lb. lean ground beef (90% lean)
- 1   Tbsp. canola oil
- 2   cups water
- 1   envelope reduced-sodium onion soup mix
- 2   Tbsp. all-purpose flour

1. In a large bowl, combine onion, saltines, egg substitute and pepper. Add beef; mix lightly but thoroughly. Shape into 5 patties.
2. In a large skillet, heat oil over medium heat. Add patties; cook 3-4 minutes on each side or until lightly browned. Remove patties from pan and keep warm; discard drippings.
3. Combine water, soup mix and flour; stir into skillet. Bring to a boil. Return patties to skillet. Reduce heat; simmer, covered, 5-7 minutes or until meat is no longer pink.

Freeze option: Freeze individual cooled steak with some gravy in an airtight container. To use, partially thaw in refrigerator overnight. Microwave, covered, on high in a microwave-safe dish until heated through, gently stirring and add water if necessary.

1 patty with ¼ cup gravy: 233 cal., 10g fat (3g sat. fat), 45mg chol., 418mg sod., 14g carb. (3g sugars, 1g fiber), 20g pro. **Diabetic exchanges:** 2 lean meat, 1 starch, 1 fat.

BACON-CHEESEBURGER RICE

After tasting a skillet dish that lacked pizazz, my husband and I created this tastier version. I've had teenage nieces and nephews request the recipe after their first bite.

—Joyce Whipps, West Des Moines, IA

- -

TAKES: 30 min. • **MAKES:** 4 servings

- 1 lb. ground beef
- 1¾ cups water
- ⅔ cup barbecue sauce
- 1 Tbsp. prepared mustard
- 2 tsp. dried minced onion
- ½ tsp. pepper
- 2 cups uncooked instant rice
- 1 cup shredded cheddar cheese
- ⅓ cup chopped dill pickles
- 5 bacon strips, cooked and crumbled

1. In a large skillet over medium heat, cook beef until no longer pink; drain. Add the water, barbecue sauce, mustard, onion and pepper.

2. Bring to a boil; stir in the rice. Sprinkle with cheese. Reduce heat; cover and simmer for 5 minutes. Sprinkle with pickles and bacon.

1½ cups: 579 cal., 27g fat (13g sat. fat), 110mg chol., 995mg sod., 48g carb. (6g sugars, 2g fiber), 34g pro.

DID YOU KNOW?

Instant rice is regular rice that's been cooked and then dehydrated. When you "cook" instant rice, you're just rehydrating the grains and heating them up again.

GROUND BEEF SPAGHETTI SKILLET

I remember my grandma making this stovetop supper many times—we always loved granny's spaghetti! My husband and I now enjoy making this for our supper. You can easily substitute ground turkey for the ground beef if that's what you have on hand.

—Jill Thomas, Washington, IN

- -

TAKES: 30 min. • **MAKES:** 4 servings

- 1 lb. ground beef
- 1 medium green pepper, chopped
- 1 small onion, chopped
- 2 garlic cloves, minced
- 1½ cups water
- 1 can (14½ oz.) diced tomatoes, undrained
- 1 can (8 oz.) tomato sauce
- 1 Tbsp. chili powder
- 1 Tbsp. grape jelly
- ½ tsp. salt
- 6 oz. uncooked thin spaghetti, halved

1. In a Dutch oven, cook beef, green pepper, onion and garlic over medium heat until beef is no longer pink and vegetables are tender, 8-10 minutes; crumble beef; drain.

2. Add water, tomatoes, tomato sauce, chili powder, jelly and salt. Bring to a boil. Stir in spaghetti. Reduce heat; simmer, covered, until spaghetti is tender, 6-8 minutes.

1½ cups: 431 cal., 15g fat (5g sat. fat), 70mg chol., 843mg sod., 47g carb. (10g sugars, 5g fiber), 28g pro.

SOUTHWEST FRITO PIE

I got a real culture shock when we moved to New Mexico several years ago, but we grew to love the food. We've since moved back to South Carolina, but we still crave New Mexican dishes. This is one of my go-to favorites.
—*Janet Scoggins, North Augusta, SC*

PREP: 20 min. • **COOK:** 25 min.
MAKES: 6 servings

- 2 lbs. lean ground beef (90% lean)
- 3 Tbsp. chili powder
- 2 Tbsp. all-purpose flour
- 1 tsp. salt
- 1 tsp. garlic powder
- 2 cups water
- 1 can (15 oz.) pinto beans, rinsed and drained, optional
- 4½ cups Fritos corn chips
- 2 cups shredded lettuce
- 1½ cups shredded cheddar cheese
- ¾ cup chopped tomatoes
- 6 Tbsp. finely chopped onion
  Optional: Sour cream and minced fresh cilantro

1. In a 6-qt. stockpot, cook the beef over medium heat until no longer pink; crumble meat; drain.
2. Stir in chili powder, flour, salt and garlic powder until blended. Gradually stir in water and, if desired, beans. Bring to a boil. Reduce heat; simmer, uncovered, 12-15 minutes or until thickened, stirring occasionally.
3. To serve, divide chips among 6 serving bowls. Top with beef mixture, lettuce, cheese, tomatoes and onion. If desired, top with sour cream and cilantro.
1 serving: 615 cal., 38g fat (16g sat. fat), 143mg chol., 915mg sod., 25g carb. (2g sugars, 3g fiber), 43g pro.

CHILI NACHOS

This creamy, chili-like dish is so warm and filling that we often prepare it when on skiing trips to Colorado. We keep it warm in a slow cooker to serve as a hearty dip at parties. It can also be served over corn chips and eaten with a fork.
—*Laurie Withers, Wildomar, CA*

TAKES: 20 min. • **MAKES:** 16 servings

- 2½ lbs. ground beef
- 3 cans (15 oz. each) tomato sauce
- 2 cans (15 oz. each) pinto beans, rinsed and drained
- 1 can (10 oz.) diced tomatoes and green chiles, undrained
- 2 envelopes chili mix
- 2 lbs. Velveeta, cubed
- 1 cup heavy whipping cream
- 2 pkg. (16 oz. each) corn chips
  Optional: Sour cream, sliced jalapeno and lime wedges

In a Dutch oven, cook beef until no longer pink; crumble beef; drain. Add tomato sauce, beans, tomatoes and chili mix; heat through. Add cheese and cream; cook until the cheese is melted. Serve over chips. If desired, top with sour cream, sliced jalapeno and lime wedges.
1 serving: 550 cal., 36g fat (16g sat. fat), 91mg chol., 1379mg sod., 28g carb. (6g sugars, 3g fiber), 28g pro.

READER REVIEW

"This is so great on a night where the kids have sports or Scouts after dinner. Boy, do guys love this mixture over big corn chips—it's like they died and went to heaven!"

LSHAW, TASTEOFHOME.COM

MEATBALL SKILLET MEAL

With colorful vegetables and nicely seasoned meatballs, this tasty, hearty dinner offers a lot of flavor for not a lot of money.
—*Donna Smith, Victor, NY*

- -

TAKES: 30 min. • **MAKES:** 6 servings

- ½ cup finely chopped fresh mushrooms
- ⅓ cup quick-cooking oats
- 2 Tbsp. finely chopped green pepper
- 2 Tbsp. finely chopped onion
- 2 Tbsp. dried parsley flakes
- 1 tsp. dried basil
- 1 tsp. dried oregano
- ½ tsp. dried thyme
- ½ tsp. salt
- ¼ tsp. pepper
- 1 lb. ground beef
- 4 medium carrots, sliced
- 1 small zucchini, sliced
- 1 can (14½ oz.) diced tomatoes, undrained
- 4 cups hot cooked rice

1. In a large bowl, combine first 10 ingredients. Crumble beef over mixture and mix lightly but thoroughly. Shape into 1¼-in. balls.
2. In a large skillet, cook meatballs over medium heat until no longer pink; drain.
3. Add carrots and zucchini; cook, uncovered, for 5 minutes or until vegetables are tender. Stir in tomatoes; heat through. Serve with rice.
1 serving: 312 cal., 8g fat (3g sat. fat), 37mg chol., 352mg sod., 42g carb. (6g sugars, 4g fiber), 18g pro.

ONE-POT BACON CHEESEBURGER PASTA

When the weather's too chilly to grill, I whip up a big pot of this cheesy pasta. Believe it or not, it tastes just like a bacon cheeseburger, and it's much easier for my young children to enjoy.
—*Carly Terrell, Granbury, TX*

- -

PREP: 15 min. • **COOK:** 35 min.
MAKES: 12 servings

- 8 bacon strips, chopped
- 2 lbs. ground beef
- ½ large red onion, chopped
- 12 oz. uncooked spiral pasta
- 4 cups chicken broth
- 2 cans (15 oz. each) crushed tomatoes
- 1 can (8 oz.) tomato sauce
- 1 cup water
- ¼ cup ketchup
- 3 Tbsp. prepared mustard
- 2 Tbsp. Worcestershire sauce
- ¼ tsp. salt
- ¼ tsp. pepper
- 2 cups shredded cheddar cheese, divided
- ⅓ cup chopped dill pickle
  Optional: Chopped tomatoes, shredded lettuce, sliced pickles and sliced red onion

1. In a 6-qt. stockpot, cook the bacon over medium heat, stirring occasionally, until crisp, 6-8 minutes. Remove with a slotted spoon; drain on paper towels. Discard drippings.
2. In the same pot, cook ground beef and onion over medium heat until the meat is no longer pink, 6-8 minutes; crumble the meat; drain.
3. Add the next 10 ingredients; bring to a boil. Reduce heat; simmer, covered, until pasta is al dente, stirring occasionally, about 10 minutes.
4. Stir in 1 cup cheese, the pickle and bacon; cook and stir until cheese is melted. Serve with the remaining 1 cup cheese and, if desired tomatoes, lettuce, pickles and red onions.
1⅓ cups: 390 cal., 18g fat (8g sat. fat), 73mg chol., 1023mg sod., 31g carb. (7g sugars, 3g fiber), 25g pro.

ONE-POT DUTCH OVEN PASTA BAKE

I was in a hurry one night, so I went on a pantry search. I found penne pasta and decided I'd go Italian! This is now one of our weeknight faves. It's so satisfying and easy, and it's a timesaver since the pasta cooks in the same pot.
—*Tammy Reid, Oklahoma City, OK*

PREP: 15 min. • **COOK:** 30 min.
MAKES: 4 servings

- 1 lb. ground beef
- ½ medium onion, chopped
- 2 garlic cloves, minced
- 1 can (8 oz.) tomato sauce
- 3 cups uncooked penne pasta
- 1 cup beef broth
- 3 cups water
- 1 can (14 oz.) diced tomatoes
- 1 tsp. onion powder
- 1 Tbsp. Italian seasoning
- 1 package (5 oz.) fresh spinach
  Shredded Parmesan cheese, optional

1. Heat a Dutch oven over medium heat; add ground beef and onion. Cook and stir until beef is no longer pink, 5-7 minutes; crumble meat; drain. Add garlic; cook 1 minute longer.
2. Add tomato sauce, pasta, broth, water, diced tomatoes and seasonings. Stir; bring to a boil. Cover, reduce heat and simmer until pasta is tender, stirring occasionally.
3. Top with spinach; cover just until wilted. Stir. If desired, sprinkle with Parmesan cheese.
1¼ cups: 287 cal., 10g fat (3g sat. fat), 49mg chol., 1061mg sod., 29g carb. (7g sugars, 3g fiber), 19g pro.

SALISBURY STEAK SUPREME

This recipe was one of my mom's go-to meals for busy nights; now it's one of my husband's favorites. It also makes a fast and satisfying solution when I need something special to serve to unexpected company.
—*Patricia Swart, Galloway, NJ*

PREP: 20 min. • **COOK:** 15 min.
MAKES: 4 servings

- 2 medium red onions, divided
- ½ cup soft bread crumbs
- ¾ tsp. salt-free seasoning blend
- ½ tsp. pepper
  Dash ground nutmeg
- 1 lb. lean ground beef (90% lean)
- 1 tsp. cornstarch
- 1 tsp. reduced-sodium beef bouillon granules
- ½ cup cold water
- 2 tsp. butter
- 1½ cups sliced fresh mushrooms

1. Thinly slice 1½ onions, set aside. Finely chop remaining onion half. Toss bread crumbs with the chopped onion and seasonings. Add beef; mix lightly but thoroughly. Shape into four ½-in.-thick oval patties.
2. In a lightly oiled large nonstick skillet over medium heat, cook patties 5-6 minutes on each side or until a thermometer reads 160°. Remove from pan. Discard drippings.
3. In a small bowl, mix cornstarch, bouillon and water until smooth. In same skillet, heat butter over medium-high heat. Add mushrooms and sliced onions; cook and stir for 5-7 minutes or until the onions are tender.
4. Stir in cornstarch mixture. Bring to a boil; cook and stir 1-2 minutes or until thickened. Return patties to pan, turning to coat with sauce; heat through.
Note: To make soft bread crumbs, tear bread into pieces and place in a food processor or blender. Cover and pulse until crumbs form. A slice of bread yields ½-¾ cup crumbs.
1 serving: 244 cal., 12g fat (5g sat. fat), 76mg chol., 192mg sod., 10g carb. (3g sugars, 1g fiber), 24g pro. **Diabetic exchanges:** 3 lean meat, 1 starch, ½ fat.

Ground Beef

SLOW-COOKER MEALS

What happens if you combine popular ground beef with the convenience of a slow cooker? You get the savory sensations found here. It's never been easier to simmer a winner!

SAUSAGE, ARTICHOKE & SUN-DRIED TOMATO RAGU

This thick and hearty spaghetti sauce is simple to make and, like all good spaghetti sauces, it tastes even better the next day. If you prefer celery or bell pepper in your sauce, go ahead and throw them in!
—*Aysha Schurman, Ammon, ID*

PREP: 20 min. • **COOK:** 6 hours
MAKES: 10 servings (about 2 qt.)

1   lb. bulk Italian sausage
½   lb. lean ground beef (90% lean)
1   medium onion, finely chopped
3   cans (14½ oz. each) diced tomatoes, undrained
1   cup oil-packed sun-dried tomatoes, chopped
2   cans (6 oz. each) Italian tomato paste
1   jar (7½ oz.) marinated quartered artichoke hearts, drained and chopped
3   garlic cloves, minced
2   tsp. minced fresh rosemary
1   tsp. pepper
½   tsp. salt
1   bay leaf
3   Tbsp. minced fresh parsley
    Hot cooked spaghetti
    Grated Parmesan cheese, optional

1. In a large skillet, cook sausage, beef and onion over medium-high heat until meat is no longer pink, 4-6 minutes; crumble meat; drain. Transfer to a 5- or 6-qt. slow cooker. Stir in tomatoes, tomato paste, artichokes, garlic, rosemary, pepper, salt and bay leaf.
2. Cook, covered, on low until it is heated through, 6-8 hours. Remove bay leaf. Stir in parsley. Serve with spaghetti. If desired, top with grated Parmesan.
Freeze option: Freeze cooled sauce in freezer containers. To use, partially thaw in refrigerator overnight. Heat through in a saucepan, stirring occasionally.
¾ cup: 259 cal., 17g fat (5g sat. fat), 39mg chol., 1535mg sod., 17g carb. (9g sugars, 3g fiber), 11g pro.

EASY CHOW MEIN

Some years ago, our daughter welcomed me home from a hospital stay with this easy Asian dish and a copy of the recipe. Now I freeze the leftovers for fast future meals.

—Kay Bade, Mitchell, SD

- -

PREP: 15 min. • **COOK:** 4 hours
MAKES: 8 servings

- 1 lb. ground beef
- 1 medium onion, chopped
- 1 bunch celery, sliced
- 2 cans (14 oz. each) Chinese vegetables, drained
- 2 envelopes brown gravy mix
- 2 Tbsp. soy sauce
  Hot cooked egg noodles or rice

In a large skillet, cook beef and onion over medium heat until meat is no longer pink; crumble beef; drain. Transfer to a 3-qt. slow cooker. Stir in the celery, Chinese vegetables, gravy mix and soy sauce. Cover and cook on low until celery is tender, 4-6 hours, stirring occasionally. Serve with noodles.

1 cup: 361 cal., 6g fat (2g sat. fat), 28mg chol., 897mg sod., 56g carb. (6g sugars, 4g fiber), 18g pro.

TEST KITCHEN TIP
Round out this entree, and keep the kitchen cool, with frozen egg rolls prepared quickly and easily in the air fryer.

SLOW-COOKER MEAT LOAF

That old standby meat loaf gets some Mexican flair and a simple preparation method with this slow-cooked recipe. Boost the flavor by serving it with taco sauce or salsa.

—Julie Sterchi, Campbellsville, KY

- -

PREP: 10 min. • **COOK:** 6 hours
MAKES: 8 servings

- 1 large egg, beaten
- ⅓ cup taco sauce
- 1 cup coarsely crushed corn chips
- ⅓ cup shredded Mexican cheese blend or cheddar cheese
- 2 Tbsp. taco seasoning
- ½ tsp. salt, optional
- 2 lbs. lean ground beef (90% lean)
  Additional taco sauce or salsa

In a large bowl, combine the first 6 ingredients. Crumble beef over mixture and mix lightly but thoroughly. Shape into a round loaf; place in a 3-qt. slow cooker. Cover and cook on low until a thermometer reads 160°, 6-8 hours. Serve with the taco sauce or salsa.

1 piece: 258 cal., 11g fat (5g sat. fat), 86mg chol., 471mg sod., 14g carb. (1g sugars, 1g fiber), 24g pro.

SLOW-COOKED ENCHILADA CASSEROLE

Tortilla chips and a side salad turn this savory casserole into a fun and festive meal.
—*Denise Waller, Omaha, NE*

- -

PREP: 20 min. • **COOK:** 6 hours
MAKES: 6 servings

1	lb. ground beef
2	cans (10 oz. each) enchilada sauce
1	can (10¾ oz.) condensed cream of onion soup, undiluted
¼	tsp. salt
1	pkg. (8½ oz.) flour tortillas, torn into 3-inch pieces
3	cups shredded cheddar cheese

1. In a skillet, cook beef over medium heat until no longer pink; crumble meat; drain. Stir in enchilada sauce, soup and salt.
2. In a 3-qt. slow cooker, layer a third of the beef mixture, tortillas and cheese. Repeat the layers twice. Cover and cook on low until heated through, 6-8 hours.
1 serving: 568 cal., 35g fat (16g sat. fat), 105mg chol., 1610mg sod., 30g carb. (4g sugars, 3g fiber), 31g pro.

MEAT LOVER'S PIZZA HOT DISH

I make this hearty casserole for the men who help us out during harvesttime. Every year they say it's the best—hands down. Throw in any pizza toppings your family likes—Canadian bacon, black olives and green peppers are some of our picks.
—*Brook Bothun, Canby, MN*

- -

PREP: 25 min. • **COOK:** 3¼ hours
MAKES: 10 servings

1	lb. ground beef
1	lb. bulk Italian sausage
1	medium onion, chopped
1	cup sliced fresh mushrooms
4	cans (8 oz. each) no-salt-added tomato sauce
2	cans (15 oz. each) pizza sauce
1	pkg. (16 oz.) penne pasta
1	cup water
1	can (6 oz.) tomato paste
1	pkg. (3½ oz.) sliced pepperoni
1	tsp. Italian seasoning
2	cups shredded part-skim mozzarella cheese, divided
2	cups shredded cheddar cheese, divided

1. In a large skillet, cook beef, sausage, onion and mushrooms over medium heat until meat is no longer pink and vegetables are tender, 10-12 minutes; crumble meat; drain.
2. Transfer meat mixture to a greased 6-qt. slow cooker. Stir in tomato sauce, pizza sauce, pasta, water, tomato paste, pepperoni and Italian seasoning. Cook, covered, on low until pasta is tender, 3-4 hours.
3. Stir thoroughly; mix in 1 cup mozzarella cheese and 1 cup cheddar cheese. Sprinkle remaining cheese over top. Cook, covered, until cheese is melted, 15-20 minutes longer.
1⅓ cups: 653 cal., 35g fat (14g sat. fat), 99mg chol., 1482mg sod., 52g carb. (9g sugars, 6g fiber), 36g pro.

SLOW-COOKED PIZZA CASSEROLE

A friend from church gave me the recipe for this tasty slow-cooker casserole. It's always one of the first dishes emptied at potlucks, and it can easily be adapted to personal tastes. You will love it!
—*Julie Sterchi, Campbellsville, KY*

PREP: 25 min. • **COOK:** 4 hours
MAKES: 12 servings

- 3 lbs. ground beef
- ½ cup chopped onion
- 1 jar (24 oz.) pasta sauce
- 2 jars (4½ oz. each) sliced mushrooms, drained
- 1 tsp. salt
- ½ tsp. garlic powder
- ½ tsp. dried oregano
  Dash pepper
- 1 pkg. (16 oz.) wide egg noodles, cooked and drained
- 2 pkg. (3½ oz. each) sliced pepperoni
- 2 cups shredded cheddar cheese
- 2 cups shredded part-skim mozzarella cheese

1. In a Dutch oven, brown beef and onion over medium heat until the meat is no longer pink; crumble meat; drain. Add spaghetti sauce, mushrooms, salt, garlic powder, oregano and pepper; heat mixture through.
2. Spoon half the mixture into a 5-qt. slow cooker. Top with half the noodles, pepperoni and cheeses. Repeat layers. Cover and cook on low for 4-5 hours or until the cheese is melted.
1 serving: 534 cal., 26g fat (13g sat. fat), 131mg chol., 1009mg sod., 36g carb. (6g sugars, 3g fiber), 37g pro.

READER REVIEW

"I jazz up this recipe by sneaking in lots of veggies, like peppers and shredded carrots, and the boys still love it!"

RUBYH85, TASTEOFHOME.COM

MOO SHU LETTUCE CUPS

I took ordinary ground beef and turned it into a new classic. With sweet and savory flavors, this dish will be a dinnertime favorite. We love this served in flour tortillas, too!
—*Christine Keating, Norwalk, CA*

PREP: 25 min. • **COOK:** 3 hours
MAKES: 4 servings

- ¼ cup apricot preserves
- 3 Tbsp. hoisin sauce
- 2 Tbsp. soy sauce
- 1 Tbsp. honey
- ½ tsp. sesame oil
- ¼ tsp. crushed red pepper flakes, optional
- 1 lb. lean ground beef (90% lean)
- ½ cup chopped onion
- 3 garlic cloves, minced
- 1 tsp. minced fresh gingerroot
- 1 cup sliced fresh mushrooms
- 1 medium carrot, diced
- 1 celery rib, diced
- ½ cup chopped sweet red pepper
- 12 Bibb lettuce leaves
  Sliced green onions

1. Mix first 5 ingredients and, if desired, pepper flakes. In a large skillet, cook beef, onion, garlic and ginger over medium heat until no longer pink, about 5-7 minutes; crumble the meat. Transfer to a 3- or 4-qt. slow cooker. Add the mushrooms, carrot, celery and pepper; stir in sauce mixture.
2. Cook, covered, on low until vegetables are tender and flavors are blended, 3-4 hours. Serve mixture in lettuce leaves; sprinkle with green onions.
3 filled lettuce cups: 311 cal., 11g fat (4g sat. fat), 71mg chol., 744mg sod., 29g carb. (19g sugars, 2g fiber), 25g pro.

SLOW-COOKER GOLOMBKI

I modified my mom's classic Polish dish to fit my hectic life. Instead of boiling the cabbage and then filling it with beef, I just toss ingredients in the slow cooker. It's much easier and tastes just as delicious.
—*Mary Walker, Clermont, FL*

PREP: 25 min. • **COOK:** 6 hours
MAKES: 8 servings

- 1 lb. ground beef
- 1 small onion, chopped
- 1 cup uncooked converted rice
- ¾ tsp. salt
- ¼ tsp. pepper
- 1 jar (24 oz.) meatless spaghetti sauce
- 2 cans (10¾ oz. each) condensed tomato soup, undiluted
- 1 cup water
- ½ tsp. sugar
- 1 medium head cabbage, chopped

1. In a large skillet, cook beef and onion over medium heat until the meat is no longer pink; crumble beef; drain. Stir in the rice, salt and pepper. In a large bowl, combine the spaghetti sauce, soup, water and sugar.
2. In a 5-qt. slow cooker, layer a third of the sauce, half of the beef mixture and a third of the cabbage. Repeat layers; top with remaining sauce and cabbage.
3. Cook, covered, on low until cabbage and rice are tender, 6-8 hours.
1¼ cups: 307 cal., 7g fat (3g sat. fat), 35mg chol., 1166mg sod., 45g carb. (15g sugars, 6g fiber), 16g pro.

MEATY SPAGHETTI SAUCE

My homemade spaghetti sauce always got rave reviews, but it was so time-consuming to make on the stovetop. My family loves this flavorful slow-cooker version.
—*Arlene Sommers, Redmond, WA*

- -

PREP: 15 min. • **COOK:** 8 hours
MAKES: 12 servings

1   lb. lean ground beef (90% lean)
1   lb. bulk Italian sausage
1   medium green pepper, chopped
1   medium onion, chopped
8   garlic cloves, minced
3   cans (14½ oz. each) Italian diced tomatoes, drained
2   cans (15 oz. each) tomato sauce
2   cans (6 oz. each) tomato paste
⅓   cup sugar
2   Tbsp. Italian seasoning
1   Tbsp. dried basil
2   tsp. dried marjoram
1   tsp. salt
½   tsp. pepper
    Hot cooked spaghetti
    Shredded Parmesan cheese, optional

1. In a large skillet over medium heat, cook the beef and sausage until no longer pink, 10-12 minutes, crumble meat; drain. Transfer to a 5-qt. slow cooker. Stir in green pepper, onion, garlic, tomatoes, tomato sauce, paste, sugar and seasonings.
2. Cover and cook on low for 8 hours or until bubbly. Serve with the spaghetti. Top with Parmesan if desired.
½ cup: 264 cal., 12g fat (4g sat. fat), 44mg chol., 1119mg sod., 26g carb. (17g sugars, 3g fiber), 15g pro.

> **TEST KITCHEN TIP**
> Add a layer of flavor to this sauce by replacing the sugar with lightly packed brown sugar.

SPICY STUFFED BANANA PEPPERS

Banana peppers can be very tricky: Sometimes they're hot and sometimes they're not. Try using bianca peppers—they're sweeter.
—*Danielle Lee, Sewickley, PA*

- -

PREP: 45 min. • **COOK:** 3½ hours
MAKES: 4 servings

6   Tbsp. water
3   Tbsp. uncooked red or white quinoa, rinsed
½   lb. bulk spicy Italian sausage
½   lb. lean ground beef (90% lean)
½   cup tomato sauce
2   green onions, chopped
2   garlic cloves, minced
1½   tsp. Sriracha chili sauce
½   tsp. chili powder
¼   tsp. salt
⅛   tsp. pepper
16   mild banana peppers
2   cups reduced-sodium spicy V8 juice

1. In a small saucepan, bring water to a boil. Add quinoa. Reduce heat; simmer, covered, until the liquid is absorbed, 12-15 minutes. Remove from heat; fluff with a fork.
2. In a large bowl, combine sausage, beef, tomato sauce, green onions, garlic, chili sauce, chili powder, salt, pepper and cooked quinoa. Cut and discard tops from peppers; remove seeds. Fill the peppers with the meat mixture.
3. Stand peppers upright in a 4-qt. slow cooker. Pour V8 juice over top. Cook, covered, on low until peppers are tender, 3½-4½ hours.
Freeze option: Freeze cooled stuffed peppers and sauce in freezer containers. To use, partially thaw in refrigerator overnight. Microwave, covered, on high in a microwave-safe dish until heated through.
4 stuffed peppers: 412 cal., 22g fat (7g sat. fat), 74mg chol., 965mg sod., 29g carb. (11g sugars, 13g fiber), 26g pro.

ITALIAN STUFFED PEPPERS

Making stuffed peppers in a slow cooker is convenient and the long simmering process gives the flavors time to blend.
—Taste of Home *Test Kitchen*

PREP: 25 min. • **COOK:** 4 hours
MAKES: 6 servings

- 6   large green or sweet red peppers
- 1   lb. lean ground beef (90% lean)
- 2   cups cubed part-skim mozzarella cheese (¼-in. cubes)
- 1   cup uncooked converted rice
- 1   small onion, chopped
- 2   garlic cloves, minced
- 1   tsp. minced fresh parsley
- 1   tsp. salt
- ½   tsp. pepper
- 1   can (28 oz.) crushed tomatoes
- 1   cup beef broth
- ½   cup grated Parmesan cheese
       Additional minced fresh parsley

1. Cut tops off peppers and remove seeds; set aside. In a large bowl, combine the beef, mozzarella cheese, rice, onion, garlic, parsley, salt and pepper; spoon into peppers. Transfer to an oval 5- or 6-qt. slow cooker. Pour the tomatoes over peppers; pour broth around the sides.
2. Cover and cook on low for 4-5 hours or until a thermometer reaches 160° and the peppers are tender. Sprinkle with Parmesan cheese and additional parsley.
1 stuffed pepper: 470 cal., 17g fat (9g sat. fat), 67mg chol., 1033mg sod., 45g carb. (5g sugars, 6g fiber), 35g pro.

CUBAN PICADILLO

Most of the traditional recipes out there have numerous variations. Picadillo is no exception. This is my take on the Cuban classic. For added convenience, I adapted it for the slow cooker.
—*Sanford Brown, Covington, GA*

PREP: 30 min. • **COOK:** 4½ hours
MAKES: 8 servings

- 2   large onions, chopped
- 2   Tbsp. olive oil
- ¾   cup white wine or beef broth
- 2   lbs. lean ground beef (90% lean)
- 1¼   cups crushed tomatoes
- 1   can (8 oz.) tomato sauce
- ⅓   cup tomato paste
- 4   garlic cloves, minced
- 2   tsp. dried oregano
- ½   tsp. salt
- ½   tsp. ground cinnamon
- ½   tsp. ground cloves
- ½   tsp. pepper
- 1   cup raisins
- 2   Tbsp. chopped seeded jalapeno pepper
- 1   medium green pepper, chopped
- ¾   cup pimiento-stuffed olives, coarsely chopped
        Hot cooked brown rice

1. In a large skillet, cook onions in oil over low heat for 15-20 minutes or until brown, stirring occasionally. Add wine; cook and stir 2 minutes longer. Transfer to a 3- or 4-qt. slow cooker.
2. In the same skillet, cook beef over medium heat until no longer pink; crumble meat; drain. Add to slow cooker. Combine the tomatoes, tomato sauce, tomato paste, garlic and seasonings; pour over top. Cover and cook on low for 4-6 hours or until heated through.
3. Place raisins in a small bowl. Cover with boiling water; let stand for 5 minutes; drain. Stir the raisins, jalapeno, green pepper and olives into the slow cooker. Cover and cook 30 minutes longer. Serve with rice.
Note: Wear disposable gloves when cutting hot peppers; the oils can burn skin. Avoid touching your face.
1 cup: 331 cal., 14g fat (4g sat. fat), 56mg chol., 685mg sod., 27g carb. (15g sugars, 4g fiber), 24g pro.

COUNTRY BACON-BEEF MAC & CHEESE

This extra-meaty mac and cheese is super easy to make in the slow cooker. Kids love it, so I like to sneak in some veggies.
—Nancy Heishman, Las Vegas, NV

PREP: 35 min. • **COOK:** 1½ hours
MAKES: 8 servings

- 5 bacon strips, chopped
- 1½ lbs. ground beef
- 1 medium onion, chopped
- 3 garlic cloves, minced
- 1 medium sweet red pepper, chopped
- 1 large carrot, coarsely grated
- 1 Tbsp. dried parsley flakes
- ¼ tsp. salt
- 1 tsp. pepper
- 3 cups uncooked protein-enriched or whole wheat elbow macaroni
- 1 can (14½ oz.) reduced-sodium beef broth
- 1 cup sour cream
- 2 cups shredded sharp cheddar cheese
- 2 cups shredded part-skim mozzarella cheese

1. In a large skillet, cook the bacon over medium heat until crisp, stirring occasionally, 5-6 minutes. Remove with a slotted spoon; drain on paper towels. Discard all but 1 Tbsp. of drippings. Brown ground beef in drippings; crumble beef; remove from pan. Add onion to the skillet; cook and stir until translucent, 2-3 minutes. Add garlic; cook 1 minute more.
2. Combine red pepper, carrot, seasonings and pasta in a 4-qt. slow cooker. Layer with ground beef, bacon and onion mixture (do not stir). Pour in broth.
3. Cook, covered, on low for about 1 hour, or until meat and vegetables are tender. Thirty minutes before serving, stir in sour cream and cheeses.
1½ cups: 591 cal., 36g fat (17g sat. fat), 113mg chol., 719mg sod., 29g carb. (5g sugars, 3g fiber), 38g pro.

SLOW-COOKED BEEF SPAGHETTI SAUCE

Down-home and delicious, this sauce simmers fuss-free for hours, leaving you time to enjoy the day without worrying about making dinner.
—Kim Stewart, North Little Rock, AR

PREP: 15 min. • **COOK:** 8 hours • **MAKES:** 2 qt.

- 2 lbs. lean ground beef (90% lean)
- 1 large green pepper, chopped
- 1 large onion, chopped
- 1½ cups water
- 1 can (14½ oz.) diced tomatoes, undrained
- 1 can (8 oz.) tomato sauce
- 1 can (6 oz.) tomato paste
- 2 garlic cloves, minced
- 4 bay leaves
- 2 Tbsp. Italian seasoning
- 1 tsp. salt
- 1 tsp. sugar
- 1 tsp. dried parsley flakes
- ½ tsp. pepper
- ¼ tsp. dried rosemary, crushed
     Hot cooked spaghetti

In a large skillet over medium heat, cook beef until no longer pink; crumble meat; drain. Transfer to a 5-qt. slow cooker. Stir in the green pepper, onion, water, tomatoes, tomato sauce, paste, garlic and seasonings. Cover and cook on low for 8 hours or until bubbly. Discard bay leaves; serve over spaghetti.
¾ cup: 186 cal., 8g fat (3g sat. fat), 56mg chol., 452mg sod., 9g carb. (5g sugars, 2g fiber), 20g pro. **Diabetic exchanges:** 3 vegetable, 3 lean meat,

SLOW-COOKER SPANISH RICE

Here's an economical dish with authentic Tex-Mex flavor.
—*Sharon Tipton, Casselberry, FL*

- -

PREP: 30 min. • **COOK:** 4 hours
MAKES: 8 servings

- 1½ lbs. ground beef
- 2 medium onions, chopped
- 1 medium green pepper, chopped
- 1 celery rib, chopped
- 2 garlic cloves, minced
- 1½ cups uncooked converted rice (not instant)
- 1 can (28 oz.) diced tomatoes, drained
- 1 can (6 oz.) tomato paste
- 1 tsp. salt
- 1 tsp. sugar
- 1 tsp. chili powder
-    Dash pepper
- 1½ cups water
- 1 can (2¼ oz.) sliced ripe olives, drained
- ½ cup shredded cheddar cheese

1. In a large skillet over medium-high heat, cook the beef, onions, pepper and celery 7-8 minutes or until no longer pink, crumble meat. Add garlic; cook 1 minute longer. Drain and transfer meat mixture to a 4- or 5-qt. slow cooker. Add next 8 ingredients.
2. Cook, covered, on low until the rice and vegetables are tender, 4-5 hours, stirring once. Top with olives and cheese before serving.
1¼ cups: 378 cal., 13g fat (5g sat. fat), 60mg chol., 632mg sod., 42g carb. (7g sugars, 3g fiber), 22g pro.

SLOW-COOKER LASAGNA

Lasagna is a popular meal, but it's hard to find time to fix it. This slow-cooker version will allow you to enjoy time with your family and still put a delicious dinner on the table.
—*Kathryn Conrad, Milwaukee, WI*

- -

PREP: 25 min. • **COOK:** 4 hours + standing
MAKES: 8 servings

- 1 lb. ground beef
- 1 Tbsp. olive oil
- ½ cup chopped onion
- ½ cup chopped zucchini
- ½ cup chopped carrot
- 1 jar (24 oz.) marinara sauce
- 2 tsp. Italian seasoning
- ½ tsp. red pepper flakes, optional
- 2 cartons (15 oz. each) part-skim ricotta cheese
- 1 cup grated Parmesan cheese
- 4 large eggs
- ½ cup loosely packed basil leaves, chopped
- 12 no-cook lasagna noodles
- 3 cups shredded part-skim mozzarella cheese
-    Optional: Quartered grape tomatoes and additional chopped fresh basil

1. Cut three 25x3-in. strips of heavy-duty foil; crisscross so they resemble spokes of a wheel. Place strips on bottom and up sides of a 5-qt. slow cooker. Coat strips with cooking spray.
2. In a 6-qt. stockpot, cook beef over medium heat until beef is no longer pink, 6-8 minutes; crumble meat; drain. Set beef aside.
3. In same pot, heat oil over medium-high heat. Add onion, zucchini and carrot; cook and stir until just tender, 2-3 minutes. Stir in beef mixture, marinara sauce, Italian seasoning and if desired, crushed red pepper. In a large bowl, combine ricotta, Parmesan, eggs and basil.
4. Spread ½ cup meat sauce into the bottom of the slow cooker. Layer with 4 noodles, breaking as needed to fit. Top with 1½ cups meat mixture, 1⅔ cups cheese mixture and 1 cup mozzarella cheese. Repeat layers twice. Cook, covered, on low until noodles are tender, about 4 hours. Let stand 30 minutes. If desired, top with grape tomatoes and additional basil.
1 slice: 631 cal., 32g fat (15g sat. fat), 199mg chol., 1074mg sod., 40g carb. (8g sugars, 3g fiber), 43g pro.

KATHRYN CONRAD
Milwaukee, WI

SLOW-COOKER ITALIAN SLOPPY JOES

These tasty sloppy joes have plenty of mass appeal and are perfect for a gathering. If you're taking them to an event later in the day, simplify your morning by cooking the beef mixture and stirring in other ingredients the night before. Cool the meat sauce in shallow bowls in the fridge, then cover and refrigerate them overnight. The next day, transfer the meat mixture to the slow cooker to keep it warm for the party.
—*Hope Wasylenki, Gahanna, OH*

PREP: 30 min. • **COOK:** 4 hours
MAKES: 36 servings

- 2   lbs. lean ground beef (90% lean)
- 2   lbs. bulk Italian sausage
- 2   medium green peppers, chopped
- 1   large onion, chopped
- 4   cups spaghetti sauce
- 1   can (28 oz.) diced tomatoes, undrained
- ½   lb. sliced fresh mushrooms
- 1   can (6 oz.) tomato paste
- 2   garlic cloves, minced
- 2   bay leaves
- 36 hamburger buns, split

1. Cook the beef, sausage, peppers and onion in a Dutch oven over medium heat until meat is no longer pink; crumble meat; drain. Transfer to a 6-qt. slow cooker. Stir in spaghetti sauce, tomatoes, mushrooms, tomato paste, garlic and the bay leaves.

2. Cover and cook on high until flavors are blended, 4-5 hours. Discard the bay leaves. Serve on buns, with ½ cup meat mixture.

Freeze option: Freeze cooled meat mixture in freezer containers. To use, partially thaw in refrigerator overnight. Heat through in a saucepan, stirring occasionally; add broth or water if necessary.

1 sandwich: 246 cal., 9g fat (3g sat. fat), 29mg chol., 522mg sod., 27g carb. (6g sugars, 2g fiber), 13g pro. **Diabetic exchanges:** 2 starch, 2 lean meat.

SLOW-COOKED SPICY GOULASH

Ground cumin, chili powder and a can of Mexican diced tomatoes jazz up my goulash recipe. Even the macaroni is prepared in the slow cooker.
—*Melissa Polk, West Lafayette, IN*

PREP: 25 min. • **COOK:** 5½ hours
MAKES: 8 servings

- 1 lb. lean ground beef (90% lean)
- 4 cans (14½ oz. each) Mexican diced tomatoes, undrained
- 2 cans (16 oz. each) kidney beans, rinsed and drained
- 2 cups water
- 1 medium onion, chopped
- 1 medium green pepper, chopped
- ¼ cup red wine vinegar
- 2 Tbsp. chili powder
- 1 Tbsp. Worcestershire sauce
- 2 tsp. beef bouillon granules
- 1 tsp. dried basil
- 1 tsp. dried parsley flakes
- 1 tsp. ground cumin
- ¼ tsp. pepper
- 2 cups uncooked elbow macaroni

1. In a large skillet, cook beef over medium heat until no longer pink, crumble beef; drain. Transfer to a 5-qt. slow cooker. Stir in the tomatoes, beans, water, onion, green pepper, vinegar, chili powder, Worcestershire sauce, bouillon and seasonings. Cover and cook on low for 5-6 hours or until heated through.
2. Stir in macaroni; cover and cook 30 minutes longer or until macaroni is tender.
1½ cups: 315 cal., 6g fat (2g sat. fat), 35mg chol., 915mg sod., 44g carb. (11g sugars, 9g fiber), 23g pro.

SMOKY GARLIC MEAT LOAF

Chopped onion and garlic plus spicy seasonings add outstanding flavor to this slow-cooked meat loaf.
—*Taste of Home Test Kitchen*

PREP: 25 min. • **COOK:** 4 hours
MAKES: 8 servings

- 6 Tbsp. ketchup, divided
- 2 Tbsp. Worcestershire sauce
- 12 saltines, crushed
- 1 medium onion, finely chopped
- 6 garlic cloves, minced
- 1 tsp. paprika
- ½ tsp. salt
- ½ tsp. pepper
- ⅛ tsp. cayenne pepper
- 2 lbs. lean ground beef (90% lean)

1. Cut three 20x3-in. strips of heavy-duty foil; crisscross so they resemble spokes of a wheel. Place strips on the bottom and up the sides of a 3-qt. slow cooker. Coat the strips with cooking spray.
2. In a large bowl, combine 2 Tbsp. ketchup, Worcestershire sauce, saltines, onion, garlic, paprika, salt, pepper and cayenne. Crumble the beef over mixture and mix lightly but thoroughly.
3. Shape into a round loaf. Place in the center of the strips. Cover and cook on low until no pink remains and a thermometer reads 160°, 4-5 hours.
4. Using foil strips as handles, remove the meat loaf to a platter.
5. Spread remaining ketchup over top of loaf.
1 piece: 222 cal., 10g fat (4g sat. fat), 71mg chol., 447mg sod., 10g carb. (5g sugars, 1g fiber), 23g pro. **Diabetic exchanges:** 3 lean meat, ½ starch.

CHILI MAC

This recipe has regularly appeared on my family menus for more than 40 years, and it's never failed to please at potlucks and bring-a-dish gatherings. Sometimes I turn it into soup by adding a can of beef broth.

—*Marie Posavec, Berwyn, IL*

PREP: 15 min. • **COOK:** 6 hours
MAKES: 6 servings

- 1 lb. lean ground beef (90% lean), cooked and drained
- 2 cans (16 oz. each) hot chili beans, undrained
- 2 large green peppers, chopped
- 1 large onion, chopped
- 4 celery ribs, chopped
- 1 can (8 oz.) no-salt-added tomato sauce
- 2 Tbsp. chili seasoning mix
- 2 garlic cloves, minced
- 1 pkg. (7 oz.) elbow macaroni, cooked and drained
   Salt and pepper to taste
   Optional: Shredded pepper jack cheese and sliced jalapeno pepper

In a 5-qt. slow cooker, mix together the first 8 ingredients. Cover and cook mixture on low for 6 hours or until heated through. Stir in the macaroni. Season with salt and pepper. Top servings with cheese and jalapenos if desired.

1 serving: 348 cal., 8g fat (3g sat. fat), 47mg chol., 713mg sod., 49g carb. (8g sugars, 12g fiber), 27g pro. **Diabetic exchanges:** 3 starch, 3 lean meat.

EASY STROGANOFF

I especially like to use my slow cooker on hot summer days when I want to keep my kitchen cool. I'm always trying new recipes for different events, but beef Stroganoff is a favorite I turn to time and again.

—*Roberta Menefee, Walcott, NY*

PREP: 15 min. • **COOK:** 7 hours
MAKES: 6 servings

- 2 lbs. ground beef, cooked and drained
- 2 medium onions, chopped
- 1 cup beef consomme
- 1 can (4 oz.) mushroom stems and pieces, drained
- 3 Tbsp. tomato paste
- 2 garlic cloves, minced
- 1½ tsp. salt
- ¼ tsp. pepper
- 2 Tbsp. all-purpose flour
- ¾ cup sour cream
   Hot cooked egg noodles

In a 3-qt. slow cooker, mix together the first 8 ingredients. Cover and cook on low for 6 hours. In a small bowl, combine flour and sour cream until smooth; stir into beef mixture. Cover and cook 1 hour longer or until thickened. Serve over noodles.

1 serving: 348 cal., 19g fat (10g sat. fat), 96mg chol., 1056mg sod., 11g carb. (6g sugars, 2g fiber), 31g pro.

SLOW-COOKED TAMALE CASSEROLE

I've been making this recipe for years because my family really likes it. I'll make it on busy Saturdays when we want a comforting and filling dinner. Stirring the cornmeal into the beef creates a thick, savory filling.
—*Diana Briggs, Veneta, OR*

PREP: 15 min. • **COOK:** 4 hours
MAKES: 6 servings

- 1 lb. ground beef
- 1 large egg, beaten
- 1½ cups 2% milk
- ¾ cup cornmeal
- 1 can (15¼ oz.) whole kernel corn, drained
- 1 can (14½ oz.) diced tomatoes, undrained
- 1 can (2¼ oz.) sliced ripe olives, drained
- 1 envelope chili seasoning
- 1 tsp. seasoned salt
- 1 cup shredded cheddar cheese

1. In a skillet, cook beef over medium heat until no longer pink; crumble beef; drain. In a large bowl, combine the egg, milk and cornmeal until smooth. Add the corn, tomatoes, olives, chili seasoning, seasoned salt and beef.
2. Transfer to a greased 3-qt. slow cooker. Cover and cook on high for 3 ¾ hours. Sprinkle with cheese; cover and cook 15 minutes longer or until the cheese is melted.
1 serving: 386 cal., 17g fat (9g sat. fat), 101mg chol., 1255mg sod., 31g carb. (9g sugars, 4g fiber), 24g pro.

MUSHROOM-BEEF SPAGHETTI SAUCE

I got the recipe for this sauce in a recipe exchange, and wish I could credit the person who gave it to me. My children love it! I added mushrooms, but if you'd like it even chunkier, add bell pepper and other veggies, too.
—*Meg Fisher, Marietta, GA*

PREP: 20 min. • **COOK:** 6 hours
MAKES: 12 servings

- 1 lb. lean ground beef (90% lean)
- ½ lb. sliced fresh mushrooms
- 1 small onion, chopped
- 2 cans (14½ oz. each) diced tomatoes, undrained
- 1 can (12 oz.) tomato paste
- 1 can (8 oz.) tomato sauce
- 1 cup reduced-sodium beef broth
- 2 Tbsp. dried parsley flakes
- 1 Tbsp. brown sugar
- 1 tsp. dried basil
- 1 tsp. dried oregano
- 1 tsp. salt
- ¼ tsp. pepper
  Hot cooked whole wheat spaghetti
  Shredded Parmesan cheese, optional

1. In a large nonstick skillet, cook the beef, mushrooms and onion over medium heat until meat is no longer pink; drain. Transfer to a 3-qt. slow cooker.
2. Stir in the tomatoes, tomato paste, tomato sauce, broth, parsley, brown sugar, basil, oregano, salt and pepper. Cover and cook on low for 6-8 hours. Serve with spaghetti. Sprinkle with cheese if desired.
½ cup: 115 cal., 3g fat (1g sat. fat), 19mg chol., 493mg sod., 12g carb. (8g sugars, 3g fiber), 10g pro. **Diabetic exchanges:** 2 vegetable, 1 lean meat.

BEEF & BARLEY

I like to serve this to company. I'm not sure where the recipe originated for this country-style dish, but I've had it for years and rely on it when I'm hosting a meal for a group.
—*Linda Ronk, Melbourne, FL*

PREP: 15 min. • **COOK:** 4 hours
MAKES: 8 servings

- 2 lbs. ground beef
- 2 Tbsp. butter
- 1 cup quick-cooking barley
- 1 can (15 oz.) diced carrots, undrained
- 1 can (14½ oz.) diced tomatoes, undrained
- 1 can (10¾ oz.) condensed tomato soup, undiluted
- 2 celery ribs, finely chopped
- ½ cup water
- 1½ to 2 tsp. salt
- ½ tsp. pepper
- ½ tsp. chili powder
- 1 tsp. Worcestershire sauce
- 1 bay leaf
- 1 cup soft bread crumbs
- 1 cup shredded cheddar cheese
  Minced fresh parsley, optional

1. In a large skillet, cook beef over medium heat until no longer pink, 10-12 minutes; crumble beef; drain. Add to a 3-qt. slow cooker. In same skillet, melt butter over medium-high heat. Add barley, cook and stir until lightly browned, 3-5 minutes. Add to slow cooker. Stir in next 10 ingredients. Sprinkle with bread crumbs and cheese.
2. Cover and cook on high until heated through and barley is tender, about 4 hours. Discard the bay leaf before serving. Garnish with fresh parsley if desired.
1 cup: 409 cal., 18g fat (9g sat. fat), 78mg chol., 990mg sod., 34g carb. (9g sugars, 7g fiber), 28g pro.

DID YOU KNOW?
There is research that suggests that choosing a diet high in barley can lead to lower cholesterol levels. It can also help to reduce the risk of Type 2 diabetes as well as certain cardiovascular problems.

SLOW-COOKED PIZZAIOLA MEAT LOAF

I like to add Italian Castelvetrano olives to my meat loaf mixture. They're bright green, very mild and fruity, and available in the deli section of the grocery store.
—*Ann Sheehy, Lawrence, MA*

PREP: 35 min. • **COOK:** 4 hours
MAKES: 8 servings

- 2 Tbsp. canola oil
- 1 large onion, chopped
- 1 cup chopped sweet red, yellow or green peppers
- 1½ cups sliced fresh mushrooms
- 2 garlic cloves, minced
- 2 large eggs, lightly beaten
- 1 cup seasoned bread crumbs
- 1 cup shredded Italian cheese blend
- 1 tsp. Italian seasoning
- ½ tsp. salt
- 1¼ lbs. ground turkey
- 1 lb. meat loaf mix (equal parts ground beef, pork and veal)
  Optional: Pizza sauce and shredded Parmesan cheese

1. Cut three 25x3-in. strips of heavy-duty foil; crisscross them so they resemble the spokes of a wheel. Place strips on bottom and up sides of a 5- or 6-qt. slow cooker. Coat the strips with cooking spray.
2. In a large skillet, heat oil over medium-high heat. Add onion, peppers and mushrooms; cook and stir until tender, 4-6 minutes. Add garlic; cook 1 minute longer. Remove from the heat and cool slightly.
3. In a large bowl, combine the eggs, bread crumbs, cheese, Italian seasoning, salt and reserved cooked vegetables. Add turkey and meat loaf mix and mix lightly but thoroughly. Shape into a round loaf; transfer to slow cooker. Cook, covered, on low until a thermometer reads at least 160°, 4-5 hours.
4. Using the foil strips as handles, remove the meat loaf to a platter. If desired, serve with pizza sauce and Parmesan.
1 piece: 356 cal., 19g fat (6g sat. fat), 139mg chol., 551mg sod., 14g carb. (3g sugars, 1g fiber), 31g pro.

ZESTY GOULASH

Ground cumin, chili powder and a can of Mexican diced tomatoes jazz up my goulash recipe. Even the elbow macaroni is prepared in the slow cooker.
—*Melissa Polk, West Lafayette, IN*

PREP: 25 min. • **COOK:** 5½ hours
MAKES: 12 servings

- 1 lb. lean ground beef (90% lean)
- 4 cans (14½ oz. each) Mexican diced tomatoes, undrained
- 2 cans (16 oz. each) kidney beans, rinsed and drained
- 2 cups water
- 1 medium onion, chopped
- 1 medium green pepper, chopped
- ¼ cup red wine vinegar
- 2 Tbsp. chili powder
- 1 Tbsp. Worcestershire sauce
- 2 tsp. beef bouillon granules
- 1 tsp. dried basil
- 1 tsp. dried parsley flakes
- 1 tsp. ground cumin
- ¼ tsp. pepper
- 2 cups uncooked elbow macaroni

1. In a large skillet, cook beef over medium heat until no longer pink; crumble beef; drain. Transfer to a 5-qt. slow cooker. Stir in the tomatoes, beans, water, onion, green pepper, vinegar, chili powder, Worcestershire sauce, bouillon and seasonings.
2. Cover and cook on low for 5-6 hours or until heated through.
3. Stir in macaroni; cover and cook 30 minutes longer or until macaroni is tender.
1 cup: 222 cal., 5g fat (2g sat. fat), 23mg chol., 585mg sod., 30g carb. (7g sugars, 6g fiber), 15g pro. **Diabetic exchanges:** 2 lean meat, 1½ starch, 1 vegetable.

ANN SHEEHY
Lawrence, MA

ZIPPY SPAGHETTI SAUCE

This thick and hearty sauce goes a long way to satisfy my hungry family. They enjoy leftovers ladled over thick slices of grilled garlic bread. To make sure I have the ingredients on hand, I keep a bag of chopped green pepper in my freezer and minced garlic in my fridge—always!
—*Elaine Priest, Dover, PA*

PREP: 20 min. • **COOK:** 6 hours • **MAKES:** 3 qt.

- 2 lbs. ground beef
- 1 cup chopped onion
- ½ cup chopped green pepper
- 2 cans (15 oz. each) tomato sauce
- 1 can (28 oz.) diced tomatoes, undrained
- 1 can (12 oz.) tomato paste
- ½ lb. sliced fresh mushrooms
- 1 cup grated Parmesan cheese
- ½ to ¾ cup dry red wine or beef broth
- ½ cup sliced pimiento-stuffed olives
- ¼ cup dried parsley flakes
- 1 to 2 Tbsp. dried oregano
- 2 tsp. Italian seasoning
- 2 tsp. minced garlic
- 1 tsp. salt
- 1 tsp. pepper
  Hot cooked spaghetti

1. In a large skillet, cook the beef, onion and green pepper over medium heat until meat is no longer pink; crumble meat; drain.
2. Transfer to a 5-qt. slow cooker. Stir in the tomato sauce, tomatoes, paste, mushrooms, cheese, wine, olives, parsley, oregano, Italian seasoning, garlic, salt and pepper. Cover and cook on low for 6-8 hours. Serve with spaghetti.
1 cup: 255 cal., 13g fat (4g sat. fat), 52mg chol., 930mg sod., 16g carb. (7g sugars, 4g fiber), 20g pro.

CABBAGE ROLL STEW

A head of cabbage seems like it never ends. Here's a delicious way to use it up. My husband is this stew's biggest fan.
—*Pamela Kennemer, Sand Springs, OK*

PREP: 25 min. • **COOK:** 5 hours
MAKES: 8 servings (3 qt.)

- 2 cans (14½ oz. each) petite diced tomatoes, drained
- 1 can (14½ oz.) reduced-sodium beef broth
- 1 can (8 oz.) tomato sauce
- 1 Tbsp. cider vinegar
- 1 Tbsp. Worcestershire sauce
- 1 tsp. garlic powder
- 1 tsp. Cajun seasoning
- ½ tsp. salt
- ½ tsp. pepper
- 1 medium head cabbage (about 2 lbs.), cut into 1½-in. pieces
- 1½ lbs. ground beef
- ½ lb. bulk Italian sausage
- 1 medium onion, chopped
- 3 garlic cloves, minced
  Optional: Hot cooked rice and chopped fresh parsley

1. Mix first 9 ingredients; set aside. Place the cabbage in a 5- or 6-qt. slow cooker.
2. In a large skillet, cook beef and sausage with onion and garlic over medium-high heat until no longer pink, 7-9 minutes; crumble meat; drain. Spoon over the cabbage; top with the tomato mixture.
3. Cook, covered, on low until the cabbage is tender and flavors are blended, 5-6 hours. If desired, serve with cooked rice and sprinkle with parsley.
Freeze option: Freeze cooled meat mixture in freezer containers. To use, partially thaw in refrigerator overnight. Heat through in a saucepan, stirring occasionally.
1½ cups cabbage mixture: 195 cal., 11g fat (4g sat. fat), 46mg chol., 564mg sod., 11g carb. (6g sugars, 4g fiber), 14g pro.

DID YOU KNOW?
Cabbage is a low-calorie food that really bulks up meals such as this stew. After all, a generous 1½ cups of the stew is less than 200 calories.

Ground Beef

AIR FRYER & INSTANT POT®

When you couple ground beef with the these timesaving kitchen appliances, you're sure to set hot, hearty meals on the table—even on your busiest nights!

PRESSURE-COOKER FIVE-BEAN CHILI

A hearty bowl of chili always reminds me of my mom's cooking. While I love this classic recipe, I wanted a faster way to cook the dried beans. I decided to make it in my pressure cooker. Now we get to enjoy the same from-scratch recipe, but in a fraction of the time.
—*Courtney Stultz, Weir, KS*

- -

PREP: 20 min. • **COOK:** 40 min.
MAKES: 12 servings (3 qt.)

- 2   lbs. ground beef
- 1   carton (32 oz.) beef broth
- 1   can (28 oz.) diced tomatoes, undrained
- 1   can (15 oz.) tomato sauce
- 1   small onion, chopped
- ½   cup each dried black beans, kidney beans, great northern beans, pinto beans and cannellini beans
- 1   Tbsp. paprika
- 2   tsp. chili powder
- 2   garlic cloves, minced
- 1   tsp. dried oregano
- 1   tsp. ground cinnamon
- 1   tsp. baking cocoa
- ½   tsp. sea salt
- ½   tsp. ground cumin
- ½   tsp. cayenne pepper
    Optional: Shredded cheddar cheese and sliced jalapeno

1. Select saute or browning setting on a 6-qt. electric pressure cooker; adjust for medium heat. Cook half the beef until no longer pink, 7-9 minutes; crumble meat. Remove the beef and drain the liquid from the pressure cooker. Repeat with the remaining ground beef. Press cancel.
2. Return all beef to the pan. Stir in the next 14 ingredients. Lock lid; close pressure-release valve. Adjust to pressure-cook on high for 40 minutes.
3. Quick-release pressure. Stir before serving. If desired, serve with cheese and jalapenos.
1 cup: 308 cal., 10g fat (3g sat. fat), 47mg chol., 704mg sod., 31g carb. (4g sugars, 9g fiber), 24g pro. **Diabetic exchanges:** 2 starch, 2 medium-fat meat.

AIR-FRYER QUICK TATER TOTS BAKE

I like to prepare this dish when I'm short on time. You can also make the bake a little fancier by assembling it in individual ramekins instead of one large baking dish.
—*Jean Ferguson, Elverta, CA*

PREP: 15 min. • **COOK:** 30 min.
MAKES: 4 servings

- ¾ to 1 lb. ground beef or turkey
- 1 small onion, chopped
  Salt and pepper to taste
- 1 pkg. (16 oz.) frozen Tater Tots
- 1 can (10¾ oz.) condensed cream of mushroom soup, undiluted
- ⅔ cup 2% milk or water
- 1 cup shredded cheddar cheese

1. Preheat air fryer to 350°. In a large skillet, cook beef and onion over medium heat until meat is no longer pink; crumble beef; drain. Season with salt and pepper.
2. Transfer to a greased 2-qt. baking dish that will fit in the air-fryer basket. Top with Tater Tots. Combine soup and milk; pour over the potatoes. Sprinkle with cheese. Place the baking dish on tray in air-fryer basket. Cook, uncovered 30-40 minutes or until heated through.
1½ cups: 570 cal., 35g fat (12g sat. fat), 87mg chol., 1357mg sod., 37g carb. (5g sugars, 4g fiber), 26g pro.

STUFFED PEPPERS IN THE PRESSURE COOKER

Traditional stuffed peppers get a southwestern twist in this easy recipe. The filling also makes a delicious meat loaf that we even like when it's served cold in a sandwich with Mexican-blend or cheddar cheese, mayo and salsa.
—*Traci Wynne, Denver, PA*

PREP: 20 min. • **COOK:** 15 min. + releasing
MAKES: 2 servings

- 2 medium sweet red, orange and/or yellow peppers
- 1 large egg, beaten
- ½ cup crushed tortilla chips
- ½ cup salsa
- ¼ cup finely chopped onion
- 2 Tbsp. minced fresh cilantro
- ½ tsp. ground cumin
- ½ tsp. seeded and finely chopped red chili pepper
- ¼ tsp. minced garlic
- ¼ lb. lean ground beef (90% lean)
- ¼ cup shredded Mexican cheese blend
  Sour cream

1. Place trivet insert and 1 cup water in a 3- or 6-qt. electric pressure cooker.
2. Cut and discard tops from peppers; remove seeds. In a small bowl, combine egg, chips, salsa, onion, cilantro, cumin, chili pepper and garlic. Crumble beef over mixture and mix lightly but thoroughly; spoon into peppers. Set peppers on trivet.
3. Lock lid; close pressure-release valve. Adjust to pressure-cook on high for 12 minutes. Allow pressure to release naturally. Sprinkle peppers with cheese. Serve with sour cream and, if desired, additional salsa.
1 stuffed pepper: 319 cal., 15g fat (5g sat. fat), 141mg chol., 458mg sod., 25g carb. (8g sugars, 4g fiber), 20g pro. **Diabetic exchanges:** 3 medium-fat meat, 1 starch, 1 vegetable.

> **TEST KITCHEN TIP**
> Keep your pressure cooker's little condensation cup clean with a quick wipedown every now and then. Most are safe to pop in the dishwasher as well.

TAMI KUEHL
Loup City, NE

SWEET & SPICY AIR-FRYER MEATBALLS

I am always on a quest for speedy meatballs that pack a sweet and savory punch. These are a snap to pull together and can be served over rice or buttered noodles.
—Tami Kuehl, Loup City, NE

- -

PREP: 30 min. • **COOK:** 15 min./batch
MAKES: 3 dozen meatballs (about 1 cup sauce)

⅔ cup quick-cooking oats
½ cup crushed Ritz crackers
2 large eggs, lightly beaten
1 can (5 oz.) evaporated milk
1 Tbsp. dried minced onion
1 tsp. salt
1 tsp. garlic powder
1 tsp. ground cumin
1 tsp. honey
½ tsp. pepper
2 lbs. lean ground beef (90% lean)

SAUCE
⅓ cup packed brown sugar
⅓ cup honey
⅓ cup orange marmalade
2 Tbsp. cornstarch
2 Tbsp. soy sauce
1 to 2 Tbsp. Louisiana-style hot sauce
1 Tbsp. Worcestershire sauce

1. Preheat air fryer to 380°. In a large bowl, combine the first 10 ingredients. Add beef; mix lightly but thoroughly. Shape into 1½-in. balls.
2. In batches, arrange meatballs in a single layer on greased tray in air-fryer basket. Cook until they are lightly browned and cooked through, 12-15 minutes.
3. In a small saucepan, combine the sauce ingredients. Cook and stir over medium heat until thickened. Serve with the meatballs.
1 meatball with 1½ tsp. sauce: 90 cal., 3g fat (1g sat. fat), 27mg chol., 170mg sod., 10g carb. (7g sugars, 0 fiber), 6g pro.

INSTANT POT CHILI CON CARNE

Although multicookers can't replace every tool in the kitchen, they sure are coming close. Chili con carne is a classic all-time favorite dish to prepare in them. This cooks up fast but it tastes as if it simmered all day!
—Taste of Home *Test Kitchen*

- -

TAKES: 30 min. • **MAKES:** 7 cups

1 can (16 oz.) pinto beans, rinsed and drained
1 can (14½ oz.) Mexican diced tomatoes, undrained
1 can (8 oz.) tomato sauce
1 medium green pepper, chopped
1 medium onion, chopped
1 cup beef broth
1 jalapeno pepper, seeded and minced
2 Tbsp. chili powder
¼ tsp. salt
¼ tsp. pepper
1½ lbs. lean ground beef (90% lean)
Optional: Sour cream and sliced jalapeno

1. Combine the first 10 ingredients in a 6-qt. electric pressure cooker. Crumble beef over top; stir to combine. Lock lid; close pressure-release valve. Adjust to pressure-cook on high for 5 minutes.
2. Allow pressure to naturally release for 10 minutes, then quick-release any remaining pressure. Stir chili. If desired, serve with sour cream and additional jalapenos.
1 cup: 248 cal., 9g fat (3g sat. fat), 61mg chol., 687mg sod., 18g carb. (5g sugars, 5g fiber), 24g pro. **Diabetic exchanges:** 3 lean meat, 1 starch.

MINI CHIMICHANGAS FROM THE AIR FRYER

My family raves over these Mexican-inspired bites. Infused with green chile, the beefy snacks are guaranteed to liven up the party!
—*Kathy Rogers, Hudson, OH*

- -

PREP: 1 hour • **COOK:** 10 min./batch
MAKES: 14 servings

- 1 lb. ground beef
- 1 medium onion, chopped
- 1 envelope taco seasoning
- ¾ cup water
- 3 cups shredded Monterey Jack cheese
- 1 cup sour cream
- 1 can (4 oz.) chopped green chiles, drained
- 14 egg roll wrappers
- 1 large egg white, lightly beaten
  Cooking spray
  Salsa

1. In a large skillet, cook beef and onion over medium heat until the meat is no longer pink; crumble meat; drain. Stir in taco seasoning and water. Bring to a boil. Reduce heat; simmer, uncovered, for 5 minutes, stirring occasionally. Remove from heat; cool slightly.

2. Preheat air fryer to 375°. In a large bowl, combine cheese, sour cream and chiles. Stir in beef mixture. Place an egg roll wrapper on work surface with a corner facing you. Place ⅓ cup filling in center. Fold bottom third of wrapper over filling; fold in sides.

3. Brush top point with egg white; roll up to seal. Repeat with remaining wrappers and filling. (Keep the remaining egg roll wrappers covered with waxed paper to keep them from drying out.)

4. In batches, place chimichangas in a single layer on greased tray in air-fryer basket; spritz with cooking spray. Cook until golden brown, 3-4 minutes on each side. Serve warm with salsa and additional sour cream.

1 chimichanga: 294 cal., 15g fat (8g sat. fat), 48mg chol., 618mg sod., 23g carb. (1g sugars, 1g fiber), 16g pro.

PRESSURE-COOKER GROUND BEEF STROGANOFF

My mother gave me this recipe 40 years ago. It's a wonderfully tasty dish that's perfect for a pressure cooker.
—*Sue Mims, Macclenny, FL*

PREP: 25 min. • **COOK:** 10 min.
MAKES: 8 servings

2	lbs. ground beef
1½	tsp. salt
1	tsp. pepper
1	Tbsp. butter
½	lb. fresh mushrooms, sliced
2	medium onions, chopped
2	garlic cloves, minced
2	Tbsp. tomato paste
1	can (10½ oz.) condensed beef consomme, undiluted
⅓	cup all-purpose flour
⅓	cup water
1½	cups sour cream
	Optional: Hot cooked noodles and minced fresh parsley

1. Select saute setting on a 6-qt. electric pressure cooker and adjust for medium heat. Add half of the ground beef, salt and pepper. Cook and stir until no longer pink, 6-8 minutes; crumble beef. Remove meat; drain any liquid from pressure cooker. Repeat with remaining ground beef, salt and pepper.
2. Add the butter, mushrooms and onions to pressure cooker; saute until onions are tender and mushrooms have released their liquid and are beginning to brown, 6-8 minutes. Add the garlic; cook 1 minute longer. Return meat to cooker; add tomato paste and consomme. Press cancel.
3. Lock lid; close the pressure-release valve. Adjust to pressure-cook on high for 5 minutes. Quick-release pressure.
4. Select saute setting and adjust for low heat. In a small bowl, whisk together flour and water. Pour over meat mixture; stir to combine. Cook and stir until thickened. Stir in sour cream; cook until heated through. If desired, serve with noodles and minced parsley.
1 serving: 356 cal., 24g fat (11g sat. fat), 84mg chol., 780mg sod., 10g carb. (4g sugars, 1g fiber), 25g pro.

AIR-FRIED CHEESEBURGER ONION RINGS

This new take on burgers will have your family begging for seconds. Serve the cheeseburger onion rings with spicy ketchup or your favorite dipping sauce.
—*Taste of Home Test Kitchen*

PREP: 25 min. • **COOK:** 15 min./batch
MAKES: 8 servings

1	lb. lean ground beef (90% lean)
⅓	cup ketchup
2	Tbsp. prepared mustard
½	tsp. salt
1	large onion
4	oz. cheddar cheese, cut into 8 squares
¾	cup all-purpose flour
2	tsp. garlic powder
2	large eggs, lightly beaten
1½	cups panko bread crumbs
	Cooking spray
	Spicy ketchup, optional

1. Preheat air fryer to 335°. In a small bowl, combine beef, ketchup, mustard and salt, mixing lightly but thoroughly. Cut onion into ½-in. slices; separate into rings. Fill 8 slices with half of the beef mixture (save remaining onion rings for another use). Top each with a square of cheese and remaining beef mixture.
2. In a shallow bowl, mix flour and garlic powder. Place eggs and breadcrumbs in separate shallow bowls. Dip filled onion rings in flour to coat both sides; shake off excess. Dip in egg, then in bread crumbs, patting to help coating adhere.
3. In batches, place onion rings in a single layer on greased tray in air-fryer basket; spritz with cooking spray. Cook until golden brown and a thermometer inserted into beef reads 160°, 12-15 minutes. If desired, serve rings with spicy ketchup.
1 onion ring: 258 cal., 11g fat (5g sat. fat), 96mg chol., 489mg sod., 19g carb. (4g sugars, 1g fiber), 19g pro.

AIR-FRYER BEEFY SWISS BUNDLES

Kids and adults alike will devour these unusual—yet comforting—pockets. With creamy mashed potatoes, gooey cheese and flavorful seasonings, what's not to love?
—Taste of Home *Test Kitchen*

PREP: 20 min. • **COOK:** 10 min./batch
MAKES: 4 servings

- 1 lb. ground beef
- 1½ cups sliced fresh mushrooms
- ½ cup chopped onion
- 1½ tsp. minced garlic
- 4 tsp. Worcestershire sauce
- ¾ tsp. dried rosemary, crushed
- ¾ tsp. paprika
- ½ tsp. salt
- ¼ tsp. pepper
- 1 sheet frozen puff pastry, thawed
- ⅔ cup refrigerated mashed potatoes
- 1 cup shredded Swiss cheese
- 1 large egg
- 2 Tbsp. water

1. Preheat air fryer to 375°. In a large skillet, cook beef, mushrooms and onion over medium heat until meat is no longer pink and vegetables are tender, 8-10 minutes; crumble meat. Add garlic; cook 1 minute longer. Drain. Stir in Worcestershire sauce and seasonings. Remove from heat; set aside.
2. On a lightly floured surface, roll puff pastry into a 15x13-in. rectangle. Cut into four 7½x6½-in. rectangles. Place about 2 Tbsp. potatoes on each rectangle; spread to within 1 in. of the edges. Top each with ¾ cup beef mixture; sprinkle with ¼ cup cheese.
3. Beat egg and water; brush wash over pastry edges. Bring opposite corners of pastry over each bundle; pinch seams to seal. Brush with remaining egg mixture. In batches, place pastries in a single layer on tray in air-fryer basket; cook until bundles are golden brown, 10-12 minutes.

Freeze option: Freeze unbaked pastries on a parchment-lined baking sheet until firm. Transfer to an airtight container; return to freezer. To use, cook frozen pastries as directed until golden brown and heated through, increasing time to 15-20 minutes.
1 bundle: 706 cal., 42g fat (15g sat. fat), 147mg chol., 809mg sod., 44g carb. (2g sugars, 6g fiber), 35g pro.

PRESSURE-COOKER BEEFY CABBAGE BEAN STEW

While we were on a small-group quilting retreat, one of my friends made this wonderful recipe for dinner. We all loved it and have since passed the recipe around for others to enjoy. Now I'm passing it on to you.
—Melissa Glancy, La Grange, KY

PREP: 30 min. • **COOK:** 5 min.
MAKES: 6 servings

- ½ lb. lean ground beef (90% lean)
- 3 cups shredded cabbage or angel hair coleslaw mix
- 1 can (16 oz.) red beans, rinsed and drained
- 1 can (14½ oz.) diced tomatoes, undrained
- 1 can (8 oz.) tomato sauce
- ¾ cup water
- ¾ cup salsa or picante sauce
- 1 medium green pepper, chopped
- 1 small onion, chopped
- 3 garlic cloves, minced
- 1 tsp. ground cumin
- ½ tsp. pepper

1. Select saute or browning setting on a 6-qt. electric pressure cooker; adjust for medium heat. Cook the beef until no longer pink, 6-8 minutes, breaking into crumbles; drain. Press cancel. Return beef to pressure cooker.
2. Stir in the remaining ingredients. Lock lid; close pressure-release valve. Adjust to pressure-cook on high for 3 minutes. Quick-release pressure.

Freeze option: Freeze cooled stew in freezer containers. To use, partially thaw in refrigerator overnight. Heat through in a saucepan, stirring occasionally; add a little water if necessary.
1 cup: 177 cal., 4g fat (1g sat. fat), 24mg chol., 591mg sod., 23g carb. (5g sugars, 7g fiber), 13g pro. **Diabetic exchanges:** 2 lean meat, 1 starch, 1 vegetable.

AIR-FRYER STUFFED MEAT LOAF SLICES

This is a family favorite requested for special occasions. We received the recipe from a fellow faculty member when my husband and I were in our first years of teaching.
—Judy Knaupp, Rickreall, OR

- -

PREP: 30 min. + chilling
COOK: 15 min./batch
MAKES: 6 servings

- 2 cups mashed potatoes (with added milk and butter)
- 2 hard-boiled large eggs, chopped
- ½ cup Miracle Whip
- ⅓ cup grated Parmesan cheese
- ¼ cup chopped celery
- 1 green onion, chopped
- ¼ tsp. salt
- ¼ tsp. ground mustard
- ¼ tsp. pepper

MEAT LOAF
- 1 large egg, lightly beaten
- ¼ cup dry bread crumbs
- 1 tsp. salt
- 1¼ lbs. ground beef

SAUCE
- ½ cup Miracle Whip
- ¼ cup 2% milk
- 1 green onion, sliced

1. For filling, mix first 9 ingredients. In a large bowl, combine beaten egg, bread crumbs and salt. Add beef; mix lightly but thoroughly. On a large piece of heavy-duty foil, pat mixture into a 14x8-in. rectangle. Spread filling over top to within 1 in. of the edges. Roll up jelly-roll style, starting with a short side, removing foil as you roll. Seal seam and ends; place on a large plate. Refrigerate, covered, overnight.
2. Preheat air fryer to 325°. Cut the roll into 6 slices. In batches, place slices on greased tray in the air-fryer basket with cut sides up. Cook until a thermometer reads at least 160°, 12-15 minutes. Mix sauce ingredients; serve with meat loaf.

1 slice with 4 tsp. sauce: 439 cal., 28g fat (9g sat. fat), 167mg chol., 1187mg sod., 20g carb. (5g sugars, 1g fiber), 24g pro.

❄ 🍎 🥫

PRESSURE-COOKER SPICY BEEF VEGETABLE STEW

This zesty ground beef and vegetable soup is flavorful and comes together so quickly. It makes a complete meal when served with cornbread, sourdough or French bread—if you can squeak in a few more calories.
—Lynnette Davis, Tullahoma, TN

- -

PREP: 10 min. • **COOK:** 5 min. + releasing
MAKES: 8 servings (3 qt.)

- 1 lb. lean ground beef (90% lean)
- 3½ cups water
- 1 jar (24 oz.) meatless pasta sauce
- 1 pkg. (16 oz.) frozen mixed vegetables
- 1 can (10 oz.) diced tomatoes and green chiles, undrained
- 1 cup chopped onion
- 1 cup sliced celery
- 1 tsp. beef bouillon granules
- 1 tsp. pepper

Select saute setting on 6-qt. electric pressure cooker; adjust for medium heat. Cook beef until no longer pink, 6-8 minutes; crumble beef; drain. Press cancel. Stir in remaining ingredients. Lock lid; close pressure-release valve. Adjust to pressure-cook on high for 5 minutes. Allow pressure to release naturally.
Freeze option: Freeze cooled stew in freezer containers. To use, partially thaw stew in refrigerator overnight. Heat through in a saucepan, stirring occasionally; add water if necessary.
1½ cups: 177 cal., 5g fat (2g sat. fat), 35mg chol., 675mg sod., 19g carb. (8g sugars, 5g fiber), 15g pro. **Diabetic exchanges:** 2 lean meat, 1 starch.

PRESSURE-COOKER BEEF & VEGGIE SLOPPY JOES

Because I'm always looking for ways to serve my family healthy and delicious food, I started experimenting with my go-to veggies and ground beef. I came up with this favorite that my kids actually request!
—Megan Niebuhr, Yakima, WA

- -

PREP: 35 min. • **COOK:** 5 min.
MAKES: 10 servings

2	lbs. lean ground beef (90% lean)
4	medium carrots, shredded
1	medium yellow summer squash, shredded
1	medium zucchini, shredded
1	medium sweet red pepper, finely chopped
2	medium tomatoes, seeded and chopped
1	small red onion, finely chopped
½	cup ketchup
¼	cup water
3	Tbsp. minced fresh basil or 3 tsp. dried basil
2	Tbsp. cider vinegar
2	garlic cloves, minced
½	tsp. salt
½	tsp. pepper
3	Tbsp. molasses
10	whole wheat hamburger buns, split

1. Select saute or browning setting on a 6-qt. electric pressure cooker; adjust for medium heat. Cook beef until no longer pink, 8-10 minutes, breaking into crumbles; drain. Return to pressure cooker. Press cancel. Add carrots, summer squash, zucchini, red pepper, tomatoes, onion, ketchup, water, basil, vinegar, garlic, salt and pepper (do not stir).
2. Lock lid; close pressure-release valve. Adjust to pressure-cook on high for 5 minutes.
3. Quick-release pressure. Stir in molasses. Using a slotted spoon, serve beef mixture on buns.

Freeze option: Freeze cooled meat mixture and juices in freezer containers. To use, partially thaw in refrigerator overnight. Heat through in a saucepan, stirring occasionally; add a little water if necessary.

1 sandwich: 316 cal., 10g fat (3g sat. fat), 57mg chol., 566mg sod., 36g carb. (15g sugars, 5g fiber), 22g pro. **Diabetic exchanges:** 3 lean meat, 2.500 starch.

BEEF WELLINGTON AIR-FRIED WONTONS

These tasty appetizers scale down classic beef Wellington to an ideal party size. They feel fancy and fun!
—*Dianne Phillips, Tallapoosa, GA*

PREP: 35 min. • **COOK:** 10 min./batch
MAKES: 3½ dozen

- ½ lb. lean ground beef (90% lean)
- 1 Tbsp. butter
- 1 Tbsp. olive oil
- 2 garlic cloves, minced
- 1½ tsp. chopped shallot
- 1 cup each chopped fresh shiitake, baby portobello and white mushrooms
- ¼ cup dry red wine
- 1 Tbsp. minced fresh parsley
- ½ tsp. salt
- ¼ tsp. pepper
- 1 pkg. (12 oz.) wonton wrappers
- 1 large egg
- 1 Tbsp. water
   Cooking spray

1. Preheat air fryer to 325°. In a small skillet, cook beef over medium heat until no longer pink, 4-5 minutes; crumble meat. Transfer to a large bowl. In the same skillet, heat butter and olive oil over medium-high heat. Add the garlic and shallot; cook 1 minute. Stir in the mushrooms and wine. Cook until mushrooms are tender, 8-10 minutes; add to beef. Stir in parsley, salt and pepper.
2. Place about 2 tsp. filling in the center of each wonton wrapper. Combine egg and water. Moisten wonton edges with the egg mixture; fold opposite corners over filling and press to seal.
3. In batches, arrange wontons in a single layer on greased tray in air-fryer basket; spritz with cooking spray. Cook until lightly browned, 4-5 minutes. Turn; spritz with cooking spray. Cook until wontons are golden brown and crisp, 4-5 minutes longer. Serve warm.
Freeze option: Cover and freeze unbaked wontons on parchment-lined baking sheets until firm. Transfer to freezer containers; return to the freezer. To use, cook wontons as directed.
1 wonton: 42 cal., 1g fat (0 sat. fat), 9mg chol., 82mg sod., 5g carb. (0 sugars, 0 fiber), 2g pro.

AIR-FRIED HERB & CHEESE-STUFFED BURGERS

Tired of the same old ground beef burgers? These quick air-fryer hamburgers, with their creamy cheese filling, are sure to wake up your taste buds.
—*Sherri Cox, Lucasville, OH*

PREP: 20 min. • **COOK:** 15 min./batch
MAKES: 4 servings

- 2 green onions, thinly sliced
- 2 Tbsp. minced fresh parsley
- 4 tsp. Dijon mustard, divided
- 3 Tbsp. dry bread crumbs
- 2 Tbsp. ketchup
- ½ tsp. salt
- ½ tsp. dried rosemary, crushed
- ¼ tsp. dried sage leaves
- 1 lb. lean ground beef (90% lean)
- 2 oz. cheddar cheese, sliced
- 4 hamburger buns, split
   Optional: Lettuce leaves, sliced tomato, mayonnaise and additional ketchup

1. Preheat air fryer to 375°. In a small bowl, combine the green onions, parsley and 2 tsp. mustard. In another bowl, mix bread crumbs, ketchup, seasonings and the remaining 2 tsp. mustard. Add beef to bread crumb mixture; mix lightly but thoroughly.
2. Shape mixture into 8 thin patties. Place sliced cheese in center of 4 patties; spoon green onion mixture over cheese. Top with remaining patties, pressing edges together firmly, taking care to seal completely.
3. In batches, place burgers in a single layer on tray in air-fryer basket. Cook 8 minutes. Flip; cook until a thermometer inserted in burger reads 160°, 6-8 minutes longer. Serve burgers on buns, with toppings af desired.
1 burger: 369 cal., 14g fat (6g sat. fat), 79mg chol., 850mg sod., 29g carb. (6g sugars, 1g fiber), 29g pro.

PRESSURE-COOKED SPANISH CHILI

I like to prepare this Spanish chili on weekends so I have an instant weeknight dinner on hand. I've come to love my pressure cooker because it makes mealtime a breeze.
—*Lynn Faria, Southington, CT*

- -

TAKES: 25 min. • **MAKES:** 8 servings

1	lb. ground beef
1	medium onion, chopped
1	medium sweet red pepper, chopped
1	medium green pepper, chopped
1	can (15 oz.) tomato sauce
1	can (14½ oz.) diced tomatoes, undrained
1	tsp. packed brown sugar
2	tsp. chili powder
1	envelope Goya Sazon with coriander and annatto (1 tsp.)
1	tsp. baking cocoa
½	tsp. pepper
¼	tsp. salt
¼	tsp. cayenne pepper
1	can (16 oz.) chili beans, undrained
2	tsp. red wine vinegar
	Optional: Sour cream and green onions

1. Select saute or browning setting on a 6-qt. electric pressure cooker; adjust for medium heat. Cook the beef until no longer pink, 5-7 minutes; crumble meat; drain. Press cancel. Stir in onion, sweet red pepper, green pepper, tomato sauce, diced tomatoes, brown sugar, chili powder, Sazon, cocoa, pepper, salt and cayenne. Lock lid; close pressure-release valve. Adjust to pressure-cook on high for 8 minutes. Let pressure release naturally.
2. Select saute setting and adjust for low heat. Stir in beans and vinegar. Simmer, stirring occasionally, until heated through and chili reaches desired consistency. If desired, serve with optional toppings.
1 cup: 194 cal., 8g fat (3g sat. fat), 35mg chol., 699mg sod., 20g carb. (6g sugars, 6g fiber), 15g pro. **Diabetic exchanges:** 2 medium-fat meat, 1 starch.

AIR-FRYER TACO TWISTS

Why serve tacos only in ordinary flour or corn tortillas? For a mouthwatering change of pace, bake the taco beef in flaky, golden crescent rolls. My family enjoys these for a warm lunch or light dinner.
—*Carla Kreider, Quarryville, PA*

- -

PREP: 15 min. • **COOK:** 20 min.
MAKES: 4 servings

- ⅓ **lb. ground beef**
- 1 **large onion, chopped**
- ⅔ **cup shredded cheddar cheese**
- ⅓ **cup salsa**
- 3 **Tbsp. canned chopped green chiles**
- ¼ **tsp. garlic powder**
- ¼ **tsp. hot pepper sauce**
- ⅛ **tsp. salt**
- ⅛ **tsp. ground cumin**
- 1 **tube (8 oz.) refrigerated crescent rolls**
  Optional: Shredded lettuce, sliced ripe olives, chopped tomatoes and sliced seeded jalapeno pepper

1. Preheat air fryer to 300°. In a large skillet, cook beef and onion over medium heat until meat is no longer pink; crumble meat; drain. Stir in cheese, salsa, chiles, garlic powder, hot pepper sauce, salt and cumin.

2. Unroll crescent roll dough and separate into 4 rectangles; press perforations to seal. Place ½ cup meat mixture in the center of each rectangle. Bring 4 corners to the center and twist; pinch to seal. In batches, place in a single layer on greased tray in air-fryer basket. Cook until golden brown, 18-22 minutes. If desired, serve with toppings of your choice.

1 taco twist: 371 cal., 21g fat (5g sat. fat), 42mg chol., 752mg sod., 30g carb. (8g sugars, 1g fiber), 16g pro.

TEST KITCHEN TIP
It's important to air-fry items such as these twists in a single layer to allow enough air circulation to take place. This results in even cooking and crispy foods.

TACO PASTA FROM THE PRESSURE COOKER

This dish is a welcome change from the usual Taco Tuesday. I've taken all the flavors of tacos and created an easy pasta dish. Kids love the taste, and Mom loves how quick and easy it comes together in the Instant Pot®. To lighten things up, you can use ground turkey.
—*Christine Hadden, Whitman, MA*

- -

TAKES: 25 min. • **MAKES:** 4 servings

- 1 **lb. lean ground beef (90% lean)**
- 1 **envelope taco seasoning**
- 2 **cups beef broth**
- 1 **can (8 oz.) tomato sauce**
- 8 **oz. uncooked medium pasta shells**
- 1½ **cups shredded Mexican cheese blend**
  Optional: Sour cream, cilantro, chopped tomatoes and black olives

1. Select the saute setting on a 6-qt. electric pressure cooker and adjust for medium heat; cook beef until no longer pink, 6-8 minutes; crumble meat; drain. Add the taco seasoning; stir to combine. Add the beef broth, tomato sauce and pasta. Press cancel.

2. Lock lid; close the pressure-release valve. Adjust to pressure-cook on high for 5 minutes. Quick-release pressure. Stir; top with cheese. Let stand until cheese melts, about 1 minute. If desired, serve with toppings.

2 cups: 598 cal., 25g fat (11g sat. fat), 108mg chol., 1845mg sod., 53g carb. (3g sugars, 3g fiber), 40g pro.

AIR-FRYER KETO MEATBALLS

I have been following a keto diet for a year and a half and have lost 130 pounds. With this recipe for tasty air-fried meatballs, you won't miss the bread crumbs at all! I like to eat these saucy meatballs on their own, but they're also great over zucchini noodles.
—*Holly Balzer-Harz, Malone, NY*

PREP: 30 min. • **COOK:** 10 min.
MAKES: 4 servings

- ½ cup grated Parmesan cheese
- ½ cup shredded mozzarella cheese
- 1 large egg, lightly beaten
- 2 Tbsp. heavy whipping cream
- 1 garlic clove, minced
- 1 lb. lean ground beef (90% lean)

SAUCE
- 1 can (8 oz.) tomato sauce with basil, garlic and oregano
- 2 Tbsp. prepared pesto
- ¼ cup heavy whipping cream

1. Preheat air fryer to 350°. In a large bowl, combine the first 5 ingredients. Add beef; mix lightly but thoroughly. Shape into 1½-in. balls. Place in a single layer on greased tray in the air-fryer basket; cook until lightly browned and cooked through, 8-10 minutes.
2. Meanwhile, in a small saucepan, mix the sauce ingredients; heat through. Serve with the meatballs.
Freeze option: Freeze cooled meatballs in freezer containers. To use, partially thaw in refrigerator overnight. Preheat air fryer to 350°. Reheat until heated through, 3-5 minutes. Make sauce as directed.
4 meatballs with ⅓ cup sauce: 404 cal., 27g fat (13g sat. fat), 162mg chol., 799mg sod., 7g carb. (3g sugars, 1g fiber), 31g pro.

AIR-FRIED BACON CHEESEBURGERS

This juicy burger only takes minutes to cook in your air fryer. I enjoy topping it with crispy bacon and my special fry sauce.
—*Elisabeth Larsen, Pleasant Grove, UT*

PREP: 25 min. • **COOK:** 10 min.
MAKES: 4 servings

- 1 tsp. Worcestershire sauce
- 1 garlic clove, minced
- ½ tsp. seasoned salt
- ¼ tsp. pepper
- 1 lb. ground beef
- 4 slices sharp cheddar cheese
- ¼ cup mayonnaise
- 2 Tbsp. ketchup
- 1 Tbsp. cider vinegar
- 1 Tbsp. honey
- 4 hamburger buns, split and toasted
- 8 cooked bacon strips
- ½ cup french-fried onions
  Optional: Lettuce leaves and sliced tomato

1. Preheat air fryer to 350°. In a large bowl, combine the Worcestershire sauce, garlic, seasoned salt and pepper. Add the beef; mix lightly but thoroughly. Shape into four ½-in.-thick patties.
2. In batches, place burgers in a single layer on tray in the air-fryer basket. Cook until a thermometer reads 160°, 8-10 minutes, turning halfway through cooking. Remove burgers from basket. Top with cheese; cover until cheese is melted, 1-2 minutes.
3. Meanwhile, in a small bowl, combine the mayonnaise, ketchup, vinegar and honey; spread over cut sides of buns. Top the bun bottoms with bacon, burgers, french-fried onions and, if desired, lettuce and tomato. Replace tops.
1 burger: 708 cal., 46g fat (16g sat. fat), 124mg chol., 1277mg sod., 33g carb. (10g sugars, 1g fiber), 39g pro.

HOLLY BALZER-HARZ
Malone, NY

Ground Beef

MORE BEEFY FAVORITES

Breakfast, lunch, dinner—even dessert!—these tasty and surprising recipes prove ground beef can pop up in every meal with delectable results.

BEEFY HUEVOS RANCHEROS

This quick, easy and oh-so-tasty recipe works for breakfast, lunch or dinner and is delicious served in flour tortillas with fruit or salad on the side. Guests can top them however they like.
—*Sandra Leonard, Peculiar, MO*

- -

PREP: 15 min. • **COOK:** 20 min.
MAKES: 6 servings

1	lb. lean ground beef (90% lean)
1	small onion, finely chopped
2	cans (14½ oz. each) diced tomatoes
1	cup frozen corn
1	can (4 oz.) chopped green chiles
½	tsp. salt
6	large eggs
¼	tsp. pepper
6	Tbsp. shredded cheddar cheese
6	flour tortillas (8 in.), warmed
	Optional: Reduced-fat sour cream, guacamole, salsa and chopped green onions

1. In a large cast-iron or other heavy skillet, cook beef and onion over medium heat until beef is no longer pink and onion is tender, 6-8 minute; crumble beef. Drain and return to the pan.
2. Drain tomatoes, reserving ½ cup liquid. Stir tomatoes, reserved liquid, corn, chiles and salt into beef mixture; bring to a simmer.
3. With the back of a spoon, make 6 wells in the beef mixture; add an egg to each well. Sprinkle with pepper. Cook, covered, until egg whites are completely set, 5-7 minutes.
4. Sprinkle with cheese. Serve with tortillas and toppings as desired.
1 serving: 434 cal., 17g fat (6g sat. fat), 241mg chol., 879mg sod., 41g carb. (6g sugars, 5g fiber), 29g pro.

BREAKFAST SUPREME

Friends shared this recipe many years ago when we spent the night at their home. After one taste, you'll understand why this breakfast is supreme.
—*Laurie Harms, Grinnell, IA*

- -

PREP: 20 min. + chilling
BAKE: 35 min. + standing • **MAKES:** 12 servings

1   lb. bulk pork sausage
1   lb. ground beef
1   small onion, chopped
¾   cup sliced fresh mushrooms
½   cup chopped green pepper
1   to 1½ tsp. salt
¼   to ½ tsp. pepper
2   Tbsp. butter, melted
2   cups shredded cheddar cheese, divided
12 large eggs, lightly beaten
⅔   cup heavy whipping cream

1. In a large skillet, cook the sausage, beef, onion, mushrooms and green pepper over medium heat until meat is no longer pink; crumble meat; drain. Stir in salt and pepper; set aside.
2. Pour butter into an ungreased 13x9-in. baking dish. Sprinkle with 1 cup cheese. Pour eggs over cheese. Top with the meat mixture. Pour the cream over meat mixture. Sprinkle with remaining 1 cup cheese. Cover and refrigerate for 8 hours or overnight.
3. Preheat oven to 325°. Remove from the refrigerator 30 minutes before baking. Bake, uncovered, for 35-40 minutes or until a knife inserted in the center comes out clean. Let stand 10 minutes before cutting.
1 piece: 344 cal., 28g fat (14g sat. fat), 288mg chol., 578mg sod., 3g carb. (2g sugars, 0 fiber), 20g pro.

HEARTY RICE DRESSING

This satisfying dressing has always been received well at church socials and family reunions. The recipe feeds a crowd—I cut back if I'm serving a smaller group.
—*Ruth Hayward, Lake Charles, LA*

- -

PREP: 25 min. • **BAKE:** 1 hour
MAKES: 50 servings

3   lbs. ground beef
2   lbs. ground pork
2   large onions, chopped
3   celery ribs, chopped
1   large green pepper, chopped
1   jar (4 oz.) diced pimientos, drained
5   cups water
2   cans (10¾ oz. each) condensed cream of chicken soup, undiluted
2   cans (10½ oz. each) condensed French onion soup
1   can (10¾ oz.) condensed cream of mushroom soup, undiluted
2   Tbsp. Creole seasoning
1   tsp. salt
1   tsp. pepper
½   tsp. cayenne pepper
4   cups uncooked long grain rice

1. Combine beef, pork and onions. Divide mixture evenly among several large Dutch ovens or stockpots; cook over medium heat until no longer pink; crumble meat; drain.
2. In a large bowl, combine celery, green pepper and pimientos. Add water, soups and seasonings. Stir into the meat mixture, dividing vegetable-soup mixture evenly among the Dutch ovens. Bring to a boil; stir in rice.
3. Preheat oven to 350°. Carefully transfer mixture to 3 greased 13x9-in. baking dishes. Cover and bake for 30 minutes; stir. Cover and bake 30-40 minutes longer or until rice is tender.
Note: If you don't have Creole seasoning, make your own using ¼ tsp. each of salt, garlic powder and paprika and a pinch each of dried thyme, ground cumin and cayenne pepper.
¾ cup: 153 cal., 6g fat (2g sat. fat), 26mg chol., 293mg sod., 14g carb. (1g sugars, 1g fiber), 10g pro.

BREAKFAST SCRAMBLE

One weekend morning, my husband and I wanted a breakfast without the traditional sausage or bacon. I reached for the ground beef and tossed in other ingredients as I went. This was the mouthwatering result.
—Mary Lill, Rock Cave, WV

PREP: 10 min. • **COOK:** 45 min.
MAKES: 6 servings

1	lb. ground beef
1	medium onion, chopped
3	cups diced peeled potatoes
½	cup water
	Salt and pepper to taste
1	can (14½ oz.) diced tomatoes, undrained
4	large eggs, lightly beaten
4	oz. Velveeta, sliced

1. In a large skillet, cook beef and onion over medium heat until the meat is no longer pink; crumble the beef; drain. Add the potatoes, water, salt and pepper. Cover and simmer for 20 minutes or until potatoes are tender.
2. Add tomatoes; cook for 5 minutes. Pour eggs over mixture. Cook and stir until eggs are completely set. Top with cheese. Cover and cook for 1 minute or until the cheese is melted.
1 serving: 310 cal., 15g fat (7g sat. fat), 191mg chol., 408mg sod., 21g carb. (5g sugars, 2g fiber), 23g pro.

TASTY TACO CHOPPED SALAD

My friends and I love Mexican food, but we try to eat healthy. My mom taught me how to make this tasty taco salad for my friends.
—Matthew Smith, Knippa, TX

TAKES: 25 min. • **MAKES:** 6 servings

1	lb. lean ground beef (90% lean)
1	envelope reduced-sodium taco seasoning
⅔	cup water
1	can (15 oz.) Ranch Style beans (pinto beans in seasoned tomato sauce)
1	head iceberg lettuce, chopped (about 8 cups)
1	cup shredded Colby-Monterey Jack cheese
1	large tomato, chopped
2	cups corn chips
½	cup Catalina salad dressing

1. In a large skillet, cook beef over medium heat, 6-8 minutes or until no longer pink; crumble meat; drain.
2. Stir in taco seasoning, water and beans; bring to a boil. Reduce the heat; simmer, uncovered, 3-4 minutes, or until thickened, stirring occasionally.
3. Serve remaining ingredients in separate bowls; add as desired.
1 serving: 471 cal., 25g fat (9g sat. fat), 64mg chol., 1193mg sod., 37g carb. (12g sugars, 5g fiber), 24g pro.

TEST KITCHEN TIP
Add more veggies, swap spinach for iceberg lettuce, skip the cheese and top with a few crunchy chips for a less-guilty yet delicious form of this potentially indulgent salad.

BEEF-STUFFED POTATOES
This is a stuffed potato with a tasty twist. The combo of green chiles and cheese is always popular with teenagers.
—*Kay Scheidler, Bull Shoals, AR*

PREP: 20 min. • **BAKE:** 70 min.
MAKES: 6 servings

6	medium baking potatoes
1	lb. ground beef
2	Tbsp. chopped onion
⅓	cup sour cream
1	can (4 oz.) chopped green chiles
3	Tbsp. butter
1	Tbsp. Worcestershire sauce
1	tsp. salt
½	tsp. garlic powder
½	tsp. chili powder
¾	cup shredded cheddar cheese

1. Bake potatoes at 375° for 1 hour or until tender. Cool. Meanwhile, in a large skillet, cook the beef and onion over medium heat until the meat is no longer pink; crumble beef; drain.
2. Cut a thin slice off the top of each potato. Carefully scoop out the pulp, leaving a thin shell; place pulp in a bowl. Add sour cream, chiles, butter, Worcestershire sauce, salt, garlic powder and chili powder; mash or beat. Stir in the meat mixture until combined. Stuff into the potato shells.
3. Place filled potatoes on an ungreased baking sheet. Sprinkle with cheese. Bake at 350° for 10-15 minutes or until heated through.
1 filled potato: 422 cal., 19g fat (11g sat. fat), 76mg chol., 711mg sod., 41g carb. (4g sugars, 4g fiber), 21g pro.

BREAKFAST BURGER

My husband is big on eggs and bacon, so I wanted to merge his breakfast favorites with a grilled burger for an over-the-top treat. Topping it with my homemade blackberry jam sealed the deal.
—*Tina Janssen, Walworth, WI*

PREP: 25 min. • **GRILL:** 30 min.
MAKES: 4 servings

- 1 lb. ground beef
- 1 Tbsp. Worcestershire sauce
- 1 tsp. Montreal steak seasoning
- ½ tsp. salt, divided
- ½ tsp. pepper, divided
- 3 Tbsp. butter, softened and divided
- 8 slices Texas toast
- 2 Tbsp. canola oil
- 2½ cups frozen shredded hash brown potatoes, thawed
- 4 large eggs
- ¼ cup seedless blackberry spreadable fruit
- 4 slices American cheese
- 8 cooked bacon strips

1. Combine ground beef, Worcestershire sauce, steak seasoning, ¼ tsp. salt and ¼ tsp. pepper; mix lightly but thoroughly. Shape into four ½-in.-thick patties. Grill burgers, covered, on a greased grill rack over medium heat until a thermometer reads 160°, 4-5 minutes on each side.
2. Spread 2 Tbsp. butter over 1 side of toast slices. Grill, butter side down, until golden brown. Remove burgers and toast from heat; keep warm.
3. Increase heat to high. Heat oil in a large skillet placed on the grill rack. Drop hash browns by ½ cupfuls into oil; press to flatten. Sprinkle with remaining salt and pepper. Fry, covered, until golden brown and crisp, 12-15 minutes on each side; add oil as needed. Remove and keep warm.
4. Reduce heat to medium. In same skillet, heat the remaining 1 Tbsp. butter. Add eggs; fry over easy.
5. Spread the blackberry spread over 4 slices of toast. Layer each slice with 1 hash brown patty, 1 burger, 1 fried egg, 1 cheese slice and 2 bacon strips. Top with remaining toast slices.
1 burger: 859 cal., 49g fat (19g sat. fat), 307mg chol., 1703mg sod., 55g carb. (13g sugars, 2g fiber), 45g pro.

EASY CUBAN PICADILLO

My girlfriend gave me this delicious recipe years ago. I've made it ever since for family and friends. My daughter says it's the best dish I make and loves to take the leftovers to school for lunch the next day.
—*Marie Wielgus, Wayne, NJ*

TAKES: 25 min. • **MAKES:** 4 servings

- 1 lb. lean ground beef (90% lean)
- 1 small green pepper, chopped
- ¼ cup chopped onion
- 1 can (8 oz.) tomato sauce
- ½ cup sliced pimiento-stuffed olives
- ¼ cup raisins
- 1 Tbsp. cider vinegar
- 2 cups hot cooked rice
  Fresh cilantro leaves, optional

1. In a large skillet, cook beef with pepper and onion over medium-high heat until no longer pink, 5-7 minutes; crumble beef.
2. Stir in the tomato sauce, olives, raisins and vinegar; bring to a boil. Reduce heat; simmer, uncovered, until the raisins are softened, 5-6 minutes.
3. Serve with rice. If desired, top with fresh cilantro to serve.
1 cup beef mixture with ½ cup rice: 363 cal., 13g fat (4g sat. fat), 71mg chol., 683mg sod., 36g carb. (7g sugars, 2g fiber), 26g pro.
Diabetic exchanges: 3 lean meat, 2½ starch, 1 fat.

GROUND BEEF STROGANOFF

Ever since my mother-in-law gave me this recipe many years ago, it's been a staple in my meal planning. The creamy, beefy noodles pair nicely with a side of green beans or a tossed salad.

—*Marjorie Kriegle, Nampa, ID*

TAKES: 30 min. • **MAKES:** 2 servings

½ lb. lean ground beef (90% lean)
¼ cup chopped onion
1 Tbsp. butter
¼ cup sliced fresh mushrooms
1 Tbsp. all-purpose flour
1 garlic clove, minced
¼ tsp. salt
⅛ tsp. pepper
2 Tbsp. chili sauce
¼ tsp. Worcestershire sauce
⅓ cup sour cream
   Hot cooked noodles

1. In a large skillet, cook beef and onion in butter over medium heat until meat is no longer pink; crumble beef.
2. Stir in mushrooms, flour, garlic, salt and pepper. Cook and stir for 5 minutes. Add chili sauce and Worcestershire sauce. Reduce heat; cook, uncovered, for 10 minutes.
3. Stir in sour cream just before serving; heat through (do not boil). Serve with noodles.
1 serving: 341 cal., 21g fat (12g sat. fat), 98mg chol., 685mg sod., 11g carb. (6g sugars, 1g fiber), 24g pro.

DID YOU KNOW?
Beef Stroganoff was named after a 18th-century Russian nobleman, Count Pavel Stroganov. Stroganov was a diplomat to Britain and a highly decorated general in the Napoleonic Wars. But his name is mostly remembered for its culinary association. He was born in Paris, and his chef merged French and Russian flavors to create a new dish in his honor.

HEARTY PITA SPINACH SALAD

Greek flavors combine in perfect harmony for a main dish you won't be able to stop munching. Serve this with a tall glass of lemonade or iced tea and enjoy it al fresco some summer night.

—*Taste of Home Test Kitchen*

TAKES: 25 min. • **MAKES:** 4 servings

2 whole pita breads
2 Tbsp. olive oil
¼ tsp. salt
¼ tsp. pepper
¾ lb. ground beef
¾ cup Greek vinaigrette, divided
1 pkg. (6 oz.) fresh baby spinach
2 medium tomatoes, cut into wedges
4 oz. feta cheese, cubed
1 cup pitted Greek olives
1 small red onion, thinly sliced

1. Preheat oven to 400°. Cut pita breads into strips; arrange in a single layer on an ungreased baking sheet. In a small bowl, combine the oil, salt and pepper; brush over pita strips. Bake for 8-10 minutes or until crisp, turning once.
2. Meanwhile, in a large skillet, cook beef over medium heat until no longer pink; crumble beef; drain. Add ¼ cup vinaigrette. Arrange the spinach on a serving platter; top with tomatoes, cheese, olives, onion and beef mixture.
3. Drizzle the remaining ½ cup vinaigrette over the salad. Serve immediately with toasted pita strips.
1 serving: 662 cal., 49g fat (12g sat. fat), 78mg chol., 1744mg sod., 30g carb. (5g sugars, 3g fiber), 24g pro.

GROUND BEEF TACO SALAD

In spring, we look for something light and refreshing after the heavier comfort food of winter; this salad is a great solution. Everyone at our house loves it.
—Muriel Bertrand, Shoreview, MN

TAKES: 25 min. • **MAKES:** 2 servings

- ½ lb. ground beef
- ⅓ cup bean dip
- 1 tsp. chili powder
- ¼ tsp. salt
- 1 cup canned diced tomatoes, plus 2 Tbsp. liquid
- 2 cups chopped lettuce
- ½ cup shredded cheddar cheese
- 2 green onions, sliced
- 2 Tbsp. sliced ripe olives
- ½ cup corn chips

1. In a large skillet, cook beef over medium heat until no longer pink; crumble meat; drain. Stir in the bean dip, chili powder, salt and tomato liquid. Remove from the heat.
2. In a large bowl, combine the tomatoes, lettuce, cheese, onions and olives. Add the beef mixture; toss to coat. Top with chips. Serve immediately.

2 cups: 469 cal., 28g fat (12g sat. fat), 107mg chol., 1007mg sod., 25g carb. (5g sugars, 4g fiber), 32g pro.

JENNIFER FISHER
Austin, TX

BEEF, POTATO & EGG BAKE

To keep my family going strong throughout the day, I start with lean ground beef and spices, then sneak some spinach into this protein-packed dish. I love that it's equally perfect for breakfast, lunch or dinner.
—Jennifer Fisher, Austin, TX

PREP: 25 min. • **BAKE:** 45 min.
MAKES: 12 servings

- 1 lb. lean ground beef (90% lean)
- 2 tsp. onion powder
- 1½ tsp. salt, divided
- 1 tsp. garlic powder
- ½ tsp. rubbed sage
- ½ tsp. crushed red pepper flakes
- 1 pkg. (10 oz.) frozen chopped spinach, thawed and squeezed dry
- 4 cups frozen shredded hash brown potatoes
- 14 large eggs
- 1 cup fat-free ricotta cheese
- ⅓ cup fat-free milk
- ¾ to 1 tsp. pepper
- ¾ cup shredded Colby-Monterey Jack cheese
- 1⅓ cups grape tomatoes, halved

1. Preheat oven to 350°. In a large skillet, cook beef with onion powder, ½ tsp. salt, the garlic powder, sage and pepper flakes over medium heat 6-8 minutes or until meat is no longer pink; crumble beef; drain. Stir in spinach. Remove from heat.
2. Spread potatoes in greased 13x9-in. baking dish; top with the beef mixture. In a large bowl, whisk eggs, ricotta cheese, milk, pepper and remaining 1 tsp. salt; pour over top. Sprinkle with cheese. Top with tomatoes.
3. Bake, uncovered, 45-50 minutes or until a knife inserted in the center comes out clean. Let stand 5-10 minutes before serving.

1 piece: 218 cal., 11g fat (5g sat. fat), 250mg chol., 489mg sod., 9g carb. (2g sugars, 1g fiber), 20g pro. **Diabetic exchanges:** 3 lean meat, ½ starch.

❄ DELUXE CHEESEBURGER SALAD

I was planning to grill burgers, and then it dawned on me: How about a cheeseburger salad? Tomato adds a fresh flavor boost.
—*Pam Jefferies, Cantrall, IL*

- -

TAKES: 30 min. • **MAKES:** 4 servings

- 1 lb. ground beef
- 2 tsp. Montreal steak seasoning
- 6 cups torn iceberg lettuce
- 2 cups shredded cheddar cheese
- 1 cup salad croutons
- 1 medium tomato, chopped
- 1 small onion, halved and thinly sliced
- ½ cup dill pickle slices
  Thousand Island salad dressing

1. In a large bowl, combine beef and steak seasoning, mixing lightly but thoroughly. Shape into twenty ½-in.-thick patties.
2. Grill burgers, covered, over medium heat for 3-4 minutes on each side or until a thermometer reads 160°.
3. In a large bowl, combine lettuce, burgers, cheese, croutons, tomato, onion and pickles. Serve with salad dressing.
Freeze option: Place patties on a waxed paper-lined baking sheet; cover and freeze until firm. Remove from sheet and transfer to an airtight container; return to freezer. To use, cook frozen patties as directed, increasing time as necessary for a thermometer to read 160°.
1 serving: 511 cal., 34g fat (17g sat. fat), 128mg chol., 1033mg sod., 14g carb. (4g sugars, 3g fiber), 36g pro.

TACO SALAD IN A JAR

Inspired by a layered taco salad by Elissa Dougherty of Babylon, New York, we created a make-and-take version for lunch on the go!
—Taste of Home *Test Kitchen*

- -

TAKES: 30 min. • **MAKES:** 4 servings

- 1 lb. lean ground beef (90% lean)
- ⅔ cup water
- 1 envelope reduced-sodium taco seasoning
- 1 medium ripe avocado, peeled and cubed
- 1 Tbsp. finely chopped red onion
- 1 garlic clove, minced
- ½ tsp. lemon juice
- ¾ cup reduced-fat sour cream
- ¾ cup salsa
- 2 medium tomatoes, chopped
- 1 can (2¼ oz.) sliced ripe olives, drained
- 1 small cucumber, peeled and chopped
- 5 green onions, chopped
- 1 cup shredded cheddar cheese
- 4 cups shredded lettuce
  Tortilla chips, optional

1. In a small skillet, cook beef over medium heat until no longer pink; crumble beef; drain. Stir in water and taco seasoning. Bring to a boil; cook and stir for 2 minutes. Cool.
2. In a small bowl, mash avocado with onion, garlic and lemon juice. In each of four 1-qt. wide-mouth canning jars, divide and layer ingredients in the following order: Sour cream, salsa, beef, tomatoes, olives, cucumber, green onions, avocado mixture, cheese and lettuce. Cover and refrigerate until serving.
3. To serve, transfer salads into bowls; toss to combine. If desired, serve with tortilla chips.
1 serving: 483 cal., 29g fat (12g sat. fat), 103mg chol., 1087mg sod., 24g carb. (11g sugars, 5g fiber), 34g pro.

BROCCOLI BEEF LO MEIN

My family craves pasta, so I'm always looking for different ways to prepare it. This dish is better than any Chinese restaurant variety I've tried.

—Joan Crandall, Burlington, CT

PREP: 10 min. • **COOK:** 25 min.
MAKES: 4 servings

- 1 lb. ground beef
- 1 large onion, thinly sliced
- 4 garlic cloves, minced
- ¾ cup bean sprouts
- 1 jar (4½ oz.) sliced mushrooms, drained
- 1 can (8 oz.) sliced water chestnuts, drained
- 6 oz. vermicelli or thin spaghetti, cooked and drained
- 2 to 3 cups broccoli florets, cooked
- ¼ cup soy sauce
- ¼ cup oyster sauce, optional
- 2 tsp. ground ginger

In a large skillet, cook beef, onion and garlic over medium heat until meat is no longer pink; crumble beef; drain. Add bean sprouts, mushrooms and water chestnuts. Cook and stir for 3-5 minutes. Stir in the vermicelli, broccoli, soy sauce, oyster sauce if desired and ginger; toss to coat. Cover and cook for 5 minutes or until heated through.

1 serving: 435 cal., 14g fat (5g sat. fat), 70mg chol., 1136mg sod., 46g carb. (6g sugars, 5g fiber), 30g pro.

DID YOU KNOW?
Mein is Chinese for "noodle"; lo mein means simply tossed noodles. Pasta is a good substitute for traditional Chinese egg noodles. Use fresh pasta if you can.

PINEAPPLE BAKED BEANS

Tangy pineapple dresses up these hearty baked beans. Brown the beef while you open cans and chop the vegetables, and it won't take long to get this dish ready for the slow cooker.

—Gladys De Boer, Castleford, ID

PREP: 15 min. • **COOK:** 6 hours
MAKES: 8 servings

- 1 lb. ground beef
- 1 can (28 oz.) baked beans
- ¾ cup pineapple tidbits, drained
- 1 jar (4½ oz.) sliced mushrooms, drained
- 1 large onion, chopped
- 1 large green pepper, chopped
- ½ cup barbecue sauce
- 2 Tbsp. reduced-sodium soy sauce
- 1 garlic clove, minced
- ½ tsp. salt
- ¼ tsp. pepper

In a large skillet, cook beef over medium heat until no longer pink; crumble beef; drain. Transfer to a 5-qt. slow cooker. Add the remaining ingredients and mix well. Cover and cook on low 6-8 hours or until bubbly.

¾ cup: 249 cal., 9g fat (3g sat. fat), 42mg chol., 1032mg sod., 28g carb. (6g sugars, 7g fiber), 17g pro.

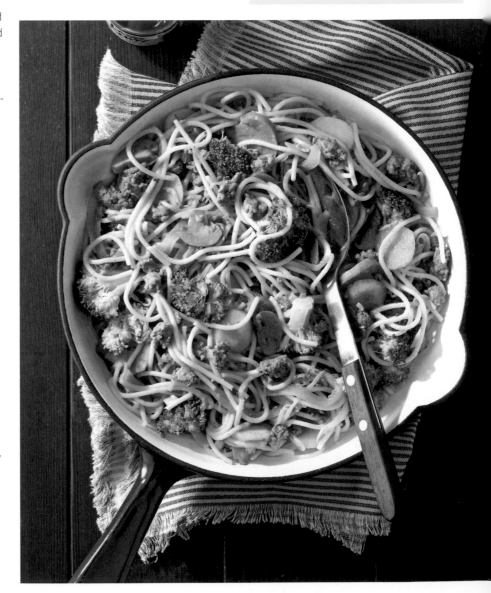

BROCCOLI BISCUIT SQUARES

With their cheesy, biscuit-like crust, these pretty squares disappear quickly at our house. We eat them for dinner or breakfast.
—*Vi Janus, Pelican Lake, WI*

PREP: 25 min. • **BAKE:** 25 min.
MAKES: 6 servings

- 1 lb. ground beef
- 1 can (4 oz.) mushroom stems and pieces, drained
- 1 small onion, chopped
- 2 cups biscuit/baking mix
- 2 cups shredded cheddar cheese, divided
- ¼ cup grated Parmesan cheese
- ½ cup water
- 3 cups frozen chopped broccoli, thawed and drained
- 4 large eggs
- ½ cup milk
- 1 tsp. salt
  Dash pepper

1. Preheat oven to 400°. In a large skillet, cook the beef, mushrooms and onion over medium heat until the meat is no longer pink; crumble beef; drain.
2. Combine biscuit mix, ½ cup cheddar cheese, Parmesan cheese and water until a soft dough forms. Press the dough onto the bottom and ½ in. up sides of greased 13x9-in. baking dish.
3. Stir remaining 1½ cups cheddar cheese into beef mixture; spread over dough. Sprinkle with the broccoli.
4. Beat eggs, milk, salt and pepper. Pour over meat mixture. Bake, uncovered, for 25 minutes or until a knife in the center comes out clean.

1 piece: 544 cal., 30g fat (13g sat. fat), 213mg chol., 1286mg sod., 36g carb. (4g sugars, 4g fiber), 33g pro.

READER REVIEW

"I prefer fresh vegetables over canned or frozen whenever available, so I used fresh mushrooms and broccoli. This recipe was easy to assemble and baked nicely!"

JARVISFAMILY, TASTEOFHOME.COM

MINCE PIES

Most people use canned mincemeat, but this is the old-fashioned way to make a mince pie. It is a sweet holiday treat that will satisfy you and your loved ones.
—*Diane Selich, Vassar, MI*

- -

PREP: 20 min. + chilling • **BAKE:** 25 min./batch
MAKES: 20 mini pies

CRUST
- 4   cups all-purpose flour
- 2   tsp. salt
- 1⅓ cups shortening
- ½   cup plus 2 Tbsp. ice water

FILLING
- ¼   lb. ground beef
- 3   medium apples, peeled and chopped
- 1   medium apricot, peeled and chopped
- ¾   cup packed light brown sugar
- ½   cup golden raisins
- ½   cup unsweetened apple juice
- 1   Tbsp. cider vinegar
- 1½ tsp. grated orange zest
- 1½ tsp. ground cinnamon
- ½   tsp. salt
- ½   tsp. ground cloves
- ¼   cup rum
- 1   large egg, beaten
- 1   to 2 Tbsp. coarse sugar

1. In a large bowl, mix flour and salt; cut in shortening until crumbly. Gradually add ice water, tossing with a fork until dough forms a ball. Divide dough in half. Shape each into a disk; wrap and refrigerate 1 hour or overnight.
2. For filling, in a large skillet or Dutch oven, cook beef over medium heat until no longer pink, 3-5 minutes; crumble beef; drain. Add apples, apricot, brown sugar, raisins, apple juice, vinegar, orange zest and seasonings. Bring to a boil; reduce heat. Simmer until apples are tender, 15-17 minutes. Stir in rum. Remove from heat; cool slightly.
3. Preheat oven to 375°. On a lightly floured surface, roll half of dough to ⅛-in. thickness. Cut 20 circles with a floured 2¾-in. round biscuit cutter. Top half the circles with 1 Tbsp. filling. Top with the remaining circles; press edges with a fork to seal. Cut slits in top. Brush tops with egg; sprinkle with coarse sugar. Repeat with remaining dough and filling.
4. Bake until crust is golden brown and filling is bubbly, 20-25 minutes. Cool on a wire rack.
1 pie: 280 cal., 14g fat (4g sat. fat), 4mg chol., 302mg sod., 34g carb. (14g sugars, 1g fiber), 4g pro.

LEMONY GREEK BEEF & VEGETABLES

I love the bright lemon flavor in this recipe. It's the latest addition to my collection of quick, healthy dinners. I'm sensitive to cow's milk, so I use goat cheese crumbles on my portion instead of Parmesan.
—*Alice Neff, Lake Worth, FL*

- -

TAKES: 30 min. • **MAKES:** 4 servings

- 1   bunch baby bok choy
- 1   lb. ground beef
- 1   Tbsp. olive oil
- 5   medium carrots, sliced
- 3   garlic cloves, minced
- ¼   cup plus 2 Tbsp. white wine, divided
- 1   can (15 to 16 oz.) navy beans, rinsed and drained
- 2   Tbsp. minced fresh oregano or 2 tsp. dried oregano
- ¼   tsp. salt
- 2   Tbsp. lemon juice
- ½   cup shredded Parmesan cheese

1. Trim and discard root end of bok choy. Coarsely chop leaves. Cut stalks into 1-in. pieces. Set aside.
2. In a large skillet, cook beef over medium-high heat until no longer pink, 5-7 minutes; crumble beef; drain. Remove from skillet and set aside.
3. In same skillet, heat oil over medium-high heat. Add carrots and bok choy stalks; cook and stir until crisp-tender, 5-7 minutes. Stir in garlic, bok choy leaves and ¼ cup wine. Cook, stirring to loosen browned bits from pan, until greens wilt, 3-5 minutes.
4. Stir in ground beef, beans, oregano, salt and enough of the remaining 2 Tbsp. wine to keep the mixture moist. Reduce heat; simmer 3 minutes. Stir in lemon juice; sprinkle with Parmesan cheese.
1½ cups: 478 cal., 21g fat (7g sat. fat), 77mg chol., 856mg sod., 36g carb. (7g sugars, 10g fiber), 36g pro.

CHEESEBURGER BOWL

This is a lighter way to enjoy an American summer staple. You can try a version of the dressing with 1 tablespoon of yellow mustard and 1 tablespoon of ketchup.
—*Laurie Rogerson, Ellington, CT*

PREP: 25 min. • **GRILL:** 10 min.
MAKES: 4 servings

- 1   lb. lean ground beef (90% lean)
- ½   tsp. salt
- ¼   tsp. pepper
- ½   cup reduced-fat ranch salad dressing
- 2   Tbsp. ketchup
- 4   cups shredded lettuce
- 4   cups torn romaine
- 1   medium cucumber, finely chopped
- 1   medium tomato, finely chopped
- ½   cup chopped dill pickles
- ¼   cup finely chopped red onion
- ¾   cup shredded cheddar cheese
      Crushed potato chips, optional

1. In a small bowl, combine beef, salt and pepper, mixing lightly but thoroughly. Shape into four ½-in.-thick patties.
2. Grill the burgers, covered, over medium heat for 4-5 minutes on each side or until a thermometer reads 160°.
3. Meanwhile, whisk the salad dressing and ketchup. In a large bowl, toss lettuces with half the dressing; divide among 4 plates. Top with burger, cucumber, tomato, pickles, onion and cheese. Serve with remaining dressing. Top with potato chips if desired.

2 cups salad with 2 Tbsp. dressing: 374 cal., 21g fat (8g sat. fat), 95mg chol., 1099mg sod., 11g carb. (7g sugars, 3g fiber), 29g pro.

TEST KITCHEN TIP
These burgers cook just as well in a grill pan on the stovetop as on an outdoor grill. Try sprinkling crumbled bacon over the salad, to imitate a bacon cheeseburger!

TACOS IN A BOWL

This easy skillet dish offers a delicious use for leftover taco meat. Garnish it with sour cream and salsa for added southwestern flavor.
—*Sue Schoening, Sheboygan, WI*

TAKES: 25 min. • **MAKES:** 2 servings

- ½   lb. lean ground beef (90% lean)
- 2   Tbsp. finely chopped onion
- ¾   cup canned diced tomatoes, drained
- 2   Tbsp. taco seasoning
- 1   cup water
- 1   pkg. (3 oz.) ramen noodles
- ¼   cup shredded cheddar or
      Mexican cheese blend
      Crushed tortilla chips, optional

1. In a small skillet, cook beef and onion over medium heat until meat is no longer pink; crumble beef; drain.
2. Stir in the tomatoes, taco seasoning and water. Bring to a boil. Add ramen noodles (discard seasoning packet or save for another use). Cook and stir until noodles are tender, 3-5 minutes.
3. Spoon into serving bowls; sprinkle with cheese and, if desired, tortilla chips.

1 cup: 480 cal., 21g fat (10g sat. fat), 85mg chol., 1279mg sod., 40g carb. (3g sugars, 2g fiber), 30g pro.

WESTERN-STYLE BEEF & BEANS

This hearty, crowd-pleasing side dish doesn't take long to make but tastes as if it simmered all day. With bread and a salad, it's an entree!
—*Jolene Lopez, Wichita, KS*

PREP: 15 min. • **BAKE:** 1 hour
MAKES: 12 servings

- 3   lbs. ground beef
- 2   medium onions, chopped
- 2   celery ribs, chopped
- 2   tsp. beef bouillon granules
- ⅔   cup boiling water
- 2   cans (28 oz. each) baked beans with molasses
- 1½ cups ketchup
- ¼   cup prepared mustard
- 3   garlic cloves, minced
- 1½ tsp. salt
- ½   tsp. pepper
- ½   lb. sliced bacon, cooked and crumbled

1. In a Dutch oven over medium heat, cook the beef, onions and celery until meat is no longer pink; crumble meat; drain. Dissolve bouillon in water; stir into beef mixture. Add the beans, ketchup, mustard, garlic, salt and pepper; mix well.

2. Transfer to an ungreased 3-qt. baking dish. Cover and bake at 375° for 60-70 minutes or until bubbly; stir. Sprinkle with bacon.
½ cup: 405 cal., 19g fat (7g sat. fat), 93mg chol., 1777mg sod., 25g carb. (10g sugars, 5g fiber), 34g pro.

MEAT BUNS

On the outside, these golden buns resemble ordinary dinner rolls, but just one bite reveals the tasty, cheesy beef filling inside.
—*Sharon Leno, Keansburg, NJ*

PREP: 25 min. + rising • **BAKE:** 20 min.
MAKES: 1 dozen

DOUGH
- 1½ tsp. active dry yeast
- ½   cup plus 1 Tbsp. warm water (110° to 115°)
- 3   Tbsp. sugar
- 1   large egg
- ½   tsp. salt
- 2   to 2¼ cups bread flour

FILLING
- 1   lb. ground beef
- 1½ cups chopped cabbage
- ½   cup chopped onion
-     Salt and pepper to taste
- ½   cup shredded cheddar cheese
- 2   Tbsp. butter, melted

1. In a large bowl, dissolve yeast in water. Add sugar, egg, salt and 1 cup flour; beat on low for 3 minutes. Add enough of the remaining flour to form a soft dough.

2. Turn dough onto a floured surface; knead until smooth and elastic, 6-8 minutes. Place in a greased bowl; turn once to grease top. Cover and let rise in a warm place until doubled, about 1 hour.

3. Meanwhile, in a large skillet, cook beef over medium heat until no longer pink; crumble meat; drain. Add cabbage, onion, salt and pepper. Cover and cook over medium heat for 15 minutes or until vegetables are tender. Stir in cheese. Remove from the heat; set aside to cool.

4. Punch the dough down and divide into 12 pieces. Gently roll out each piece into a 5-in. circle. Top each circle of dough with about ¼ cup filling. Fold dough over filling to meet in the center; pinch edges to seal.

5. Place buns seam side down on a greased baking sheet. Cover and let rise in a warm place until doubled, about 30 minutes. Brush with butter. Bake at 350° for 20 minutes or until golden brown. Serve warm.
1 bun: 199 cal., 8g fat (4g sat. fat), 53mg chol., 172mg sod., 19g carb. (4g sugars, 1g fiber), 12g pro.

SPECIAL HERB DRESSING

Here's a fabulously satisfying dressing with all the great tastes people crave: savory meat, fresh herbs, earthy mushrooms, crunchy apples and water chestnuts, and a zesty burst of tart cranberries.
—*Trudy Williams, Shannonville, ON*

PREP: 30 min. • **BAKE:** 35 min.
MAKES: 14-16 servings

- 1 lb. ground beef
- 1 lb. bulk pork sausage
- 1 lb. sliced fresh mushrooms
- 1 can (8 oz.) water chestnuts, drained and chopped
- 2 cups diced peeled apples
- 1 cup chopped onion
- ¼ cup minced fresh parsley
- ¼ cup chopped fresh celery leaves
- 1 cup chopped fresh or frozen cranberries
- 2 garlic cloves, minced
- 1½ tsp. salt
- 1 tsp. dried savory
- 1 tsp. dried thyme
- 1 tsp. rubbed sage
- ¾ tsp. pepper
  Pinch nutmeg
- 12 cups day-old bread cubes
- 1 cup chicken broth

1. Preheat oven to 350°. In a large skillet, cook beef and sausage over medium heat until no longer pink; crumble meat; drain. Add mushrooms, water chestnuts, apples, onion, parsley and celery leaves; cook 6-8 minutes, or until mushrooms and apples are tender. Add cranberries, garlic and seasonings; cook 2 minutes longer.
2. Place bread cubes in large bowl. Add the meat mixture; stir in broth. Spoon into a greased 13x9-in. baking dish. Cover and bake 35-45 minutes.
1 serving: 204 cal., 9g fat (3g sat. fat), 24mg chol., 561mg sod., 21g carb. (5g sugars, 2g fiber), 10g pro.

GROUND BEEF SNACK QUICHES

My husband, Cory, farms, so our supper can sometimes be quite late. A hearty appetizer like these meaty mini quiches is a perfect way to start the meal. They taste super made with ground beef, but I sometimes substitute bacon, ham, ground pork or sausage.
—Stacy Atkinson, Rugby, ND

- -

PREP: 15 min. • **BAKE:** 20 min.
MAKES: 1½ dozen

- ¼ lb. ground beef
- ⅛ to ¼ tsp. garlic powder
- ⅛ tsp. pepper
- 1 cup biscuit/baking mix
- ¼ cup cornmeal
- ¼ cup cold butter, cubed
- 2 to 3 Tbsp. boiling water
- 1 large egg
- ½ cup half-and-half cream
- 1 Tbsp. chopped green onion
- 1 Tbsp. chopped sweet red pepper
- ⅛ to ¼ tsp. salt
- ⅛ to ¼ tsp. cayenne pepper
- ½ cup finely shredded cheddar cheese

1. Preheat oven to 375°. In a large saucepan over medium heat, cook the beef, garlic powder and pepper until meat is no longer pink; crumble beef; drain and set aside.
2. Meanwhile, in a small bowl, combine biscuit mix and cornmeal; cut in butter until crumbly. Add enough water to form a soft dough.
3. Press dough onto the bottom and up the sides of greased miniature muffin cups. Place a teaspoon of the beef mixture into each shell.
4. In a small bowl, combine the egg, cream, onion, red pepper, salt and cayenne; pour over the beef mixture. Sprinkle with cheese.
5. Bake for 20 minutes or until a knife inserted in the center comes out clean.

1 snack quiche: 93 cal., 6g fat (3g sat. fat), 27mg chol., 137mg sod., 7g carb. (0 sugars, 0 fiber), 3g pro.

PATRIOTIC TACO SALAD

When my daughter asked to have a patriotic theme for her July birthday party, I made this refreshing dish. If you want to prepare your salad in advance, omit the layer of chips and serve them on the side so they don't get soggy.
—Glenda Jarboek, Oroville, CA

- -

PREP: 10 min. • **COOK:** 20 min.
MAKES: 8 servings

- 1 lb. ground beef
- 1 medium onion, chopped
- 1½ cups water
- 1 can (6 oz.) tomato paste
- 1 envelope taco seasoning
- 6 cups tortilla or corn chips
- 4 to 5 cups shredded lettuce
- 9 to 10 pitted large olives, sliced lengthwise
- 2 cups shredded cheddar cheese
- 2 cups cherry tomatoes, halved

1. In a large skillet, cook beef and onion over medium heat until meat is no longer pink; crumble beef; drain. Stir in water, tomato paste and taco seasoning. Bring to a boil. Reduce heat; simmer, uncovered, for 20 minutes.
2. Place chips in an ungreased 13x9-in. dish. Spread beef mixture evenly over top. Cover with lettuce. For each star, arrange 5 olive slices together in the upper left corner. To form stripes, add cheese and tomatoes in alternating rows. Serve immediately.

1 cup: 357 cal., 20g fat (9g sat. fat), 63mg chol., 747mg sod., 24g carb. (4g sugars, 2g fiber), 20g pro.

CLASSIC RED BEANS & RICE

After living where Cajun cooking is common, we rely on this staple dish. Even If you've never tried red beans and rice, you'll like this recipe!
—*Jackie Turnage, New Iberia, LA*

PREP: 10 min. • **COOK:** 2¼ hours + standing
MAKES: 8 servings

- 1 lb. dried kidney beans
- 8 cups water
- 1 ham hock
- 2 bay leaves
- 1 tsp. onion powder
- 1 lb. ground beef
- 1 large onion, chopped
- 1 tsp. salt
- ½ tsp. pepper
- 1 garlic clove, minced
  Hot cooked rice
  Chopped fresh parsley, optional

1. Sort beans and rinse with cold water. Place beans in a Dutch oven; add water to cover by 2 in. Bring to a boil; boil for 2 minutes. Remove from the heat; cover and let stand until beans are softened, 1-4 hours.
2. Drain and rinse beans, discarding liquid. Return beans to Dutch oven. Add water, ham hock, bay leaves and onion powder. Bring to a boil. Reduce heat; cover and simmer for 1 hour.
3. In a large cast-iron or other heavy skillet, cook the beef, onion, salt and pepper over medium heat until the meat is no longer pink; crumble beef. Add garlic; cook 1 minute longer. Drain.
4. Add beef to the bean mixture. Simmer, uncovered, 1 hour. Discard bay leaves.
5. Remove ham hock; allow to cool. Remove meat from bone; discard bone. Cut meat into bite-sized pieces and return to broth. Heat through. Serve with rice and, if desired, top with chopped fresh parsley.
1 serving: 309 cal., 7g fat (3g sat. fat), 35mg chol., 346mg sod., 37g carb. (4g sugars, 9g fiber), 25g pro.

> **TEST KITCHEN TIP**
> Smoked or cured ham hocks are usually available in your grocer's meat department. If you can't find them, ask your butcher for some leftover ham bones.

BISCUIT-BOWL CHILI

Kids love to help make these biscuit bowls almost as much as they love to eat them. For another weeknight option, fill the cups with taco-flavored or sloppy joe meat.
—*Cassy Ray, Parkersburg, WV*

PREP: 20 min. • **COOK:** 30 min.
MAKES: 8 servings

- 1 tube (16.3 oz.) large refrigerated flaky biscuits
- 2 tsp. cornmeal
- 1 lb. lean ground beef (90% lean)
- ½ cup chopped onion
- 1 can (16 oz.) kidney beans, rinsed and drained
- 1 can (11½ oz.) V8 juice
- 1 cup ketchup
- 2 tsp. chili powder
- ½ tsp. salt
- ¼ to ½ tsp. cayenne pepper
- ¼ tsp. crushed red pepper flakes
- ¼ tsp. pepper
- ½ cup shredded cheddar cheese

1. Preheat oven to 350°. Place 2 muffin tins upside down; spray bottoms and sides of 8 alternating muffin cups. On a work surface, roll or press biscuits into 4-in. circles. Sprinkle both sides with cornmeal, pressing lightly to adhere. Place biscuit circles over greased muffin cups, shaping biscuits around the cups.
2. Bake for 11-13 minutes or until lightly browned. Carefully remove biscuit bowls from muffin cups to a wire rack to cool.
3. Meanwhile, in a large skillet, cook beef and onion over medium heat until the beef is no longer pink, 6-8 minutes; crumble beef; drain. Stir in beans, V8 juice, ketchup and seasonings. Bring to a boil. Reduce heat; simmer, covered, for 10 minutes. Serve in biscuit bowls; top with shredded cheese.
1 biscuit bowl with ½ cup chili and 1 Tbsp. cheese: 395 cal., 15g fat (5g sat. fat), 35mg chol., 1357mg sod., 44g carb. (16g sugars, 4g fiber), 20g pro.